Incredible BARN FINDS

The Highly Entertaining Stories Behind 50 Treasured Cars

(Valued today at over 50 million dollars!)

Wallace A. Wyss

Enthusiast Books

Enthusiast Books
1830A Hanley Road
Hudson, Wisconsin 54016 USA

Visit www.enthusiastbooks.com

© 2013 Wallace A. Wyss

Iconografix books are offered at a discount when sold in quantity for promotional use. Businesses or organizations seeking details should write to the Marketing Department, Enthusiast Books, at the above address.

Library of Congress Control Number: 2013944859

ISBN-13: 978-1-58388-305-1
ISBN-10: 1-58388-305-3

13 14 15 16 17 18 6 5 4 3 2 1

Printed in The United States of America

Incredible
BARN
FINDS

Table of Contents:

Foreword by Tom Tjaarda

In 1959, with a fresh degree from the University of Michigan, I set off for Italy to work on a one year assignment for the famous design house Carrozzeria Ghia.

I stayed at Ghia for a couple of years before being hired at Pininfarina—then with De Tomaso and Ford for ten years—and finally setting up my own practice in 1986 up to now. During this time span I have designed around 85 automobiles—prototypes, show cars and production cars.

I met Wallace Wyss in 1970 when he was a brand new reporter for *Motor Trend*. Ford had a little intro of the DeTomaso Pantera in Dearborn, a car I had designed while head designer of Ghia, and Wally and I sat down for lunch at the Dearborn Inn, a historic old hotel built by the first Henry Ford and talked about how it was an American was chief designer of an Italian carrozzeria.

I am glad to see that, though Wallace went on to write three books on Cobras that he still retains a strong interest in Italian cars, and when he contacted me and told me he was working on a new book that would discuss some of the cars I've designed among those found by barn hunters, I was all for it.

The irony of many of the cars he has chosen to feature is that many were built purely to be prototypes or concept cars. Nobody building them ever envisioned they would see them on the road afterwards, especially many decades afterward. They were like a Broadway play—you design the sets, you perform the play to the end of the show's run, you tear down the sets and go on to planning a new show.

But, as Wallace shows here, these cars have a way of surviving even when they were supposed to be destroyed. Every so often, I get a phone call from someone somewhere who has found one of these cars and, no matter how decrepit it has become, they have assigned themselves the mission of bringing the car back to their former glory.

I applaud them. It is believers with that mindset that are filling in the blank spots of automotive history—we get to see what almost happened, the roads not taken.

It is especially gratifying when I see one of these cars at a concours, say the Mercedes 230SL I did for Pininfarina, or the Pantera II (7X) I did for Ghia at a high quality show like the Pebble Beach or Villa d'Este concours. People come up and comment on the car and it's like I'm back there at the car's debut 30-40 years ago. It makes me feel like a movie director who is attending a retrospective of his best films!

Wallace has told me he is already started on the second in the series and I can see why he's so enthusiastic—it's a natural subject. Car collectors dream of finding a rare car but Wallace is picking the rarest of the rare to write about. I like his comment about his criterion that the cars he picks must be worth "a life-changing amount."

So, enjoy his recounting of the great hunt.

Tom Tjaarda
Torino, Italy
January 2013

Introduction

This book could just as well be called "Confessions of a Car-o-holic" because I have been hooked on cars for over five decades. It wasn't always that way. Originally, back in high school, I had a literary bent, even published poetry and short stories. Then there was my artistic period. I blame a single life-changing moment for becoming a raging car nut. It was while in the library at Wayne State U that I came across an article on the Iso Grifo A3C racecar. That one picture of low-slung exotic racing car turned me into a car nut. I had to know more and began devouring every issue of *Road & Track* and the occasional English magazine.

I later became an advertising copywriter (writing muscle car ads for Chevrolet) and then in 1970 moved to California to become associate editor of *Motor Trend*. Moving to California was an eye-opener. I would see things like Ferrari 250Ps and Cobra Daytona coupes, cars that could go almost 200 mph at Le Mans, being used on the streets. There were one-off show cars on used car lots. It was heaven on earth!

When I had the idea for this book, it was, to tell the truth, based a little bit on Jerry Heasley's RARE FINDS books. But where he includes some of what I call "ordinary cars," I decided to set a baseline, and establish a different criterion for my book. It stems from when I tried to buy a Bentley Mk. VI in N. California for $7,000 and got turned down because the seller said it was not what he considered a "life changing" amount. I understood what he meant, so I've picked $100,000 as a life-changing amount, because outside of California or Hawaii or NYC, that's still hopefully enough for a down payment on a 2 bedroom home.

I also chose to include racecars on the street, always an exciting subject for me, and a fantasy I have seen realized many times.

And dream cars. Well, now they call them "concept cars," but, back in my day, when Harley Earl ruled the styling roost at GM, they were "dream cars." The dream of owning one, I found out eventually, is not that impossible. Call me a contrarian, but

I like to point out again and again that dream cars do not always go to the crusher. Sometimes they go to private owners' garages. Garages we can buy them from.

I became a fine artist in 2007, some 40 years after I last took an art class. That opened up to me a new appreciation of color, of texture, of the flow of design. So I can now say honestly that I have become even more of a car enthusiast as the beauty of prewar cars interests me more, as some of them—particularly the French-bodied ones of the late '30s—are among the most flamboyant of all cars.

The best part of doing this book has been meeting in person or interviewing by phone the successful car hunters, guys who had a dream and followed it through thick and thin. Some of them got to keep their cars, some of them didn't; but, damn it, they followed their dream.

I hope they inspire you as they did me.

Wallace Wyss, Cobra Ranch
Mendocino, California March 2013

Acknowledgements

The author would like to thank Richard Bartholomew, and the team of Mr. & Mrs. E. Musarra, all graphic consultants, the archivists at the Detroit Public Library Automotive History Collection, the Nethercutt Museum, and the El Segundo Automobile Driving Museum. Also the author would like to thank auction companies Gooding, Mecum and RM for providing information on some of their most historical car sales. Also the author would like to personally thank car collectors Brian Winer and Al Axelrod for advice on what makes a good car history.

Chapter 1
"Wankel, Wankel, Little Star"
(GM's Italian Corvette)

Wherein sometimes you get
what you ask for...

This story is one of incredible luck, and because of the purchase price paid, perhaps the best story in the book as far as to what was paid in order to secure a barn-find treasure.

It all starts with Ed Cole, former President of GM, who was an engineer through and through (credited with the design of the famous Chevy small block V8 introduced in 1955). He became enamored of the rotary engine devised by Dr. Felix Wankel over in Germany and, after seeing how successful Mazda was with the R-100, the RX-2 and the like in the early '70s, pushed GM to hop on the bandwagon.

Cole talked GM's board into buying a license to create rotary engines from the U.S. license holder, Curtiss-Wright. GM spent approximately $50 million on developing their own rotary engine and was almost ready to introduce them in a new series of cars when they decided, hey, why not build a show car that sensationalizes the rotary engine?

That's when Kip Wasenko and another designer were assigned to do a mid-engined car. They came up with a sensational design that, for some reason (probably security) was mocked up at GM's Opel subsidiary in Germany. The design even wore Opel badges originally, so if anyone accidentally saw it being tested, they would think it was a future Opel design and not connect it with GM in the U.S.

Then the famed design house of Pininfarina, at that time designing most of Ferrari's models, was contracted to do the actual building of a running, driving steel-bodied prototype.

This was no surprise as the assistant GM Design chief Charles "Chuck" Jordan was a big Ferrari fan and this gave him an excuse to see what else they were doing in the Ferrari Dept. every time he went to check on the progress of GM's rotary-engine car.

After its show debut at the 1978 Frankfurt Auto Show, the Two Rotor was rapidly de-emphasized as if it were a popular movie star who suddenly got busted on a morals charge. The show car minus engine and transaxle was put in storage in the UK after its British Motor Show debut and pretty soon GM was touting the all-American-designed-and-built Four Rotor Corvette, the name of which was a bit of an exaggeration because it was in actuality two twin-rotor GM rotaries lashed together with a Rube Goldberg-type use of chain drive. It didn't really run except up on the rotating display and any reporter who said he drove it is a flat out liar.

The Two Rotor not only ran, I drove it and I can remember it had a rorty exhaust sound, cornered well and I only lament it had a Toronado-sourced automatic (GM being loathe to tool up millions for a transaxle when maybe only 15-25% of the buyers of such a car would order a manual). But then disaster struck. Just as the Two Rotor and Four Rotor were being touted, suddenly Europe and the U.S. were in danger of being cut off from Mideast oil due to some aggressive action by the organization of petroleum producers.

Suddenly any car that used even the tiniest excess of oil was regarded with suspicion. GM, who at the start of their Wankel engine project had one scientist who bragged "the Wankel rotary engine is nothing but an extension of air pump technology," had labored mightily to come up with an engine that, surprise, surprise, used a quart of oil every 1,000 miles. That was too much. The 180-hp twin rotor engine was dropped. Plus GM secretly hated the idea of having to pay a license fee per engine if they put it into production. After all, they weren't paying the heirs of the Otto-cycle piston engine which all of their other engines were based on.

THE PRIDE OF SNODLAND

Now we come to the barn find part. In 1982, Englishman Tom Falconer, a car collector and auto historian, had an interview appointment with Chuck Jordan at the GM Tech Center in Warren, Michigan. The reason was to talk about the new Cadillac Seville as Falconer, a dealer in used Corvettes, was also an author, with an assignment for a book.

As he was sitting there sipping coffee, Falconer got a phone call from his bosom buddy, Geoff Lawson, a designer over at Vauxhall in the UK (later to become famous as the designer of the Jaguar XK8). Lawson told him he was at that moment in time on the roof of the Vauxhall building and some blokes there were intent on making more storage room by throwing away the boxes on the roof.

Lawson had peeked into a large box and recognized the Two Rotor Corvette. Why would they want to throw it away? Well, that is kind of embarrassing. Lawson didn't spell it out but it was a secret inside the industry that that Zora Arkus-Duntov, the famous Corvette engineer, while in his cups during an interview, had let slip that, underneath that sexy Italianate body of the Two Rotor, was nothing more than the chassis of a Porsche 914/6.

That revelation meant GM had spent 2 million dollars to build the world's most expensive custom Porsche! So, naturally after Duntov let the cat out of the bag, GM wanted to expunge the Two Rotor from their Corvette bloodline. It was rather like the tabloids coming out with a story that proved a Royal family of Europe heir to the throne was actually fathered by, say, the Royal riding instructor. So the heir is cast off; exiled as a "pretender to the throne." Lawson knew Falconer was in Detroit and told him that this was a perfect opportunity to ask Jordan if he could save the car. After all, he had a Corvette business and could be considered to be the UK's most stalwart defender of the marque.

Amazingly, Jordan said "yes."

Two weeks later Falconer was back in Blighty, driving his Citroen wagon, pulling a trailer up on the ramp to the roof of the Vauxhall building. He had help rolling the car onto the trailer, secured it, drove down the ramp and to his country home, amazed that it had been so easy. Once he got to his shop, he installed a four-cylinder Vauxhall Cavalier engine and automatic gearbox merely to get it drivable. In 1997, it was fitted with a Mazda 13B rotary engine matched to a Cadillac front-wheel drive automatic gearbox.

Another report said he was later on offered a Two Rotor GM engine, probably one of hundreds of experimental ones built and discarded by the firm, but at that point he turned it down because he didn't want to re-engineer the car. More's the pity, a running Two Rotor with the original engine and trans would—in this writer's view—be worth about $2 million dollars. Nonetheless, even with the wrong engine, today the car is the pride of his showroom, in the improbably-named village of Snodland, Kent, England. Lesson learned? Hey, it never hurts to ask.

Chapter 2
Der Snakemeister's Own (Twin Paxton 427)

When Shelby built one for himself, it was hold on, Molly!

Let's say, back in the mid-'60s, you were a boutique automaker, making just a few hundred cars a year, and you belonged to a club of aging gentlemen whose wont was to occasionally skedaddle from the civilized environs of Los Angeles to the wild frontiers of Nevada to cavort.

By "wild" I'm talking an area where packing heat on your hip was Jake and you didn't have to even wait 'til night to meet the Ladies of the Evening.

And, hell, blasting through town in an old racecar at 170 mph to rattle the windows was just your way of sayin' Howdy.

In this case, the man was Cobra creator Carroll Hall Shelby. For this annual expedition of the *Conquistadores Visatores*, he had a very special car built for himself. He wanted the fastest 427 Cobra in the world.

He started with an S/C Cobra, a fairly early one. The car had been made on September 7, 1965. That's the date CSX 3015 was shipped and invoiced to Ford Advanced Vehicles. It arrived just when the big block Cobra's future was darkening. You see, back in '63 and '64, Ford was glad the small block 289 Cobra was out there flying the flag for Ford and winning races; but the problem was that the Cobra, with a top speed of 180 mph (in the Daytona coupe form) was not fast enough to win the 24 Hours of Le Mans. And winning at Le Mans was Ford's goal.

So in '64 they started making the mid-engine GT40, a car that would top 200 mph with ease, and thus their enthusiasm for a big block 427 Cobra faded commensurately. Though they had given Shelby the money to build 100 427 Cobras to homologate them (a task he failed at in '65), they were hoping he would sell to private teams so they wouldn't have to support a race program for the big block 427 Cobra that would rob dollars from the Ford GT program.

The big block Cobra's future was further endangered when Shelby failed to get enough built by the time the FIA (Federation International d'Automobile) inspector showed up and began counting cars and found Shelby had only finished 52 of them, whereas the inspector needed to count 100 of them lined up for the 427 Cobra to be homologated as a production car. That meant buyers of the ones they had already built would have to run against prototype cars, which were at least 40 mph faster.

Fortunately some sales whiz in the office thought "well, all we have to do is slap some road equipment on these racecars and we can sell them for the street." Thus was born the S/C. Anyhow, records show that the car sat around Shelby's shop for some time (the racecars being difficult to unload because of the homologation problem), until Shelby gave the order for it to be transformed into the so-called "Super Snake"—one of the most crude but also most awesome sports cars ever built.

Oh, not only did it have the fearsome side-oiler FE series 427-cubic-inch V8 (some 427 Cobras had 428 engines which, despite being larger, were less fearsome than the 427 side-oiler), but this one for *Der Snakemeister* had twin Paxton superchargers which allowed it to crank out something like 800 hp. The engine was coupled to a super stout three-speed automatic transmission from a Lincoln.

Why an automatic? Well, it turned out, way back, before WWII, when just a lad, Shelby had been a motorcycle courier and dumped his bike with subsequent injuries to a leg. So even though he went on to become a noted sports car driver (winning the 24 Hours of Le Mans, no less), he decided that, for his own private cars, he would let an automatic transmission do the work. The Ford-brand trans couldn't take the torque of the twin blower 427, hence the Lincoln M6.

To clear the engine, with its twin blowers and twin carburetor covers, a sinister hood scoop was devised. Inside the car there was a separate set of gauges which might have been meant to scare the passenger by seeing just how fast the driver was going. Of course, to Shelby, having been a pilot since before WWII, duplicate instrumentation was normal.

In addition to using it around town as his personal automobile, Shelby was able to field it in the annual run from Los Angeles to Elko, Nevada. Your author, on assignment from *Car & Driver* (for a story never run) infiltrated one of the runs by flying there ahead of them by private plane and showing up at their celebratory dinner in Elko. There, around the table in turn, each participant regaled the group of his adventure along the way. I saw Shelby's group even had a CHP official in uniform at the table, who had been counted on to turn a blind eye as the group collectively nailed their throttles leaving California. In Nevada, at that time, out in the country, there was no speed limit. In the run the author attended, other participant's steeds included a Maserati Bora, a Lamborghini Miura, and other assorted foreign tin. Once they hit that Nevada border, it was pedal-to-the-metal, devil take the hindmost.

On one of the runs, ol' Shel might have gotten a little carried away with the Cobra's 180-mph potential. He blew the engine. He left the car smoking by the side of the road, unstretched his lanky frame from the car, and stood up just in time to flag down another Conquistadore who was driving one of those new-fangled sideways-engine V12 Lambo Miuras. Shelby hopped in and they were off.

Leave a one-off car sitting on the shoulder? Hey, they had business in Elko. After all, to Shelby it was just an old used car.

Of course the car was recovered forthwith and eventually sold to a songwriter who wrote some of the best-selling songs in history. But the songwriter ran afoul of the IRS who, as is their wont, began confiscating what assets they could find.

The author recalls coming across the car years later, hidden in a restorer's shop in Simi Valley North of Los Angeles. The shop owner said the car had been there for 17 years. Well, eventually the Feds glommed onto it and the author remembers the Feds running a full-page ad for the car. It was sold; and years afterwards, was rescued and restored by Harley Cluxton III, a well-known Ford GT40 enthusiast and rare car dealer in Arizona. Cluxton did a full restoration, painting it blue once again (when the author discovered it, it was still black). Cluxton took it to the 36th annual Barrett-Jackson auction in 2007 where it sold for a reported $5.5 million.

But not before graciously offering Shelby, who was then in his '80s, the chance to drive his ultimate Cobra one more time. Alas, though I was on the Barrett-Jackson auction's grounds at the time, I didn't see Shelby arrive, but wonder if the car lived up to Shel's memories. (Shelby told another interviewer the car was fun "when it wasn't catching on fire.")

It was a car builder's tribute to himself, so it must have been a helluva car, equivalent to, say, William Colt making a Colt revolver especially for himself.

Of note, CSX3015 wasn't the only Twin Paxton Shelby built. While he still owned his car, after running into comedian Bill Cosby at a supermarket in Playa del Rey, California, near his condominium, Shelby chided Cosby for preferring Ferraris. Cosby reportedly retorted, "Well, you build a Cobra that will go 200 mph and I'll buy one." So Shelby drove back to his factory at LAX airport and ordered another Super Snake built.

That car, CSX 3303, was only in Bill Cosby's hands briefly. Reportedly, it scared him to death. He even recorded an album entitled "Bill Cosby at 200 mph," making light of the experience.

That car then went to S and C Motors in San Francisco, who sold it to their customer, Tony Maxey. Unfortunately, after being stopped by a cop, Maxey nailed it upon retaking the road, had a stuck throttle and plunged off a cliff into the drink. Results? Fatal. The car was rebuilt by Brian Angliss in the UK, a man who was Shelby's nemesis through his founding of CP Autokraft, a company that made Cobra replicas. (Though one Cobra expert who, for a time had the wreck before it went to the UK, said, "When I had it, it wasn't nothing but a stack of tubing.")

In the UK, the owner of the car at the time also found its original engine, which fortuitously had been sold to the builder of a hot rod in the UK. He had to buy the hot rod to get the engine so that made the rebuild a little bit more genuine—new frame, old chassis i.d. plate, new body and old engine.

Lesson to be learned? Well, during its time in the wilderness, the original first car was out there somewhere; everyone knew it had been built. And a smaller select few knew the songwriter had bought it. Even fewer knew where it was hidden.

If you were a true barn finder, and didn't mind being a rat fink, the deal to be made here was to "drop the dime" on the songwriter, and rat the car's location out to the IRS once of course you locked them into an agreement where you would be positioned to be first in line to buy it. It's a strategy, but that doesn't mean you could have pulled it off—no, the law reads confiscated material has to be offered to the highest bidder amongst the public. If they ran that ad for everybody to read, it would have been, "get in line, Buster."

Chapter 3
Quarterhorses (Mustangs)

Half Bosses/half Shelby.

There is an in-between class of prototype cars. They are based on street cars, not with hand-made from-the-ground-up chassis. These type of test mules have the most chance of surviving the buzzsaw because the automaker might have the philosophy (back in the '60s anyway) of "Hey, this car can be licensed. Let's sell it and that will help us recover some of our expenses." That might be an explanation of how the two cars known as the "Quarterhorses" survived.

Their pedigree is mighty interesting because of the shop that developed them, the legendary but little known operation known as "Kar Kraft," a shop that seemed to exist just to build Ford racecars. Some years earlier the same shop had built a model called the Ford GT Mk. II. The same exact car that, yes sir, won Le Mans in '66. So, in short, they had the ability to build anything, and a Mustang was duck soup.

Why they built the Quarterhorses takes some noodling. Let's speculate a bit and say, by 1969, Ford and Shelby were near a parting of the ways. Shelby was ornery about not being the Number 1 Trans Am team to get funding from Ford (Bud Moore, a NASCAR shop, got the lion's share of the goodies). Then, as if Shelby didn't have enough enemies at Ford, at some point Semon "Bunkie" Knudsen came over from GM and Shelby and Knudsen had previously had a little "tiff" going from back when Shelby had publicly needled Knudsen for supplying racing parts to race team owners running GM cars at a time when GM was telling the public they had quit supporting racing.

The fact is that the two Quarterhorses exist. Ford historian Steve Strange was one of the first to document these little known Mustangs, in his Boss 429 book. When one appeared at the Carlisle All-Ford Nationals in 2005, it was no longer such a mystery car.

The original Quarterhorses used '69-'70 Shelby front end fiberglass and chrome trim but the scoop and vent openings were blocked off. In late 1969, the "Composite Mustang," as it was called at Ford, was among a number of projects being developed by Kar Kraft, who were at that time building the Boss 429 on a small assembly line located in Brighton, Michigan, one where the cars moved by hand from station to station because it took a lot of work to jam such a huge engine into a Mustang.

The Boss 429 was a hot rod Mustang developed by Ford specifically because they wanted to run the 429 engine in NASCAR racing and NASCAR had a rule requiring that so many engines had to be sold before an engine could be considered a production engine. The odd part is that, for NASCAR they weren't even going to run the engine in a Mustang, but were allowed to consider it a production engine as long as they made 1,000. So they looked around at what cars they were building and figured "Those Mustang guys will buy anything" and sent some Mustangs over to Kar Kraft in January 1969 to start production of what became the "Boss 429" Mustang.

It was a ridiculously expensive operation because each car had to have a hand-assembled front engine compartment to accommodate the wider engine. Model year 1969 production ran from January 1969 through July 1969. A total of 859 units were produced. This includes two experimental 1969 Boss Cougars. Production for the second model year, 1970, started in August of 1969 and ran through December 1969. Total units produced were 500.

Total production for the Boss 429 Mustang, including the two 1969 Cougars and two 1970 Quarterhorses, was 1,359 vehicles—enough to qualify the engine for NASCAR. All of the Boss 429-powered vehicles, except for a handful of proto-types and a couple of factory drag cars, were completely assembled & fully dressed with Thermactor pollution equipment, power steering, & exhaust manifolds. To certify that they were production cars, each car had to go through a complete final inspection for equipment verification and certification prior to final shipment. Each vehicle was assigned a KK 429 Nascar production number. These KK numbers started with KK-1201 running through KK-2558. It is difficult to say when production models of the Quarter Horse would have been built if they had been greenlighted—1970 in all probability as the 1968-'69 body style ended with the 1970 model year.

The hood was supposed to be smooth, more like a 1971 Mustang with no scoops or vents (your author feels it lost a lot of Shelby identify when those vents were filled in). The front fenders and grille were lifted directly from Shelby stock. Wheels were Magnum 500s.

According to Steve Strange Boss 429 author and Ford Mustang historian (see www.BossPerformance.com), he believes the concept behind the Composite Mustangs (Quarterhorses) was quite basic; Ford was noodling on finding a replacement car for both the Boss 429 NASCAR Mustang and the Shelby GT-350/500 Mustang. It had to be a car that could be built at KK-Brighton, Ford's secret hi-performance assembly plant, located in Brighton, Michigan. Strange wrote the author, "Both production programs were scheduled to end in early 1970 and Kar-Kraft needed a future project to keep the plant going. Keep in mind, Ford's lucrative racing budget would be cut in half in January of 1970 and soon there would be a real battle going on internally for funding."

Strange described the Quarter Horse prototypes: "KK-2061 0F02Z102383 and 0F02Z104687 (no KK number was ever assigned) rolled off the line at KK-Brighton the first week of September 1969. Prior to that, the cars started life over at DAP (Dearborn Assembly Plant) as Grabber Blue (J) exterior colored Boss Mustangs with TW (semi-deluxe white interiors).

Soon after the cars arrived, Fran Hernandez and Larry Lawrence at KK-Brighton painted the 2nd car Medium Red (CandyApple Red) (T) and did the ornament mock-up work; before actual delivery to Ford Engineer Bill Humpries, for engine performance evaluations."

According to Strange, the Quarterhorses were doomed ponies from the get-go; " Interestingly enough," Strange wrote the author, " about a week later Bunkie Knudsen was fired by Henry Ford II and for all practical purposes, the Boss 429 program was DOA going forward at Ford Motor Co. But no one other than the big-dogs at Ford's glass prison knew that yet."

Despite the dismal prospects, according to Strange the Ford Design Studio, in conjunction with Kar-Kraft, proceeded on developing both Quarterhorses as a potential production project. The name Boss 429 was not part of it though is because, according to Strange, "the Boss 429 hemi engine was really not even being considered to be used going forward. Both Quarter Horse cars were fitted with 429SCJ and 429 Thunder-Jet (wedge) engines. Why? If production was to proceed with a new Composite Mustang, it needed a more reliable, cheaper, production powerplant than the Boss 429 engine. Which was not only expensive to build and install, but had racked up some very expensive warranty claims, (engine replacements) early on in it's field service with customers."

Ford wound up the Boss 429 NASCAR program the first week of January 1970 with the last of the 1970 Boss 429 Mustangs being shipped out on January 6, 1970.

About a month later, the last of the 1970 Shelby GT Mustangs left the barn area at KK-Brighton Assembly Plant for good. With Knudsen and his "private" designer Shinoda having left the building, and no major funding left to build "Special Performance Vehicles"; the future for Kar-Kraft and their secret KK-Brighton Assembly Plant looked bleak!

Both Quarter Horse prototypes somehow made it away from Ford Motor Co. One car was sent to California, to a movie production studio where it appeared in some *Dan August* TV episodes starting Burt Reynolds (who was to become much more identified with the Firebird Trans Am through the *Cannonball* movies). The second car was purchased by a Ford employee and eventually was offered for sale. In 1997 and 1999, both cars were advertised for sale in *Hemmings Motor News*.

One Quarter Horse later went to collector Randy Woods and was on display at the Boss Nationals during the Carlisle All-Ford Nationals in 2005.

The candy apple red Quarter Horse was fitted with a 429 SCJ engine. According to Steve Strange's book, *Boss 429: Performance Mustang Style*, the red Quarter Horse was used for performance tests and evaluations, clocking high 13-second quarter-miles at 103 mph. That car went to Christopher Lemp, who had the car restored by Don Goebel at Goebel's Performance Corner.

But were they found in barns? I dunno. But we heard a rumor that at least one of the two was once advertised for sale on a used car lot near Port Huron, Michigan. The used car salesman didn't know much about the car but when you looked at it, it looked like a Boss 429 with a Shelby front end. The price was only $3,600. Somebody got a deal but, with Ford publicizing the cars so little, who was to know that it was a genuine factory-built prototype and not just another backyard custom?

Fully restored, considering that a 1969 Boss 429 sold at Barrett-Jackson in Orange County in 2012 for $253,000 (with various fees, gavel price being $230,000), this author estimates the present value of a Quarter Horse at over $400,000 especially the one with the Boss 429 i.d. number because that's a Boss 429 plus a prototype engineering car. Lesson to be learned here? O.K., Michigan is a "rust bowl" State, but if it's Michigan and if it's an unusual Detroit automaker-made car you are putting on your target list, there's more of a chance it could be found in Michigan than any other State. Do your research into prototypes and concept cars and you too might be able to find the equivalent.

Chapter 4
The Green Hornet Returns (Shelby)

*They didn't make
Shelby notchbacks in
Sixties...or did they?*

When you are an automaker, before you plunge into producing a new model, you make prototypes. Actually two kinds. One is the rough and ready engineering mule that the public doesn't see. The other is the cosmetic concept car prototype you send to the big auto shows (sort of let's-run-this-flag-up-the-flagpole-and-see-who-salutes type things). More often than not the prototype is shot down as inconsistent with the current offerings, or too costly, or something that would compete against what they're already making. In that case, the prototype is cut up, or sold downriver.

This explains in a nutshell the Shelby Mustang prototype dubbed 'The Green Hornet' (after a comic book and TV show character, on account of its dark green color)—one of a very few factory Shelby prototypes to survive the always waiting crusher. You can see why it might have been shot down. Shelby had already picked the fastback coupe as the body shape for the Shelby coupe. To offer a notchback, in the view of some, would have been edging toward offering a "family" of vehicles (what's next—a station wagon?) Still, as you'll read shortly, there was a run of notchbacks but they weren't quite Shelbys yet fancier than Mustangs, sort of an in-between car.

LIL' RED THE FIRST

This was all done with the approval of Shelby and Ford, but the story actually starts first with a prototype called "Lil' Red." Fred Goodell, a Ford engineer assigned to Shelby, decided to order up a Mustang notchback created with Shelby parts, this car nicknamed "Lil' Red." This was a supercharged 428, C-6 automatic coupe dressed up in bright red paint, and a vinyl roof, intended to be more formal than the fastback Shelby Mustang coupe. It was put on display at a dealer's meeting to gauge market response as a possible Shelby Mustang. One dealer saw it as the bones of a special Mustang he wanted to build—a "California-Only Mustang."

He met with Lee Iaccoca and the decision was made to bring the car to Dearborn to develop into a limited edition Mustang for California dealers. Each one wore the name "California Special," a name it had on the car as well as badging that said GT/CS, which to the Shelby fans wasn't quite as good as saying "Shelby" but who the hell else would "CS" be? (Unless it was also for "California Special" which it said in script on the rear of the car). Other zones—such as Denver—used some elements of the bodywork for special models for their zones but in all cases it was a cosmetics-only package.

In April 1968 Goodell had a second notchback built, at a time when the GT/CS models were already being made. It was called the "EXP-500," and built by Shelby Automotive based on a GT/CS purchased from Ford that was a lime Gold 1968 Mustang hardtop with Deluxe interior and a 390/C6 drivetrain (VIN 8F01S104288).

According to an article on the *Hemmings Daily* website, it went from Ionia, Michigan (where Shelbys were built after the closure of Shelby's LAX airport facility), to Shelby's shop in California where Goodell replaced the stock C6 automatic with a C6 built to GT350 specifications. Also around that time it was temporarily fitted with an independent rear suspension using a Ford 9-inch center section and a cradle bolted into the rear leaf spring mounts. Rear disc brakes and a full Shelby front suspension completed the mechanical models. Goodell must have liked good looking cars because he switched the paint to a darker green and again had a black vinyl top.

It became a test mule, fitted with one engine after another

ending up with a 428. Among the configurations it ran under the hood was a single Paxton blower and later twin Paxtons like Shelby's famous Super Snake Cobra and still another time it ran Conelec fuel injection (this was when the only Detroit car that had offered a production "fuelie" was the Corvette and one obscure model of Pontiac Bonneville). The top speed was around 157 mph at the peak of its development. That was with a 3.0 rear axle ratio. The car also had a C6 automatic from a Lincoln and a Lincoln torque converter.

But Goodell was working in the wrong direction. The California Mustang package was a sales success because it was cosmetic and could be ordered on a car with an ordinary engine, not a high performance engine, thus cost consumers a lot less than a Shelby Mustang. Goodell's proposed mechanical changes on Lil' Red and Green Hornet flat contradicted the main philosophy of the sales guy's which is: "Put the money on the outside where you can see it."

The general trend at Shelby was a gradual watering down of the mechanically souped-up parts and a tarting up cosmetically as a reflection of this philosophy. The California Mustang program was to make cars that were different from other Mustangs but still affordable whereas the Shelby Mustangs of that time were priced as high as Corvettes. The sales guys won. After the GT/CS program, the order went out to destroy the two prototype notchbacks.

A SURVIVOR

"Green Hornet" survived. "Lil' Red" didn't. Writer Jeff Koch in *Hemmings Daily*, a website, says the chain of private owners started with Ford employee Robert Zdanowski, who worked at the Resale lot run by Ford to sell ex-FoMoCo cars. He bought it for a reported $3,000 and used it as a family car. It looked like a family car too, now that it was sans its EFI and IRS. With the heavy 428 in front it was a little light in the rear and spun its tires too much on rainy streets so he sold it to Don Darrow, a Ford dealer in Cheboygan, Michigan.

To their credit, Darrow 's son Randy realized they had something special and, after confirming its identify as a factory prototype with Goodell, they developed their own scratch-built IRS built to Goodell's recommendations and added a Holley ProJection EFI system. According to Koch, Goodell was so interested in seeing the car be reborn in the configuration he ran it in that "he rounded up components of another Conelec EFI system for the Darrows." That's the sign of a true enthusiast!

The car next came to the attention of Steve Davis, president of Barrett-Jackson, before it made its way into the collection of Craig Jackson of the famed Barrett-Jackson auctions around 2006. Mentioned in *Classic & Muscle Mustangs* is the shop of Martin Euler of Midland, Michigan, a man so skilled that he could even restore the various prototype parts except for the fuel injection—which have been on display next to the Green Hornet on a display board on occasion.

The Green Hornet was a feature car of the 2013 Barrett Jackson auction in Scottdale, Arizona, where it failed to sell despite being bid up to an astounding $1.8 million. Lesson to be learned? You wonder how many guys passed this car up before young Darrow recognized its provenance and realized what they saw before them was not just some wannabe Shelby Mustang, but a Shelby prototype that turned out to be worth more than most Shelbys will ever be.

Chapter 5
The Pantera That Never Was (Pantera 7X)

Motor Trend ran a campaign urging readers to write Ford to save the Pantera. Ford was having none of it.

If the U.S.-spec Pantera had lived beyond '74 this would have been it.

This is the story of a car that was supposed to be produced, a car where all the engineering was done, and it only needed a green light from management to make it into the showrooms and then, BAM, it was dropped like a hot potato.

It was called the Pantera 7X, the "X" meaning that no one was quite sure what model year it would be. First a little background. The way the Pantera came about was so convoluted a story, fair warning, you have to stick with us on the curves. Alejandro de Tomaso was an Argentine living in Italy, trying to make it as a race driver when he met Isabella Haskell, a tall blonde who, as they said at the time, "came with money."

They married, raced Maseratis and OSCAs together and, starting in 1959, began building racecars. The first production car was the Ghia-bodied Ford-powered mid-engined Vallelunga, of which 52 were made. Somehow, through his legendary wheeling and dealing (and a pile of his in-laws' money), DeTomaso bought Ghia, a famous name in coachbuilding, and began building a much more aggressive looking V8-powered sports car—the Mangusta—with styling by the incomparable Giorgetto Giugiaro, then a youthful designer who had not yet fully developed the legendary reputation he has today.

Ford Motor Co's chief designer at the time, Eugene Bordinat, was so intrigued with the Mangusta that he bought one. He pushed for Ford to import the car in much the same way as Ford had just a few years earlier backed Texan entrepreneur Carroll Shelby with his Cobra. But after a team of Ford designers went to Italy and saw the uneven quality of the Mangustas being built, Ford changed their mind and told DeTomaso something to the effect of: "If you come up with a car that can be easier to build, let us know."

As it turned out DeTomaso already had a follow-up design to show them, though in the form of a wooden model only 1/5th scale. Giugiaro had left Ghia Carrozzeria before the Ford visit to start his own design firm (Ital Design) and so DeTomaso had assigned an American working in Italy for Ghia, Tom Tjaarda, to design the replacement car. When the Ford people visited, the Ford representatives were afraid to go home and tell their Uber-boss, Henry Ford II, an Italian car fan, that they hadn't come back with a car, so they ordered the follow up car anyhow before the first one was built and tested. The original name for the car was "DeTomaso 351" but it was changed to Pantera.

Ford planned to sell them for only $10,000 which was about $8,000 less than a Ferrari Daytona. True, it couldn't catch the 175-mph Daytona but a Pantera would do at least 145 stock and with a few mods, would reach 165 mph. When the Panteras began to come to America as 1971 models, Ford sold them in Lincoln-Mercury showrooms with the belief that Division had "import experience" (with the Capri). It was a disaster at first as Ford had to recall the first 100 or so cars to repair the suspension but after that, Ford got the car sorted out. Actually, to give credit where credit is due, it was the two Pantera clubs in America who diagnosed most of the car's problems and devised solutions. Eventually the 6,000 or so Panteras sold in the U.S. became renowned for their easy maintenance and reliability, compared to the more expensive exotic cars with exotic engines.

Right from the get-go, Ford had a tough time dealing with the mercurial DeTomaso, whose attention span was measurable in nanoseconds; he was always off on another tangent, so in 1972 they bought him out, and wound down production though the Panteras were offered until the 1974 model year.

DeTomaso, through an escape clause in the contract he had engineered back in 1969, continued to make Panteras seemingly forever and even introduced new improved models like the GT5 and GT5-S, selling them all over the world.

Before Ford burned their bridges with DeTomaso, there was a concept car designed by Tom Tjaarda intended to be the next-generation Pantera. It was called the 7X, the "X" referring to an unknown model year in which it would be introduced. (Also in some reports it's called the Pantera II and in others "the Montella.") Based on a 1973 model, it was shown at various auto shows by Ford throughout 1974, even though Ford, internally, had soured on doing anything more with DeTomaso as early as 1972. The vehicle shared the same chassis and drivetrain from the Pantera, while incorporating a new body with many updates by Tjaarda. The biggest difference was the rear roof, (which used to have blind sail panels) being changed to two flying buttresses. The nose was also changed for a blunter look, probably to cope with upcoming bumper laws.

When first shown, it was a light metallic green. Later it was treated to a two-tone paint job, Pearl White over Metallic Bronze, reportedly at the behest of Ford designer Don De La Rossa who at one time had been President of Ghia and that is when it got the name "Montella."

One report says that DeTomaso showed the vehicle to other manufacturers in hopes of putting it into production—perhaps anticipating the split with Ford, but that report doesn't jive time-wise with the fact Ford had bought out DeTomaso's Pantera operation in '72 and wouldn't have bothered to show the 7X if it was destined for some other automaker's stable. Plus the car was identified with Ford, and not changed enough to fool anybody even if it was sold under another brand name. The one-off car was sold to a sports car dealer in Michigan in 1981.

The big name classic car auctions in Scottsdale and Monterey have a way of attracting these cars out of the woodwork and the 7X appeared at the RM auction in Monterey in 2007, where it was listed with an estimated value of $90,000–$120,000. The vehicle carried no reserve, which proved to be unnecessary as bidding reached $99,000 including buyer's premium. The car was sold, reportedly to an Italian architect who restored it with the first-hand advice of its designer Tom Tjaarda, changing the color to a warm copper which complements the car very well. They had stripped the white paint off the car and found the copper and decided that was the best color for the car.

Lesson learned about THPNNGO6114? First of all, old show cars should be followed, especially when they first leave the limelight. In a way they are like old racecars: when they aren't racing, they're thought of as "in the way" by the automaker. If they are a concept car not scheduled for production, they are usually scheduled for a date with the buzz saw, but, if you do due diligence in your search, you might intercept them before that.

I was bowled over in August 2007 when I saw it in the outer courtyard for sale at the RM Auction in downtown Monterey during "Monterey car week." First I thought it was perhaps a custom copying the 7X and then I realized, hot damn, it was the real thing—a Detroit automaker factory prototype. But nobody took much notice of it. It finally sold for $99,000. More's the pity for whoever put it up on the block as they should have fetched much more. First of all, anyone who had done their homework would realize this was a factory-built prototype, both by DeTomaso, Ghia and Ford so in a way it had the luxury of three pedigrees, not just one. Probably a lot of people going to the auction didn't realize it was a prototype.

Now that it has been repainted a beautiful copper color, it was recognized as a stunning one-off car at the Villa d'Este concours on Lake Como. The Italian owner was lucky—how often does one have to available the original designer of a prototype to advise you on its restoration?

DeTomaso cars, because of their "low-born" cast-iron V8 pushrod engines, for decades have been thought of by the high-end collectors of foreign cars as not worth collecting. Too mass market; too plentiful at over 6,000 imported to the U.S. by Ford. But those purebred snobs made a mistake when they walked right by the 7X at Monterey, as it represents a running, driving easily-maintained one-off car with a great story.

Chapter 6
The Last Cobra?

*Shel's last shot with Ford
(the first time around).*

You could argue that since this was the last prototype by Shelby in the Sixties that it was indeed the "last Cobra."

Only it wasn't called the "Cobra." Here's another case of a factory prototype once available for a song because nobody knew what it was. The sole "in-period" reference (from the Sixties) I could find to it was in a brochure put out by 3M, a company that made the reflective tape put on Shelby Mustangs. It's called the "Lone Star," a name referring to Texas' one time slogan when it tried to go it on its own minus the rest of the United States.

The car came about in the mid-'60s when Carroll Shelby was realizing the front-engined Cobra's days were numbered. He liked the GT40 but Ford's attempts to make that car a street GT40 were proving tough—the ground clearance was too little, the car was too hot, the visibility too poor. When they put the steering wheel on the left, only four LWD versions were sold (that being the Mk. III).

Shelby had Gomm Metal Development over in the UK, working with FAV, build a tub for an all-new mid-engined car and had it clothed with a svelte body that somewhat resembled a P3/4 Ferrari, the Ferrari prototype of 1967 (though considerably fatter).

Power plant was a proven Cobraized 289 connected to a ZF 5DS/25 gearbox, a variation of the 5-speed transaxle on the GT40. It had a removable roof, and bumpers like a road car.

Al Dowd, the one-time General Manager of Shelby-American, told your author that he drove it once and that for him, once was quite enough. "After I slid across the fuel tank in the rocker area I thought who the hell wants to drive a car surrounded by gasoline," he growled.

Ford did not want it. After the Cobra was produced, Ford and Shelby grew distant, finally cutting ties in 1969. Ford may have already been talking to DeTomaso, at first being intrigued with the sexy mid-engined Mangusta.

At any rate, *Motor Trend* reviewed the car, mocking it as if it were on a used car lot, which it wasn't (you know the story angle—200 mph car found on used car lot!). It was found still in the hands of Shelby by a famous Shelby historian and has been undergoing restoration for over a decade. When it's done you can expect considerable hoopla if it appears at vintage races as "the last Cobra."

Is it to be considered the last Cobra? Maybe; though there's another mid-engine racecar that Shelby made at the time that actually raced and thus could also claim that title. Suffice to say, the Lone Star was the last production car prototype developed by Shelby-American during its *original* era. The time to buy this one was when Shelby had cut his ties with Ford and was intent on starting a new adventure on The Dark Continent (see the book *SHELBY The Man, the Cars, The Legend* for more details on that).

Chapter 7

Ford's Own Cobra Coupe (Cougar II)

Yeah, Ford could've gone the Corvette route with fiberglass.

Ford certainly was enthusiastic about the Cobra when they started backing cowpoke (actually chicken farmer) Carroll Shelby in 1962. They immediately began thinking of ways of making the car more of a Corvette competitor, like with roll-up windows, air conditioning, automatic (you know stuff people actually want in American cars). So they designed this body for the Cobra small block.

They called it the "Cougar II" because they had earlier made a gull-winged prototype, the Cougar. The Cougar name was the name first selected for the car that became the Mustang, so it could have been thought of as a two-seater companion for the Cougar four-seater.

Anyway, the car was one of the hits of the '64–'65 New York World's Fair. Its styling was very American/Euro (though the rear fastback window was a little too much Barracuda) with less of the Cobra's sensuous curves. And it was fiberglass, like the Corvette, so could've given the Sting Ray some competition.

You could see Ford's reasoning in re-doing the car. The A.C. Cobra after all was an old design adapted from the A.C. Ace of 1953 which itself copied some hand-built specials which, when ordered custom built, copied the 1949 Ferrari Barchetta. Plus Ford saw Chevrolet had the Sting Ray coupe and wanted a coupe. With this aerodynamic body, the Cougar II could have reached 170 mph where the stock Cobra, with its brick-shaped body, was stuck at about 150-165 mph, depending on its state of tune.

It featured a leaf spring Cobra chassis which had been de-bodied by Ford, Rudge-Borrani wire wheels, and Ford's famous "260" engine, which the first 75 Cobras had before they went to the 289. The headlights, like the Corvette, were hidden, and, because Ford was worried that air coming through open windows would pop out the back window (not a needless worry because this actually happened to the hardtop-equipped A.C. Cobras at Le Mans in '63 practice), they designed in a pressure-relief panel in the rear deck that would open to let air out if it built up substantially at speed.

The original A.C. Cobra was a carryover from the A.C. 2.6 with similar instrumentation, so Ford saw no reason to be loyal to that and re-did the whole interior. The Cougar also had a unique spring-loaded window-lift mechanism that allowed adjustment to the curved side windows. In a press release Ford claimed it was built on Chassis CSX2004, which would mean it's an early car (though the all-important serial number was covered up by the new body so there remain disputes as to its original CSX serial number), which would have been built by A.C. with a 260-cubic-inch V8 originally. After first announcing it had a 260, they later talked about a high-performance 289 Ford engine which they said was moved rearward in the chassis.

Time-wise Ford claimed that this car was designed before the Corvette Stingray but this is balderdash because Pete Brock, while a design intern at GM in '57 built a clay model car (the Q-Corvette) that presaged the '63 Corvette coupe. So Chevy gets the nod for doing an American fastback design first though not putting it in production until late '62 as a '63 model. In another press release, Ford said the car was built at Dearborn Steel Tubing (DST Industries), a firm famous for making Ford prototypes, and then the fiberglass body was laid on according to the Shelby American Automobile Club's 2008 World Registry. The Cougar II was assigned a new chassis number, XDCO315091, "XD" presumably meaning "Experimental Design."

The car was donated to the Detroit Historical Museum when its time as a show car was over, and forgotten for many years until 2004 when Jeff Burgy, a stalwart of the Shelby-American Automobile Club and a former Ford employee, found that the Museum still had both that car and the XD Cobra, another Cobra-based car, a convertible with lift-off hardtop. He arranged to borrow them both for a car club convention being held in Michigan and spent many hours before the convention detailing them; not easy for cars that had gathered dust for decades.

Is it for sale? Ah, how crass you are; can you not admire art for just *being*? Well the answer to that would depend on the Museum; its finances and its future in a town that is half the size population-wise as it was in 1963 when this car was built. Lesson learned? Some 'lost' cars don't go very far from their makers and can be found. Whether or not you can buy them is another question…as yet unanswered in the case of these two.

The first objective of the barn-finder is to find the car (see last chapter for strategies on how to do that). And now the big question: is this car, were it purchased, more valuable with a 1962 Cobra body, or as the Cougar II? As of this writing, small block Cobras are "only" $600,000 and change. You will have to stay tuned to the auctions and the price of 260 Cobras for the answer to that question.

Chapter 8
Buried Treasure: a Sebring Winner (GT40 Spyder)

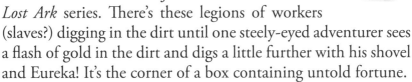

Yes, it's out there for the taking...but we can't say in what condition.

It's the beginning of at least one of the *Raiders of the Lost Ark* series. There's these legions of workers (slaves?) digging in the dirt until one steely-eyed adventurer sees a flash of gold in the dirt and digs a little further with his shovel and Eureka! It's the corner of a box containing untold fortune.

Well, there's a Ford GT like that, buried somewhere. Who's to say what condition it's in? Oh, did I mention it's a Sebring winner?

Here's the story, in brief. Ford built four GT40 roadsters, five if you want to count this big block, GT110. It is GT110 that this story is about, the one and only big block open top GT40 Spyder/targa.

Ford employed New Zealand racing hero Bruce McLaren as a test driver on the GT40 in 1964. McLaren wanted to race in the series that became Can Am. Ford wanted to see the feasibility of the GT40 chassis as a Can Am car and McLaren had been in on the GT40 program since '64 so was given the budget.

So they ordered from Abbey Panels, their British supplier of chassis to Ford Advanced Vehicles (FAV) in England, a chassis just like the steel chassis for GT40s but made out of aluminum. Originally, according to an expert who interviewed Eric Broadley at length, Broadley wanted to make all the hulls for the GT40 of aluminum instead of steel, but had been over-ruled, part of his decision to leave FAV and set up his own Lola shop again. Not only did he set it up again, but more than coincidentally right down the street (and even taking a few employees with him). Ironically the Lola T-70 that followed had all his ideas, including an alloy tub, but was far less successful than the Ford GT40s collectively.

When the two aluminum-bodied hulls from Abbey Panels arrived at FAV, one of them became the ill-fated Can Am X-1 for McLaren to run in what became the Can Am races where most of the cars had American-made V8 engines of unlimited horsepower. In Can-Am, it was run as a targa, with a roll over hoop. It had a wraparound racing windscreen that was only a few inches high instead of a full height glass windscreen like the four small block GT40s. It had the "long nose" tried earlier in testing at Le Mans and also used on the 1965 427 Le Mans Ford GT.

The engine was a 427 side-oiler and one picture this author has seen shows sidedraft Weber carbs. It was singularly unsuccessful in USRRC racing (that class became Can Am racing) with at least three races and no finishes. The problem was that the car was still, even being aluminum-hulled, too heavy compared to the aluminum-hulled purpose-built Can Am cars of their competition. And even with a big hulking 427 it did not have enough power. The Chaparrals had aluminum block big blocks and were tuned to produce almost 1,000 horsepower.

So, was that all she wrote? Not quite. Ford still believed in the aluminum-hulled big block chassis. This was contrary to what was happening at FAV where two steel hulls were finished out as big block Mk. II (though they weren't called Mk. II yet) for the 1965 Le Mans 24 hour. They both didn't finish though Phil Hill amply demonstrated they were faster than anything there and could top 210 mph down the Mulsanne straight.

After the failure of the big blocks the first year Ford put a lot of work into development and by 1966 had steel-hulled Mk. II 427-powered coupe versions of the GT40 that could win Le Mans, and they did so, in June 1966; but even before that, in February 1966 the supporters of the aluminum-hulled school got a boost when the old X-1 roadster was brought in-house at Shelby, fitted out to Mk. II specs, and rebodied with a standard GT40 MK.II nose and tail, and a full height glass windscreen. It was painted red (that last move maybe just to irk Ferrari).

Sebring that year was much anticipated. That was because, the year before, race organizer Alex Ulmann had allowed Chaparral to enter even though their car didn't fit the rules of any existing class. And the damn Chevy-powered Chaparral won! Ulmann was allowing them to enter again in '66. It was expected Ford would put up a better fight than in '65; but Alec Ulmann was worried that Ferrari would boycott the race in '66, and, without the red cars from Maranello, in his opinion, the race wouldn't be worth watching. (In 1965 Ulmann's decision to allow the light-weight Chaparrals to enter had also ticked off Enzo Ferrari, who was planning on boycotting Sebring by not sending factory entries.)

He knew Ford would be there. Henry Ford II had opened the spigots in Dearborn and the cash was flowing in all directions to build Ford GT40s. Everyone knew Ford would be at Le Mans in June but Sebring would be an opportunity for them to test what they would run at Le Mans in June.

Ford had already shown what they had at the Daytona 24-Hour Continental in February of 1966, where Fords came in 1st, 2nd, 3rd. Enzo was already yelling that all European automakers would be crushed by what he called the "American steamroller." The *Commendatore* (Ferrari's title, awarded by Mussolini) was good at shedding crocodile tears, even when his cars were every bit the match of what Ford was building.

Reportedly, hat in hand, Ulmann traveled to Maranello, to beg Ferrari to enter some cars at Sebring. In the end only one of the new factory 4-liter 330 P3s arrived to be on the grid on race day with their back-up being a private team's car, the North American Racing Team (NART) 365 P2/3. Not much to battle several 427-cubic-inch Ford GTs. Not that the Ferrari prototype was anything to sneeze at, the 330P3 engine cranked out 420 horsepower and was lighter than the big block Fords.

Ironically, one of the Ferrari drivers was ex-Shelby team member Bob Bondurant.

Ford fielded three 475-horsepower, 7-liter 427 GT40 Mark II coupes, plus the star of this story, the 427 GT40 Mark II "X-1" roadster in its new short nose body style (but still an open car), plus a couple of small block 289 GT40s entered as prototypes and seven more GT40s entered in the production car Sports 5000 category. And as back-up carrying the Ford badge, three Cobras. In all, 18 of the 64 cars that made it to the start line were Fords.

One drama of the race right at the start was that Dan Gurney's blue GT40 wouldn't start. Vapor-lock. Once he got it running, he drove like a cat on fire, passing 27 cars on the first lap alone. He was running so strong that he set a new race-day lap record of 2 minutes, 54.8 seconds with a speed of 107.09 mph, even passing teammate Ken Miles who was at the wheel of the #1 Shelby Ford X-1 roadster. That flipped out Shelby who did not like his team members in different cars racing each other. He waved a knock-off hammer at them, implying he would hit them if they kept that up.

Tragedy happened when the privately entered Comstock GT40 from Canada crashed, killing driver Bob McLean. Ferrari's biggest chance to win the race ran out around lap 172, when the P3 car piloted by Bob Bondurant didn't come around any more and Bondurant was seen arriving at the pits by motorcycle. His gearbox had packed up when he was running second. That put the pressure on Mario Andretti and Pedro Rodriguez driving the #26 NART Ferrari 365 P2/3. But, at that point they were eight laps behind. And their car was a tired old nag that had 25,000 miles on its clock.

With less than two hours left in the race, that Ferrari was rolled into the pits for Andretti to take over. He went out on the track but on the 200th lap came in with front damage, so bad that he had lost the headlamps. He had been running third at 140 mph when the gearshift gate broke and he hit first instead of third, causing the car to spin off into a sandbank. He had to drive back to the pits with no lights at night! So what happens when he comes at the pits? A flash fire starts, causing severe damage to the wiring. The car is trailered off and Andretti leaves for the airport where he has a plane waiting to go to Pennsylvania.

Later it came out that Andretti had hit a Porsche that had gone off the track, that car killing four spectators in a forbidden area. Andretti was later accused of fleeing the scene. Andretti had left for the airport believing he had only hit a sandbank.

Back to the race, it was then thought that the #2 Ford GT40 Mk. II of Dan Gurney and Jerry Grant were now a shoe-in because Ken Miles was running a full lap behind in the #1 Shelby Ford GT40 X-1; but then you have the perverse phenomenon of "Gurney Luck" where on occasion the barefoot boy with cheek takes a winning hand and turns it into a losing hand. Gurney still had another five miles to go and he runs out of gas. He starts to push the car by hand. Only to have the Ford Mk. X-1 roadster blast by with Ken Miles at the wheel to take the checkered flag. There was momentary confusion. Dan had been leading? Would he be forced to accept second place? Worse. For pushing, he was unceremoniously disqualified.

Shelby, however, was happy. The X-1, with Ken Miles and Lloyd Ruby sharing driving tasks, won. Would the car now receive a "victory tour" being taken to Ford HQ and put on display, race dirt and all? No.

Shelby's racing chief back then, Carroll Smith, confided to me years later at an interview at his house in Palos Verdes that he "couldn't wait to get the car off the track because it was falling apart and needed to be destroyed before someone was hurt." You could see his point. On many Can Am cars of that era, the aluminum sheeting they are made of can't take the load from harder steel bolts and after a single racing season the holes become so elongated it is not uncommon to "re-tub" a monocoque racing car tub (make it all over again for the next racing season).

Smith got his wish but not until three or four years later. The car was probably stored at Shelby's Gardena facility because Shelby had lost his lease in 1967 on the Shelby-American factory, which had been housed in a leased airplane hangar. According to those who knew Steele Therkelson, the New Zealand-born mechanic who wrenched on the car, the car was stripped of its engine, its transmission, and its body, then unceremoniously cut into four pieces to discourage anyone from retrieving and re-building it. It was then taken to a landfill, shoved in and dirt put atop it. Why was it destroyed? Presumably because it was unsafe according to Smith, but in reality, if Ford didn't destroy it they would have had to pay customs-duty, which would have amounted to (today) what would probably equal the cost of one wheel for the car.

The mystery deepens when you ask what happened to the second X-1 chassis, GT110A. Ronnie Spain, the historian, says it was never used. It was reported still around as a bare chassis in the mid '80s in the USA. Why would there be two with the same number? Ah, let's go back to the reason the car was created in the first place—for Bruce McLaren to experiment. Ford probably thought if he mades a major goof-up in building the first one and had to start over, he could save time by working instead on the spare chassis. Also when you are building test cars, there's the chance of a crash (McLaren was in fact later killed testing one of his own cars). One expert in GT40s says the second chassis, though accounted for in Ford records as 110A, was never numbered. Still another rumor is that the second chassis never went to Shelby—that it went to Holman & Moody instead, they being Ford's east coast racecar building operation.

So this is a story without an ending. Either someone finds the exact corner where the car is buried and uses the right metal-detecting gear that can spot aluminum, or someone finds the spare chassis and builds it out as the X-1 reborn. That second chassis might be accepted into vintage racing and might not (it's still, after all, a GT40 tub accounted for being ordered in the original FAV records). Am I launching a wild goose chase? Not at all, several other cars from the same era disappeared into the sands of time and were found.

Hey, I never said it would be easy.

Chapter 9
Super Snake (Shelby '67 GT500)

The ultimate Sixties Shelby, lost, then found.

The 1967 Shelby represented a new body style for the Shelby Mustang. And the availability of a new engine, the hulking 428-cubic-inch V8. This was the first year of the Shelby Mustang that had a big block and a small block, like the Corvette and the Cobra did.

You'll note the unusual striping scheme. Now this was purposeful and from the factory to set it apart from all of its brethren because this one was for The Boss, the Head Snakemeister, Carroll Shelby himself.

He of course deserved to have the fastest Shelby Mustang but it wasn't for his own vanity or even for promotion—the biggest reason the car was built was to test tires and the stock GT500 just wasn't fast enough to really put the load on the tires.

Here's how the car came to be: it turns out that Shelby, besides building Shelby Mustangs and Cobras and running a GT40 team for Ford at Le Mans, was also a distributor of Goodyear racing tires on the West Coast. In fact, that gig paid the bills when he was first developing the Cobra back in 1961.

In February 1967, Goodyear asked Shelby to star in a short promotional film they planned to make to show the durability of the new Thunderbolt tires. Now these were not, mind you, racing tires but regular road tires—they wanted to show what punishment the tires could take. The plan was for a Thunderbolt-shod Shelby to be driven 500 miles at high speed on the Goodyear Proving Grounds' five-mile track north of San Angelo, Texas.

Don McCain, a former Shelby General Manager at who had gone to run a dealership, encouraged Shelby to build a more muscular Shelby for this test, one that could outrun any Ferrari or Corvette available in the showroom at the time. McCain thought if the car got a lot of publicity, they could tool up to make a run of 50 of these real hot-dog big block Shelbys.

McCain had been at Shelby during the years Shelby was making waves, 1964-'66, the glory era for Cobras and Shelby Mustangs.

McCain told reporter and Mustang historian Brad Bowling: "I was picking up a Shelby for Burns [a dealer in Long Beach] when I ran into Carroll. He told me he was going to do the tire test in a regular GT500. At Dana [a performance Chevrolet dealership], we stuffed a Chevy 427 into the new Camaro; I told Carroll he needed to put a 427 race engine in his car for the test, then let me sell the car and build 50 more just like it. It would have to retail for nearly $8,000 to make any money, but it would be one of the fastest cars in the world."

Shelby, who always liked to indulge in a little one-upsmanship (for instance he had ordered up for himself a 427 Cobra with twin superchargers), accordingly went back and talked to Fred Goodell, the Ford engineer assigned to Shelby-American, and Goodell fitted a standard Shelby GT500 (SN ends in 544) with a GT40 Mk II competition engine, utilizing a lightweight 427-cubic-inch side-oiler, medium-riser V8 with aluminum heads, an aluminum water pump, solid lifters, a single Holley 780 cfm four-barrel carburetor, and a handmade exhaust which could be called "bundle of snakes" (though the area they were deployed was not enough to tune to individual length like they had been on the GT40 big blocks). Horsepower rating for the engine was 600.

The stock Toploader four-speed transmission was considered adequate to the task at hand but the rear end was changed to a 2.73:1 ratio which would give it a much higher top end.

There was some worry about durability so an external oil cooler was added, with braided metal lines.

A minor cosmetic touch to chrome the inboard headlight surrounds, which made this GT500 look like no other Shelby.

The testing was done in Texas. For the actual event the wheels were Shelby 10-spoke aluminum rims measuring 15x7 inches, shod with 7.75-15 Goodyear Thunderbolt four-ply tires, actually much narrower than the stock tires on the GT500.

An old racer's trick (used at Bonneville salt flats runs) is to put nitrogen in the tires to minimize tire heat build up and the tires were overfilled with this gas beyond recommended pressures to keep the sidewalls stiff. Shocks and springs were changed only on the passenger side because for the direction the car would be going, the weight transfer would occur on that side.

Shelby turned up, helmet in hand, and was filmed running a few laps, clocking 175-mph top speeds. He also took a few media members for a ride they would never forget.

For the actual test runs that would be recorded, though, an anonymous driver did the drudge work.

Stopping each 100 miles so the heat and wear could be recorded, the car averaged 142 miles per hour over four hours and Goodyear was able to report that the Thunderbolts still had 97 percent of their original tread at the end of those four hours.

Mission accomplished.

The second part of the plan, selling the car for a premium amount, fell through. McCain was by then with Mel Burns Ford in Long Beach. He thought that Shelby fans would clamor for this one-off car, but even though he gave it prime showroom space, it was no dice. It was just too expensive at $7,000, more than the 427 Cobra.

So it was sent back to Texas, to Dallas where two pilots went together on it as an investment, paying a mere $5,000.

The first thing the pilots, James Hadden and James Gorman (who flew for Braniff), did was to install a set of 4.10:1 gears in the back so they could get a lot of oomph off the line.

They did some drag racing but eventually sold it and other owners are lost in the sands of time until 1970 when Bobby Pierce, another Texan, purchased the GT500. Pierce kept the car for an incredible quarter century before selling it to a Florida man, David Loedenberg, who kept it seven years before passing it on to Charles Lillard of California. Now, just how many of those owners realized that it was a one-off factory-prepared car I don't know but you have to reckon that this was before the Shelby clubs sprung up, before books had been written about Shelby Mustangs (the first one besides Sheby's own book was *Shelby's Wildlife,* by yours truly, which first came out in 1977).

Around 2008, the first really qualified owner (in terms of returning it to its original glory) came along—Richard Ellis of Illinois. He bought the car with the intent of restoring it. Amazingly, even though it had been through all those owners, it still only had 26,000 miles on the clock.

According to Ellis, "the car wasn't a barn find as far as no one who owned it not being aware of its historical significance." In other words, it sold each time for what you would call 'full market price.' But what still makes it a 'barn find' in this writer's mind is that, in the span of Shelby history, that was a big block Shelby that stands out, and if it was properly documented and restored, it could be an auction superstar. Think Marilyn Monroe when she was on the production line at an aircraft factory during WWII, a brunette at the time. Then after the war, she went bottle blonde, someone took a picture and she was on a path to glory.

Ellis's approach reminds this author of the pains taken for authenticity by National Corvette Restoration Society members. I mean details-details-details, like having the correct wires and hoses under the hood or even a correct era Rotunda brand fire extinguisher.

And of course he didn't want reproduction wheels, no, he wanted a new old-stock set of Shelby 10-spoke wheels, but the really amazing thing was that he found four brand-new Thunderbolt whitewall tires in the proper size. Usually only old racing tires are saved, but these were tires for economy-minded folks so it was a real find to discover a set (in tire country, Akron,

Ohio!). That explains why, when you see the car, it has such skinny tires (whitewalls at that).

The car was scheduled for the Mecum auction in May 2013. Now, you take most folks, they show up with a car and hope for the best, but not Richard Ellis. It wasn't enough that it was the only fully documented 427 side oiler equipped '67 big blocks out of 2,048 cars. Ellis was taking no chances auction goers would divine its specialness. No, instead Ellis mounted a full-fledged educational campaign on the car, starting up to a year beforehand. He built a trailer to haul the car around, a trailer with see-through plexiglass windows. He visited various Mecum auctions, parking the car right on the auction grounds, and setting up a display of the special parts on the car, as well as having a laptop play a continuous loop video showing Shel himself flogging the car during its famous test for Goodyear. He printed a little book on the car with some period pictures and made that available to prospects. His efforts were rewarded…

The car finally rolled up on the block at the Mecum Spring Classic auction in May 2013 and the auctioneer hammered down "SOLD" on a top bid of 1.3 million dollars!

Lesson learned: if you see a vintage car where the equipment seems unoriginal, don't immediately dismiss the car as some guy's backyard custom. Even if it was never shown at an auto show by its maker, it could still be a factory car created for a special purpose like the "Super Snake" (a name Shelby reached back and adopted for a Mustang in the year 2012 as well).

Chapter 10
"Pick one and it's yours." (GT40 Roadster)

You ask, you sometimes get.

Here's another one of those million-to-one shots.

It's the 1960s. You're walking through a warehouse at Ford Motor Company with some dude, let's say a very heavyweight dude at that—a racer with muscles like coiled steel who won, oh say, a little race called Le Mans? Not to mention Indy.

This dude knows that Ford has a lot of racecars in storage and is taking you on a tour. As he enters one warehouse, he says, with a grandiose sweep of his arm, something to the effect of, "Take your choice. If you can get it in a movie, you can have one." In this case the dude talking was Anthony Joseph Foyt, winner, with Dan Gurney, of Le Mans in 1967 plus an Indy winner in '61. And that was only the first time he won Indy.

The guy listening to Foyt was customizer Dean Jeffries, creator of the Monkeymobile and numerous other movie cars. Jeffries was also a stunt driver (broke his back twice in just one movie) so if you were an automaker who gave him a car, it was pretty certain you'd gain back your monetary loss with publicity. Jeffries called Foyt's bluff and pointed a car out—a small block GT40 roadster. Now the key word here is ROADSTER. Most of the GT40s built were coupes. The roadsters were built only because Ferrari had open cars like the 250P, so Ford initially thought, if we're going to imitate Ferrari on mid-engined cars, we need roadsters too.

However, when you're talking a 24-hour race, roadsters have one big disadvantage: when it rains it pours, filling your car with water (even the GT40 coupes leaked). Besides raindrops hitting you at 200 mph, open cars lack rigidity. The design of the GT40 suspension had been based on a very rigid chassis, which the roadster lacked, so one thing you didn't want in a racecar chassis was a flexi-flyer. Such a car wouldn't hold the line through a corner consistently like a closed roof coupe. The real racecar drivers I've met always like closed cars because of increased rigidity.

Ford Advanced Vehicles Ltd (FAV) only made four small block roadsters themselves: numbers GT108 109, 111, and 112. Sharp-eyed readers will notice one missing number from this sequence—GT110—which is better known as GT40 'X-1.' (That car has its own chapter.)

The small block roadsters had an indifferent racing career. In fact, Jeffries' car—GT109—had a racing career consisting of only one race; but when that one race is the 24 Hours of Le Mans, that is indeed a heavy name to drop.

The car's history in a nutshell: Ford's 1965 GT40 Roadster, Prototype chassis GT109 (Twelve 'Ford GT' prototypes were initially made, numbers GT101 through GT112) was delivered from Abbey Panels of Coventry in October 1964 to Ford Advanced Vehicles in Slough, England, near Heathrow Airport.

FAV was originally headed up by Eric Broadley of Lola Cars Ltd. Roy Lunn was then brought in to FAV by Ford USA as the "Politician," as Broadley fondly recalls (through gritted teeth). By this time Ford had failed miserably, falling flat on their collective face with the Ford GT40 program trying to run it without Shelby so they started shipping GT40s to Shelby with the idea that he would run the GT40 program in 1965. GT109 arrived in March 1965 at the Shelby-American plant on West Imperial Highway in Los Angeles. It was tested and made ready for a race. Well, not just any race, but The Big One—The 24 Hours of Le Mans.

GT109 was shipped to France for Le Mans in June 1965. It was entered by Ford of France SA with two French drivers, Trintignant/Ligier. (Shelby liked to have at least one of his team be French at Le Mans, that way if the scrutinizers tried to kick out one of his other identical cars with American or British drivers, the French might have to then take out a French team with the same car; it was in effect buying protection of a sort.)

By 1965, Ford had abandoned running the alloy block push-rod 255-cubic-inch "Indy" engine they had started out with in '64 because of its unreliability. For '65 the small block engine was an iron block pushrod 289 per Shelby racing Cobra specs coupled to a 5-speed ZF transmission and the wheels were Hali-brand mags (though the roadsters have also been photographed running more fragile wire wheels). The future Jeffries roadster retired in only the second hour after 11 laps. The driver at the time was Maurice Trintignant, but the poor second driver, Guy Ligier, didn't even get his chance at the wheel before the car retired. Enter its savior.

OFF TO THE MOVIES?

Then it was off to the movies with Jeffries, right? Well, not immediately. (In fact, not even by 2013, many decades later.) First the car sat around Shelby's LAX plant until Shelby had to close the airport plant (the airport made noises about their not being enough aircraft activity at his shop to warrant him using an airport hanger, thence the move). The car went back to Ford in Dearborn where Foyt and Jeffries saw it and Foyt "gifted" the car.

Another source says Jacques Passino, the high Ford executive eventually put in charge of racing, gifted the car. It matters not so much in this case as to who gave the car away, but who was asking. Jeffries was "bankable" in terms of getting cars publicity, and the car wasn't doing Ford any good sitting in a warehouse. To an automaker, last year's racecars are oh-so-last-year. The irony is that just a mile or two away was the world class Henry Ford Museum at Greenfield Village. You would think a Ford racecar would be welcome there, but no, Ford had a lot more racecars than the museum had room; plus they were already displaying the Mk. IV that won Le Mans.

Back to Jeffries....You would think a guy who makes cars for movies under extreme deadlines could get that car done in a hurry, right?

Well, problem was Jeffries had a fumble-fingered employee who broke the windscreen. Problem? There weren't any replacements. The author remembers talking to Jeffries some 25 years later and he still hadn't found a replacement.

Problem no. 2: Jeffries, while involved with Indy racing, had been given a few Indy four-cam alloy block dry sump engines, most likely by Foyt. Ford had originally thought of putting this engine into a GT40 but then backed off when they had trouble with a 255-cubic-inch dry sump overhead valve version in the '64 GT40 (for those of you who doubt that there was a pushrod Indy engine, read Hans Tanner's book *The Racing Fords*, which documents the engine's evolution from pushrod to overhead cam). The Indy engine just couldn't take 24 hours of hammering. A three-hour race at Indy in a single-seater, though, was duck soup by comparison. Not that it was a bad engine. The 255 "Indy" engine "owned" the Indy 500 during the same period the GT40 "owned" Le Mans and went on winning at Indy up until 1975 with no backing from Ford, who had walked away from the program, leaving the championing of the engine to A.J Foyt.

So Jeffries, being of a similar mindset to Carroll Shelby (i.e. mule-headed as they come), decided he'd show those damn engineers in Dearborn what they should have done in the heyday of the GT40. He developed the engine even more for GT racing and dropped a four-cam version, one of three he owned as left-overs from working with Foyt on Indy cars. Putting that engine into the GT40 took considerable fabrication, like adding a dry sump lubrication system and that process stretched out another couple of decades.

Periodically, as I would drive down the Hollywood freeway and see his shop, I'd drop by. In tiny increments, the roadster was looking good. In fact, Jeffries had finally got a windscreen made, and redone the body, but then decided he had done the body all wrong and took it off and did a new body. The original body from the 1965 Le Mans race had come with the car by the way, as had the original 289 motor and crates of spare parts.

Has the car been completed? Well, Jeffries was never quite satisfied but at least it was finished enough to be loaned back to Ford for the 100th Year celebration of Ford Motor Co. in 2004 where it was shown next to the 'new Ford GT ('05-'06 model).

Now, for you profit-minded barn finders, is it for sale? Jeffries was thinking about retirement—selling it would be a nice retirement bonus. In a March 2006 *Motor Trend* article he told the editors he wanted $4 million for it. Not much of a stretch by 2012 when a Gulf-liveried GT40 went for over $11 million at Monterey and that was a coupe. It seems like a fair price when you consider that there were only five roadsters built and this one has a Le Mans history. Oh, and be sure to get the original Hi-Po 289 engine when you buy it.

Sadly, Jeffries never got to see that sale—he died in May 2013, his barn find still in his shop. And so we are at one story's ending and another story's beginning...Who will be it's next owner?

But the real lesson to be learned is one extremely basic. Just like the guy who was given the Two Rotor Corvette, if you don't ask, you don't get. Of course, *when* you ask, it always helps if you're hangin' with heavyweights like A.J. Foyt.

Chapter 11
"Destroyed in the Targa." (GT40 Roadster)

Yeah, and if you believe that I got a bridge in Brooklyn...

This is yet another story of magazine and book authors getting it wrong. And some lucky bloke getting it right.

I speak of the GT40 roadster, one of four small block roadsters made, a car that was listed as "destroyed" after the Targa Florio of 1965. When Ford started on the GT40 program they set up their own factory in England, FAV (Ford Advanced Vehicles) though they used Lola GT Mk. 6s at first to check components as they were developed.

GT/101, the first prototype, was assembled in March 1964, just in time for testing and the imminent Ford-Ferrari battle at Le Mans in June. But Ford did terrible with the GT, with ten starts and not even a finish, let alone a win. In 1965, they rethought the program and put it all under Carroll Shelby. He delivered a win at Daytona with Ken Miles and Lloyd Ruby in a GT40 coupe, GT/103, and a 2nd place at Sebring with Ken Miles and Bruce McLaren in the same car.

Four cars were sent to Le Mans for practice on April 10th and 11th, 1965. GT/103 and GT/104 came from Sebring, while GT/105 and GT/111, the car in this chapter, came from the factory, FAV, in England. GT/105 was the surviving 1964 test car, while GT/111 was a brand new roadster, the 11th of 12 pre-production GT40s. Two other roadsters had been sent to Shelby in America. By now, all four cars had iron block 289-cubic-inch Cobra tuned engines, and the two FAV cars had the first ZF five-speed gearboxes, intended to cure one of the GT40's worrisome weaknesses, the Colotti Italian-made gearbox being inadequate to the task.

Led by Surtees again, Ferrari set the top five times, but Attwood in FAV coupé GT/105 was 6th and Bondurant in GT/104 was 7th. Sir John Whitmore drove both the FAV cars but found GT/105 to be five seconds faster than the roadster. Shelby therefore elected to take GT/103 and GT104 to Monza in Italy for the 1,000 kilometer race, while John Wyer, head of Ford Advanced Vehicles, tasked Sir John Whitmore and Bob Bondurant to take the new roadster GT/111 to the Targa Florio, thinking the open cockpit would be just right for the steaming hot race run in Sicily.

The Targa Florio at that time took place over 10 laps on the island's 44-mile Little Madonie road circuit, which is mostly a series of tight, interconnected turns. The weather was daunting enough but the surface was hard as marble with a lot of loose gravel on top of that. In the race, GT/111, painted Linden Green, ran well at first, reaching as high as 3rd place, despite only firing on seven cylinders, but on the fifth lap Sir John lost a front wheel and parked the car. He set off on foot, found the wheel but some souvenir hunter had run off with the knock-off hub and he had to get a *carabineri* to lean on the hunter to give it back. When he got back to the pits, Bondurant took the wheel and was running strong until he hit aforesaid loose gravel and nailed a solid stone kilo marker, tearing off the front wheel that Whitmore had lost earlier. The car ended up on its side. Bondurant went to a nearby bar and was sitting there downing a *grappa* when Carroll Smith, the crew chief, showed up and together they walked back and looked at it and decided it couldn't be repaired in the pits.

GT/111 was shipped back to England, but the idea of making any more roadsters was killed off as production proceeded on coupes. So the car became a parts source for other cars. Finally the chassis, sans body, engine and gearbox, was sent to a nearby "breakers yard" (junkyard in the U.S.).

The story then proceeds several decades to England, to a vintage racing event called the Goodwood Revival, where mechanics from GT40 experts Gelscoe Motorsport Limited were working on a GT40 in the paddock when a passerby watching them piped up, "I've got a GT40."

Their ears pricked up but odds were it was a replica. They pricked up even more though when the bloke said: "Ours is in need of restoration. We've had it for years…this car's for sale, if you're interested."

Later, the Gelscoe reps went to see the car in a locked garage in Stratford in East London and found what was left of GT/111 resting on an old mattress. Only if you were a GT40 expert would you recognize it. The windshield had been cut away; but when they saw that all the support ribs in the pontoons were perforated steel, which was only on the 12 prototypes, they knew it was an early car. They bought it on the spot. At that point the seller produced the chassis plate GT/111, and they knew they had a winner.

They subsequently found a buyer for the car who was not daunted by the fact that it would require a major restoration. The new owner called in Ronnie Spain (a Scotsman who tracks the world's GT40s and publishes the results in a Register) and the owner agreed to buy it if Gelscoe would do the restoration. Spain actually took days to examine the car and issued a three-page report in December 2006 that absolutely pegged the car as the Targa Florio car.

Rather than be embarrassed that he himself had earlier listed this car as "destroyed" in one of his first GT40 registers, he was quoted this time as saying he was happy that "after all this time, one of the missing GT40 chassis has finally come out of the woodwork and can now be restored and join its many siblings on the historic racing circuit, where it belongs and I am grateful for having had the opportunity to examine it and being able to verify its authenticity as GT/111."

The amazing thing is that the car was restored in time for the 2007 Goodwood Revival, which was a mere nine months away. Though they could have cheated a bit by putting on roller rockers (which even Shelby snuck on Cobras from time to time) they did it right with non-roller rockers, and got a correct zero-series ZF transaxle with exposed linkage. Even the frame was painted as per original correct "Raven Blue" color and the seats covered with parachute material seats, unlike the production cars which had black upholstery.

The car was painted in the original Linden Green color it wore in the 1965 Targa Florio Race.

Of course the car had minor teething troubles as a newly refurbished car but these were solved and the car ran the Spa 6 Hour race in 2007 and 2008 and the Le Mans Classic in 2008. It also won a 3rd at the 2009 Goodwood Whitsun Trophy, a 4th in the 2009 Spa 6 Hour race and 2nd in class at the 2010 Masters Festival at Brands Hatch.

In 2011 the car rolled across the block at the auction at the prestigious Villa d'Este where it fetched a high bid of 2,100,100 euros (well over $1 million) but did not reach the seller's reserve.

Lesson to be learned? Any true believer wouldn't have been discouraged by that listing of the car being "destroyed."

How that first bloke found it hasn't been revealed to this author. Either he mounted an organized search, in concentric circles starting with the nearest junkyards near the FAV factory or he had a tip from a former race mechanic where the car might be.

Either way, he didn't believe that word "destroyed" and thus recorded one of history's all-time great barn finds.

Chapter 12
"Say, would you be interested in a GT40?"
(GT40 Mk Le Mans Winner)

Oh, and did I mention it won Le Mans?

One of the best barn-finding stories ever, bar none, concerns a Blue Mounds, Wisconsin, gentleman by the name of George Stauffer, who once collected Rolls Royces. But, as often happens with car collectors, at some point his taste moved on, in this case from Rolls Royces to Cobras and all things Shelby. Well, it turns out that one day back in the early 1980s, a chap shows up who hadn't got the word and he says something to the effect of "I heard you like Rolls Royces."

Well, I'm here to tell you that Stauffer is a true gentleman, a man of the earth with no pretension, and, despite not being that much interested in Rolls Royces anymore, he didn't summarily boot the fellow out for being out of date with his current predilections. The inquirer then spotted a car in the distance and asked, "Well, that's too bad. I wonder, I see you've got a Cobra over there, well tell me, are you by any chance interested in GT40s?" Stauffer's ears perked up. In the pecking order of that time, GT40s were worth a lot more than Cobras.

First some background. By the early 1960s the Ford Motor Company decided to adopt a more youthful image. They felt one of the best ways to do so was to go out and win races in general, and the 24 Hours of Le Mans in particular. Due to the gentleman's agreement between the three big American companies to stay out of racing, Ford desperately lacked the experience or know-how to take on the specialized, European manufacturers like Ferrari. Fortunately, the third ingredient required, money, was available in abundance.

In an attempt to get into racing quickly and easily, Ford tried to buy the entire Ferrari operation in 1962. When the negotiations turned sour, Henry Ford II's negotiators went home but did not give up, instead deciding to develop their own damn endurance racer. How hard could it be? They had already developed an Indy racer working with Colin Chapman, head of Lotus in the UK.

Ford already had a toe-hold in the endurance racing game, having written out a check as early as 1962 to Carroll Shelby to fund his Cobra racing cars, but in the end, having to share the credits with Shelby and AC Cars was not to the company's liking. Another problem was that despite the fact that the Cobra was fast, it could only go 180 mph in coupe form. From what the Ford negotiators had seen at Le Mans in '62, where the winners were clocking 200 mph on the famed Mulsanne straight, they needed to have a faster prototype to win Le Mans.

In 1963 the decision was made to build a prototype sports racer that, unlike the Cobra, was built to score overall victories. They were realistic enough to realize that outside help was needed, and after closely looking at companies like Lotus and Cooper, Ford eventually teamed up with Lola. This Eric Broadley run company had just completed a Ford-powered, mid-engined sports racer that would form the ideal basis for the new project.

A new company called Ford Advanced Vehicles (FAV) was founded, which would be responsible for the engineering and assembly of the cars. The chassis and body panels were made by specialists Abbey Panels. Broadley was responsible for the overall design, fellow Englishman Len Bailey took care of the chassis design and John Wyer was hired as team manager. Bailey's chassis design closely followed that of the Lola Mk 6 though Ford had a major difference, preferring steel in the monocoque compared to Broadley's penchant for aluminum.

Since Ford had already developed a 255-cubic-inch all-aluminum, dry-sump Ford Fairlane engine for Indy use, they thought this could work in their endurance racer, at least until they got the four cam version available. The Fairlane V8 displaced just under 4.2 liters and could crank out a reliable 350 bhp.

The Achilles heel of the design was the Italian-made Colotti four-speed gearbox. The finished car, bodied in fiberglass, stood only 40.5 inches tall, hence the nickname GT40. One novel feature was doors cut into the roof so that once you had the door open you could plop right down into the seat.

The first two were completed in time to take part in the Le Mans test day in April of 1964. Both cars crashed, one surviving enough to be re-tested in England where it was discovered the car had tail lift. The solution was a "ducktail" spoiler to add down-force to the rear, suggested by test driver Richie Ginther, who had mentioned the same to Ferrari earlier when he was a test driver there (he had learned about aerodynamics while working at an aircraft assembly line back in California).

Alas, the GT40s proved to be very fragile and in that first season not one car even lasted until the end of the race. Disgusted with the Italian gearbox, Ford put in an order for ZF's German-made five-speed gearbox for the next season. The alloy block engine also conked out, enough to force the team into using 289 Cobra engines in cast iron late in the season, the same ones used by Shelby in his Cobras. It produced more power and torque, and was only slightly heavier, once Shelby threw out the dry sump oiling.

The biggest change for the '65 GT40 program was in management. When they experienced a lack of success, Ford realized, "Hey, we've already got Shelby on our payroll" and had sent him the leftover '64 cars to develop for '65. Ford also cut ties with Eric Broadley who had annoyed them by setting up production of Lola cars next door and even hiring away some of their best workers. The move was a good one as the first race Ford entered in '65 (the 3-hour long Daytona Continental) saw a GT40 victory plus a 3rd place win with another. Back at FAV Ford continued with variations including open roadsters and cars with alloy chassis.

THE BIG BLOCK SAVES THE DAY
Two of the chassis sent to the United States were designed

from the get-go to be fitted with seven-liter, 427-cubic-inch V8 engines. This was because at some point, after too many 289 engines had blown up, an exasperated Ford official had asked, "What engine do you have around here that can take this without blowing up?" and everyone pointed to the 427 side-oiler FE series block proven in NASCAR.

The two big block chassis were so fitted, and together, with one of the small block roadsters and the first three GT40 production cars, they were all entered at Le Mans in '65. The two big blocks were the quickest in qualifying but, due to poor reliability, Ford again left the track empty-handed with none of the six GT40s managing to make it to the finish.

THE WINNING YEAR

Eventually Ford got past the 100-car production requirement with the small block Ford GT40 and those were homologated. But for '66 Ford was still intent on winning the race and put their efforts into the 427-powered chassis. The '66 generation eventually were referred to as the "MK. II" models.

No fewer than eight big block side-oiler 427 FE-powered Mark IIs were meticulously prepared for the 1966 24 Hours of Le Mans. Although the cars were entered by three different privateer teams on paper, it was Ford backing all the entries and supplying most of the personnel in the pits.

Ford's assault was further backed by five small block GT40s. By contrast, the "enemy," Ferrari, fielded only three of their latest generation prototypes. The 24-hour race proved to be particularly tough that year, and only 15 of the 55 starters even reached the finish line 24 hours later. All of the Ferraris had gone out with seven hours still left in the race, as had nine of the Fords, but the surviving three Ford GTs held together long enough to score a historic 1-2-3 photo finish.

Even though Ford had achieved their long range goal, victory in the 24 Hours, Ford continued development work on an all-new version of the GT40; nicknamed the "J-car" (because it fit appendix J of the FIA Rules), which would later become known as the Mark IV. This last car was completely developed in the United States and, with it, Ford successfully proved that European help was no longer needed in order for an American firm to score a Le Mans win. Of course this car would have never existed without the without the help of the English four years earlier.

NOW, ABOUT THAT CAR IN THE BARN...

We return to our hero, George Stauffer and the barn-find Mk. II. He cautiously responded to the man's question with the question: "Do you have one?" The guy held up three fingers. "Three, but to get them you'll have to buy my Rolls Royce too." (The guy really wanted to get rid of that Rolls Royce). The other cars included a Mk. IV Ford like the one that won Le Mans in '67 and SN1074, the Gulf team Monza-winning GT40; all stored in crates in a warehouse in Belgium.

Stauffer, whose family was in cheese production, did some rapid mental calculation. He figured, well, maybe I can resell the Rolls so when I go over to pick them up I'm not stuck with a car I don't want. One thing he couldn't figure out though, was that the man said one of the Ford GTs was a big block GT40 and Stauffer couldn't believe Ford wouldn't have that car someplace in storage or on display as it was a great museum draw.

Then Stauffer asked where the cars were and the man said "Belgium." That put a damper on it right there because Wisconsin to Brussels ain't cheap, and Stauffer knew he would have to fly in his expert Ronnie Spain from Scotland, the man who had written the "bible" on GT40s with the individual racing histories of each of the original cars. But the deal was set and they all convened in Europe, whereupon Stauffer gets a surprise.

The Mk. II isn't just any Mk. II, it is P/1046, the Ford GT that won Le Mans in 1966. Why would Ford sell it? Who knows? When Ford got out of racing after the 1967 win, they sent all the Ford GT parts to either Shelby or John Wyer at FAV. They weren't going to make Ford GTs anymore so didn't need them for promotion. So it was out the door with all that junk as far as they were concerned.

When he checked out the history even further, Stauffer found that Chassis P/1046 was a brand new car when it was built specifically for the 24 Hours of Le Mans in 1966. It was entered by Shelby American and piloted by 'Kiwis' (New Zealanders), Bruce McLaren and Chris Amon. It finished the race in second, but was classified as the winner because it had started further down the grid than the sister car that crossed the line first (A huge brouhaha was then started by fans of Ken Miles who felt robbed of victory, and Ford's decision to stage a 3-abreast finish still rankles Miles fans half a century later).

Ford used the car for promotional purposes for the next year or so, but it again saw service in a major race. Holman & Moody subsequently fielded the car in the 1967 Daytona 24 Hours. A gearbox failure resulted in an early retirement.

Ford's first Le Mans winner was sold soon after and somehow it found its way to Belgium, where Stauffer bought it. He subsequently had raced it in vintage racing, always keeping it in prime condition. It was at the 2006 Le Mans Classic where the 40th anniversary of the historic win was celebrated, together with the second and third placed cars. Stauffer finally sold the car to a wealthy collector with homes around the world, and reportedly at least one more original Ford GT in the garage. Price tag when sold? Over $9 million.

That'll buy a lot of cheese, in Wisconsin or anywhere else. And if you go to his website, you find George still has a Rolls Royce. Now what's the lessons to be learned here? First you may have to buy cars you don't want in order to get the cars you do want. So establish relations with other collector car dealers, in case this happens and you need to be ready to unload the "off brands" fast.

Secondly, and this is the significant point: don't EVER be a snob. Stauffer did not turn the man away who had come to his shop to sell a Rolls Royce, even though he was no longer interested in Rolls as much as he was in Cobras. He was polite, and that left the way open for the man to ask what eventually became the nine-million dollar question: "So, OK, are you interested in GT40s?"

Chapter 13
Early Giugiaro (1964 Alfa Romeo Canguro)

Wherein a schoolteacher (almost) realizes his dream...

If ever there was the right car coming along at the right time it was the Alfa GTZ.
The initials had a meaning—the "T" for tubolare (tube framed) and the "Z" for Zagato, one of the most famous coachbuilders in Italy whose specialty at the time was lightweight curvaceous bodywork.

First conceived in 1959 using the yet unannounced Giulia engine, Alfa thought the way to dominate racing was to first use this engine in a tubular frame car until the Giulia GTAs could be ready, these being a more mass production car. Basically the show car would function as a teaser for what would be the heavier production car.

So, in order to quality it as a production car itself, they had to make a minimum of 100 as per FIA rules.

In actuality they made 124 TZ's, and that is counting the 12 second-generation, ultra-lightweight, ultra-low TZ-2's as well. The chassis of the TZ cars was made of multiple tubes, each the diameter of a Tootsie Roll. The weight of the chassis was a mere 203 pounds in the TZ-1 and when they went all out for the less road-able (on ordinary roads) super lightweight TZ-2 they got it down to 140 pounds. You wouldn't want to take the TZ-2 on the road as it was a pure racecar. Even though the output was 170 horsepower, with the weight only 1,370 pounds (660Kg) it had a power-to-weight ratio of over 200 horsepower per ton.

While the front of the TZ-1 resembled a European GT car of the early '60s like the Ferrari GTO, with its faired-in headlamps, the back of the car was really chopped off in a dramatic way. This type of tail was called the "Coda Tronca" by the Italians which meant "cut-off tail." Those who knew about the history of car aerodynamics called it the "Kamm tail," attributed to the German aerodynamicist Dr. Wunibald Kamm, who liked the chopped-off tail only if you couldn't have a long tapered tail, which he preferred. Top speed of the GTZ-1 was 135 mph.

The TZ's all shared the Giulia 1600 engine in various stages of tune from the single plug 116-horsepower version through to the 170-horsepower twin spark plug engine that was later part of the GTA. The GTZ-1 was a long time gestating. Though started in 1959, the public didn't see the car until 1963 when it made its debut at the Geneva motor show. It immediately demonstrated its superiority in racing when it won its class in the 1964 Sebring 12-hour race in its first race of the season. This was the first of a whole string of victories topped by the outright wins in the Coupe des Alps and the Tour de Corse.

Ironically the GTZ-1 was obsolete in terms of basic concept, as it came out at a time when automakers were already realizing that mid-engine was the way to go for the ultimate sports car. Mid-engined cars cornered better and with the engine amidships, the car could be lower by not having to have a high hood line to clear the engine.

The Porsche 904GTS, a mid-engined two-seater coupe, came along in '64, so the front-engined Alfa GTZ's time in the sun was short, eclipsed by the more modern layout of the German rival. The TZ's also had the rear brakes mounted on the differential to reduce unsprung weight. The suspension was double wishbone all round. Most, but not all, TZ-1's had aluminum bodywork. A few were fiberglass. The TZ-1s were mostly raced by privateer teams, that is to say not factory-backed. Top teams were those of Jolly Club and the Scuderia Sant'Ambroeus.

GIUGIARO'S MASTERPIECE

Now we come to the car in the barn and the burning ambition of an American schoolteacher working in Europe to find a great sports car, maybe even a factory racing prototype or one-off concept car. He eventually focused on one car, a one-off TZ-1.

In 1964, Carrozzeria Bertone was given the opportunity to build two prototypes on genuine racecar chassis (some show cars are built on makeshift chassis, only sufficient to hold up the body). One of these became the Alfa Romeo Canguro, which made its debut at the 1964 Paris Motor Show. It stood out as one of the greatest designs ever put on an Alfa. It was partly due to the fact that the original dimensions of the GTZ-1 were already so classic—long nose, short rear deck, chopped-off tail.

The designer was youthful Giorgetto Giugiaro, who had started at Bertone at the tender age of 19. He made an extremely smooth design, no unsightly lumps or scoops. It was called the "Canguro," Italian for "kangaroo." Probably the most outstanding view is the side where he installed engine heat exhaust vents in the fuselage in a vertical row, all rectangular with rounded edges. The car was a sensation. Alfa might have considered it for production except that the tubolare chassis was too expensive to make in mass production. No doubt they would have had to have a more conventional chassis and no doubt, in translating the body design to another chassis, some of the beauty of his design would have been lost.

The firm that had made the chassis of the GTZ-1, Autodelta, was primarily a racecar builder. At that time they didn't have the capacity to mass-produce such a car. The roughly 100 GTZ-1's were about all they could do in one year, and even that number was stretching it considering they also had racecars to prepare.

CUSTOM BY CRUNCH

Sadly, the world would never know what could have happened if it had been produced, because not long after its debut, the one-off concept was crashed hard all the way to the windscreen during the shooting of a promotional film by Shell Oil.

The crash happened in the toughest part of the Monza track, the Parabolica Curve, where it not only crashed, but in doing so, rear-ended a second one-off Bertone concept, the 1963 Chevrolet Testudo (which was subsequently repaired, though the Corvair chassis was not anywhere near the performance platform of the GTZ-1 so nobody particularly cared that it was repaired).

Nuccio Bertone, the head of Bertone, of course knew that the Canguro could be repaired. He would almost have to start from scratch, but who was going to pay for what he estimated was going to be 15,000 hours of work? Apparently the cars weren't insured; and let's face it, the car had gotten a lot of publicity when first unveiled, so in a sense it had already done its work, completed its mission so to speak. Like a mercurial songstress who sings a boffo song at the Academy awards and then drops out of sight forever. So it was unceremoniously parked out back of the plant, left to rot.

Enter our hero, an American, Gary Schmidt, working in Germany as a schoolteacher for the U.S. Armed Forces. Schmidt had no doubt been an enthusiast when he signed up for the school teaching gig, knowing that working in Europe he could look for collector cars in his spare time. He spied the sad-looking Canguro in Italy in the Seventies and made an offer that was accepted. Alfa didn't want it because of the repair cost, and Bertone had gone on to other prototypes, so maybe Bertone's thinking was, "hey, if this guy wants to put it back on the road, it's good for us if he succeeds."

Another version of the story is that Schmidt actually bought it from Rob de la Rive Box, a Dutch journalist living on the Continent who bought and sold interesting cars. In that version of the story Box bought it for peanuts and made a profit selling the crunched car to Scmidt.

Schmidt got a good deal as well. He made some initial contacts, and got some of the mechanical bits he needed, but as often is the case with a one-off car with unique bodywork, had problems getting the new bodywork to the same look as the original. Close-but-no-cigar is not enough when you are dealing with a car everybody remembers.

Finally, around the year 2000 he had to give up on his dream and the car went to Japanese businessman and collector Shiro Kosaka. Kosaka picked up where Schmidt left off and was able to roll the fully restored car out onto the lawn of the Ville d'Este concours in 2005. This is a very prestigious concours; in fact, unlike Pebble Beach, the general public is not invited. At the Ville, it won the coveted title of "Best in Show." Sadly, Schmidt had passed on two years earlier so never got to see his dream of restoring a factory prototype to perfection realized. But he showed the way for barn-finders, proving once again prototypes can be bought even when crunched.

Lesson learned? No. 1: Concept cars are one-offs. So when one gets pranged, the builders are often loathe to fix them, especially when their show career is, for all intents and purposes, over. The Canguro had been built to promote a certain engine. It did that job so Alfa didn't need it anymore.

Right at the time an automaker makes that decision—that a given car is surplus to their needs, is the absolute best time to buy it.

Lesson No. 2: Engrave this one inside your eyelids, automakers *do* sell concept cars and prototypes. Especially when the new wears off. Be there at the right time in the right place with the money, and you could get lucky...Gary Schmidt was.

Chapter 14
Fortunes of War (Plymouth XNR)

Yes, war does indeed provide opportunities.

Back in the early 1950s, Detroit automakers didn't propose that many two-seaters, Detroit actually being unsure of what this new-fangled thing called a "sports car" was; but when urbane sophisticated Virgil Exner became head of Chrysler Design, he proposed several, including the exciting Italian-built two-seater, the XNR.

So, um, I can see you looking puzzled and asking, "what two-seater? What about the passenger seat," you ask? The answer is that it is a temporary 'Monoposto'—what the Italians call a one-seater. Back in the day, we're talking early-'50s, it was the fashion with some two-seater sports cars to cover the passenger seat with a metal or fiberglass tonneau, as if to say, "We are a two-seater to meet the rules but no passengers are allowed because we are serious racers." Another very '50s thing that is key to the design is the headrest-cum-tailfin, the likes of Jaguar's D-Type racecar.

Exner did the design in the U.S. and a Valiant chassis was sent to Ghia in Italy, where they made a wooden former for the whole car and used it to guide the shaping of each panel of the steel body. Originally you can see in the picture of the wood buck that it was supposed to have a regular glass windshield, but that was fighting the rest of the car's beauty so they succumbed to the allure of pure racecar styling and made a wraparound racing windscreen for the driver only. The car had a strong T-motif from the rear caused by the vertical back of the tailfin and the vestigial rear bumper.

The car was based on the Valiant's 106-inch wheelbase, as was frequent in styling exercises (but not so much in racecars where it added weight). The prominent overhangs stretched the car's overall length, in this case to 195 inches, close to qualifying as wretched excess. Height was just 43-46 inches high to the top of the fin, so it was a few inches taller than the low-slung Ford GT40 coupe of a few years later.

Rarely does such a sexy shape get such a lumpen proletariat engine, in this case a Valiant-sourced slant six-cylinder engine, which Chrysler claimed was "tuned to racing specs," all of 250 horses, an output Ferrari would have laughed at. Ferrrari was getting that out of engines half its size!

Chrysler also claimed the engine could wind to a heady 9,000 rpm which was about 3,000 rpm more than anyone with good sense would try in an overhead-valve American-made engine at the time. If Chrysler ever would have produced the car, they might have had to think about a real engine, not this pipe-dream stuff.

Another report says they were thinking of an aluminum block version, but then this was still the stage when Detroit auto-makers thought sports cars were boulevardiers, for mustachioed gents (think Caesar Romero) to cruise the boulevard with, eyeing the ladies and not actually going to a racetrack and driving at speed. That's the way Chevy had started with the Corvette (only to change their tune around '56), but Exner impressed the lap-dog press by having a professional driver clock just over 150 mph in it. That was a respectable speed, something the Corvette had only achieved on the packed sands of Daytona Beach (before the track was built).

However, any production possibilities were scotched by the fact it was a two-seater, didn't have a legal windshield (though the original drawings show one), or a provision for a top of any kind. Plus, the brass couldn't get around the asymmetry of it all, I mean, with a hood hump on only one side, the car was lopsided for chrissake! Most Detroit cars were decidedly balanced from side to side in an end-on view, the left half looked like the right half and so forth. Having something asymmetrical was thought of as just plain weird. It was also common knowledge around Detroit that GM lost money on the Corvette, but just built it so the dealers could suck prospects off the street and sell them a regular Chevy. They had plans for changing the styling starting in '56 so there was hope it would someday turn a profit.

So what happened with the XNR? Traditionally, once a prototype's show career is over, it will be trashed in Detroit; but Exner had the XNR shipped to the Ghia design studio where the body had been built. That might have spared Chrysler from having to pay customs duties, but was the equivalent of shipping coals to Newcastle. The last thing Ghia wanted to see arrive on their doorstep was an old obsolete show car not being shown anymore and no budget to doll it up for a return to the show arena. They summarily sold it off.

It is worth mentioning Chrysler and Ghia made a second concept car with a similar body with a full windshield on a Valiant chassis called the Asymmetrica, which was a watered-down design without the drama of the Monoposto. This second car has been restored and seen at various concours, including Pebble Beach. Ken Gross, in *Motor Trend*, adds to the rumor that several more were made, maybe as many as 25!

What happened to the XNR? One report, on a Chrysler website called Winged Warriors/National B-Body Owners Association, says it was sold to a Geneva butcher, who in turn sold it around 1968-'69 to his Royal Highness, the Shah of Iran, who was no doubt unimpressed with the weak horsepower-to-weight, when you consider he had Ferraris and Maseratis that could clock 180 mph without working up much of a sweat.

The author has a personal memory of discovering this car; remembering his shock decades ago, when he saw it pictured in a *National Geographic* article on Kuwait (some say it's the May 1969 issue). The magazine plainly identified the owner of the car as being Anwar Al-Mulla, from a leading business family (I toyed with writing the family firm but never got around to it).

Flash-forward to a recent Pebble Beach in the late 2000s. The crowd parts and suddenly I see it, the fabled often-dreamed-of XNR, now perfectly restored. Somebody else had beat me to it! Turned out that it was Lebanese car collector Karim Edde, who had employed an age-old but effective technique to find it in Beirut in the 1980s.

His "gimmick" was to pay neighborhood kids cash money if they would prowl the neighborhood in search of unusual cars. Maybe he even paid a bounty if they found one. After so many such forays, the kids came up with a winner. How it got there from the Shah's collection isn't exactly clear, but it's probably better not to ask. A lot of the Shah's cars escaped, often because he was only in love with a car for the moment. If he saw something better and bought it, he didn't miss the old love leaving.

Knowing he had found something special, Edde rescued it, though keeping it safe under wartime conditions involved hiring flat bed tow trucks to move it from one location under fire to another. The car was eventually shipped to RM Restoration in Canada, who took many months to restore it. The restoration was made easier by it having that engine, which could be found in any U.S. junkyard, but complicated by the fact much of the trim was hand-made. The car sold in 2012 at the RM auction in Monterey for close to one million dollars.

Lesson for barn finders? If I would have gotten myself energized from the moment I had seen the picture in *National Geographic*, at least I would have gotten to talk to the actual owners of the car and established a base price. Or even was it for sale? Do bears dump in the woods? That's a no-brainer. It was owned by a car dealer, for gosh sakes; who normally sell everything that rolls onto the lot.

But it was the old, gee...I don't know, the Mideast? A place I'd never been. Fear of the unknown prevented me from acting. I can't say I wasn't given a heads-up that the car was still out there, waiting to be found.

Lesson Number 2: pay off those pesky little kids on their bicycles. Tell them what kind of car you want and have them scour the neighborhoods. You never know what the tykes will find (and nowadays you can equip them with digital cameras.)

Chapter 15
Trading for a Bentley (1947 Bentley Mk. VI)

A classic all-French car for a Brit-Franco collaboration.

The British word "bespoke" is almost (subhead) unknown in America. It means "hand made to one's taste" and you can still order shoes like that in England, from Lobb.

There was a time you could order a Bentley or Rolls bodied to your taste. The Bentley this story revolves around, a 1947 Mk. VI model, is one of those cars from a practice that almost died out in the 1960s. It is identified by its serial number, B20BH. This is a saga of one temporary infatuation traded for true love (cue violins).

First some facts about the car, before I dive into the drama. Franay was a French coachbilder, ordinarily not as "flashy" as his rivals Figoni et Falaschi or Saouchik but very competent as far as the level of workmanship.

After WWII, in the early '50s, Franay did several Bentley Continentals (not the full fastbacks but notchback sedans) but, though the work was flawless, the designs were, well, uninspired, mere copies of the British styling—interesting, but not enough to stop traffic on the Champs Elysées, the main street of Paris.

Then came a discerning customer—a Monseur Gudol—who had bought a Bentley Mk. VI chassis. He wanted something special and asked Bentley to recommend an outside coachbuilder, for above all, he did not want the standard steel body. He was recommended to Franay and when Franay said they could meet his desire to have a coachbuilt alloy body with all the pre-war elegance of such cars as Delahayes and Delages, Gudol awarded them the contract.

The result was a car that was stunning, with all the elegance of the pre-war grand tourers, proving that the era of styling was not dead (though tastes might have changed). It won its first two Concours d'Elegance (Enghien and Boulogne) in the same year the car was delivered.

Monsieur Gudol did not have an exclusive, though, for records show that Franay did one other Mk. VI to the same style (the other owner capitalizing off Monsieur Gudol's good taste).

Those were the days when the owners of such coachbuilt bodies would go to a concours wearing color-matching clothes and sometimes even sporting color-matched fur on their poodle!

The car, when finished, went to the 1947 Paris Auto Show where it was a sensation, but not so much so that other French coachbuilders were willing to go back to the separate prewar-style fenders. They all thought all-enveloping bodies were the way to go, like the Americans.

Monsieur Gudol kept the car for several years before having a larger displacement, more-powerful 4.5-liter engine retrofitted in the early 1950s.

Records then indicate it went to a family in England, and, sometime in the 1950s it migrated to the U.S. where it next became the property of a Mr. Cohen of Troy, New York.

The list of owners over the next few years included an early supporter of the Pebble Beach concours, Opera tenor Sergio Franchi. Later, one of the organizers of Pebble Beach, impresario Lorin Tryon, owned it but not while it was restored.

Now, if I haven't lost you, hang on because the story takes some twists and turns involving subsequent owners including the star of our story, Gary Wales, a Southern Californian.

THE TRADE

Wales bought the car and made it a superstar. But his

path to the car was not easy. The way it happened was this: Wales, a Bentley guy, was selling parts over the phone to a guy who happened to mention that he had once owned a genuine pre-war classic—a Talbot Lago. "Back when he owned it," the man explained, "the Talbot did not have its Talbot engine but a Cadillac engine and was painted a non-stock Fire Engine red."

The Talbot had been imported from Europe by Tommy Lee, a famous Los Angeles millionaire of great taste (in cars) who had imported half a dozen Talbot Lagos. But Lee's family owned a Cadillac dealership so, wanting the car to be easy to service and drive, Lee had converted it to a Cadillac V8, plus a Cadillac trans and power steering. Lee had sold the car to a man who bought it for his wife. But in one of her first drives, she had put it in neutral to open the gate of their estate (the car not having a "park" position) and the car rolled flat over her, with fatal results.

The newly minted widower was so distraught that he gave the car to his gardener, a gentleman of color who had always admired it. That man sold the car to Gary's friend, the guy buying the parts.

Now came the second tragedy, not fatal, but nonetheless a tad off-putting. The new American owner of the Talbot spent so much on the car that his wife up and left, divorcing him. He tried to sell the bad luck car. But no one wanted it, being as it was, still in a million pieces (well, 10,000 pieces anyway). So he went back to the gardener and sold it back to him.

Flash forward 20 years. The former Talbot owner tells Gary the story of the car. Now Gary Wales, a car collector for over half a century, was not to be deterred by a few bumps in the road, one death and one divorce (hey, that was par for the course in a truly exotic car). He knew that, with cars of this stature, there's the chance they can turn a man's head more than any woman.

Wales invited the Bentley parts buyer over to his house,

which is a treat because it has a stained glass windowed library which is more like a museum for Bentley fans, and they imbibed a few glasses of high quality Scotch until Gary jumped up and said, "Let's go see if you can remember where the hell that gardener lived—if we find it and I get the car, I'll give you a $500 finder's fee."

So off they went, driving around for hours while Gary's friend tried to remember what the gardener's house looked liked. Actually, he had last seen the car at an old gas station that the gardener used for his workshop. He finally recognized the station, and they pulled up. Gary's friend saw the same black man working on something outside as they stepped out of the car. Gary's friend connected his gaze and said, "Remember me?"

By golly, he did. Gary's friend then eagerly asked the all-important follow-up question: "Do you still have the car?"

The man stopped working and slowly nodded yes, saying: "It's over at the house about a block and a half away. Would you like to see it?"

Now the good news was that the car was still there.

The bad news was that the man had stored it in a garage that had collapsed on it. Now this would be a real tragedy if the car was flattened but Wales noticed the fenders and hood were over in another area, untouched. "Now on that car the fenders and hood are about half the body," Wales says, "So I knew I would save money there."

Wales asked what the price was and when the man said "$3,000," Gary shook his head. "No way," he said, thanked the man and Wales and his friend up and left.

Then about halfway home he hit himself upside the head and said, "you fool" and went back and paid the man's price.

Wales of course still had to pay the finder's fee, but figured it was well worth it.

So Wales took the Talbot-Lago home and restored it. Not to Pebble Beach standards because in those days Pebble Beach was a car show for locals in Monterey and Wales went to Monterey strictly for the vintage car races, having been a Ferrari guy before he was a Bentley guy.

So back to the story... It is around 1979, and Gary is up at the races driving the Talbot around the pits on a Saturday. Along comes Loren Tryon, the co-producer of the Pebble Beach Concours which was set to take place the next day. Tryon sees the non-original Talbot and he says to Wales, "You know, Gary, we like to invite a few of the racers over to the concours. Why don't you bring that car over tomorrow with the others?"

This was with the understanding the new invited cars would not be judged, not even entered in the concours, just brought over to show the crowd some racecars, and "build the gate" so to speak.

Wales was pleased to accept and the next day, there's the Talbot, with non-original color, non-original engine, non-original upholstery but drawing a crowd because of its voluptuous body style, courtesy of Figoni et Falaschi, two French coachbuilders renowned for their somewhat baroque elegance and grace. It was even, Wales recalls, drawing crowds away from the meticulously correctly restored cars, which you can guarantee got a few noses bent out of shape since it was a car not even officially entered in the concours.

After the show, Tryon approached Gary and said, "You know, I kind of like that Talbot. What say we trade for it?"

Gary was amenable, but it depended on what Tryon could come up with.

"What do you have?" he countered.

"A Bentley Mk. VI, serial number B20BH. I don't know much about it, but I know it's French-bodied. And it looks rough but it's got the original engine."

So Wales went over to Tryon's house on the Peninsula and looked the Bentley over and they traded across even-steven. Gary had no regrets because he had a lot of Bentley parts already, was in three different Bentley clubs and knew that a French-coachworked Bentley was already "a car with a story."

And to win an event like Pebble Beach, it isn't enough to have a correctly restored car with flawless paint and upholstery. It helps if the car has a dramatic story (who it belonged to; who it was built for; how it was rescued, yadda-yadda).

Wales took it home. And it sat.

For ten years it sat, all the while Wales working on other cars. But the Bentley was not forgotten—he was periodically engaged in finding pictures of it in its Paris days, and finding paperwork that would prove its provenance. Finally, after 10 years he had the courage to tackle it because he knew he could "do it right." Incidentally, in the ten years that had passed in the meantime, Pebble Beach had become more of a world-class event, with world-wide entries, and much tougher judging standards, so he knew that he couldn't just do it with a color he liked.

The car was in sorry shape, the front spats (wheel well covers) were there, but the chrome was shot and that alone took 1,000 hours because Franay used chrome as a decorative element over about 10% of the body. Wales recalls, "I can't tell you how many times we would hand-fit the chrome and then have to resurface the body so it was a match within a half millimeter."

Of course, Wales being a flamboyant showman as far as concours cars, didn't stop at a dead-stock restoration. He did change one thing—the windshield. It came with a one-piece fold-down unit and Wales, figuring a black car needed that extra bit of chrome to call attention to the top of the car and brighten up the front view, replaced it with a period-correct two-piece one. He also added French-made period-correct small spotlights to each side of the windscreen, a badge bar with period correct badges, French license plates, the whole nine yards.

And then came the frog-skin upholstery. "I knew it would be controversial," he said, "but I like to give something for people to talk about," so when he redid the leather he had the inserts (inside the outer bolsters) done in 1,000 red-dyed frogskins. It looked elegant and set off the car's flamboyance. He even had identical skins put on a matched set of luggage, which would have been something a hand-crafted car owner would have done for competition in concours in Europe in the '50s.

Before the car was even done, Wales took the restored chassis to the Santa Barbara concours. Even "au natural," it was a hit. Bentley fans could hardly wait to see the car clothed with its bodywork. Wales then set a target date for the 1991 Pebble Beach Concours d'Elegance.

It was accepted and up to Pebble Beach Gary and Mrs. Wales went.

At Pebble Beach, B20BH was awarded First in Class, and then it was recalled to the judge's stand to receive the French Trophy as well. When Best of Show was awarded to another car (a 1932 Chrysler Imperial roadster), it was the only time in memory that the chief judge felt obliged to apologize for not giving the award to a particular vehicle. He commented that the Franay Bentley, indeed, had missed by just one-tenth of a point, the closest margin of victory in the event's history. It easily was the crowd favorite, drawing so many spectators that photography was nearly impossible.

On the side, Tryon told Wales that, owing to the general ambiance that the concours had developed as a homage to pre-war cars, there was "no way a post-war car was ever going to get Best of Show over a pre-war car." You can kind of see why—if postwar cars started winning "Best of Show" well, then the next year you would see Corvette owners trying to win and so forth. Wales took the decision stoically (though he may have given a French salute as he left the field).

Coincidentally that year the Rolls-Royce Owners Club annual meet was being held concurrently with the Pebble Beach event, and B20BH was named best of all post-WWII vehicles in that competition.

Directly as a result of the Pebble Beach crowd reaction, Wales received an invitation to accompany his Bentley to Germany where it was the focal point of the following year. At the 1995 Louis Vuitton (Hurlingham) Concours in London, B20BH was judged Best of Show, and at Paris (Bagatelle), it was further honored by the prestigious Connolly trophy. In addition, at the non-judged Retromobile 10-day exhibition at Paris, B20BH was designated as one of the 10 most historically important vehicles on display.

It returned to Paris to be displayed at the CIA Museum in suburban Paris until returning to the USA for the Newport Beach Rolls-Royce and Bentley Parade.

Going to all these shows got some wear and tear on it and in March 1999 the restoration was refreshed with a two-month, extensive re-restoration of the paint, top and seat upholstery.

A model car company made a scale model of it, which was sold at $200 per copy, one of the few they have done in such exquisite detail (opening lids, engine, etc.).

At Barrett-Jackson's 2006 Palm Springs auction, the car was sold for a record $1,728,000 USD plus commission to Ron Pratte. This made it the most valuable postwar Bentley on the planet.

A later owner sold it at another auction for over $2 million. Both times it was the highest price ever recorded at auction paid for a postwar Bentley. Wales, by his diligence, research and workmanship, not to mention a certain amount of flamboyance, had moved the bar up on postwar cars.

Why didn't he keep it? You have to understand—to Wales, the fun is in the finding and the restoring. Once a car is done, his interests move on. But he and his wife had many memorable moments in the car—driving it through Paris, London and other world capitals and making friends everywhere.

Everywhere the car is shown, it represents the last vestiges of coachbuilding in France along with the all-French marques like Delahaye and Delage.

Lesson learned? Note that Gary Wales had treated that original tipster right and, accordingly, the man helped him find the Talbot Lago that led to Wales finding the Bentley of his dreams.

One could say: "But wasn't he giving up a future million dollar car by giving up the Talbot?" Possibly, but you have to remember that Talbot did not at that time have the correct engine and transmission whereas the Bentley had an engine supplied from Bentley. It was duck soup for a Bentley guy to put it together.

The Talbot? It went on to be come a concours winner, and is no doubt a million dollar car as well, but this author thinks Wales made the right choice, in that the Bentley was the more complete of the two."

Chapter 16
The First Mustang (1963 Mustang Prototype)

Yeah, we know, the first Mustangs didn't come 'til '64 1/2.

Yessir. Your eyes do not deceive you. This car, technically, by my way of thinking, has to be a 1963 Mustang. I know, I know, they didn't start making the Ford Mustang until 1964, as '64 1/2 models were registered as 1965 models, but here it is. If you go to the Museum it's in now (it was last loaned to the Owls' Head Museum in Owl's Head, Maine) you can see it and maybe even touch it to prove to you that, despite what every historian on earth has written about Mustangs being 1964 models at the earliest, here's one that was running and driving in 1963 (confounding historians ever more).

However, they were prototypes. Let's go back into the Mustang history to bring you up to speed. In 1962 Ford Motor Co. was fired up to create a new car, and one way to fire up a new design is to pit one team against another, sometimes even involving teams from different countries. The design team headed by Joe Oros, Gayle Halderman and David Ash won the competition with their design, a four-seater close-coupled coupe they called the "Cougar."

While the Oros team was busy moving the design into production, Ford felt a show prototype was needed to "whet the public's appetite"

Showing your cards in advance is sometimes good if you want to see what the public reaction is to a car. The downside is that once your new design breaks cover, the competition can start on a car to counter yours. Yet Ford was willing to take the chance.

Maybe the show-going public would love it so much they would bring out their checkbooks and write a deposit (as they did with the Dodge Viper decades later). But it was a two-edged sword—once Ford showed this Mustang, dubbed the Mustang II, Chevy began to plan the Chevrolet Camaro, Pontiac started on the Firebird, American Motors had distant thoughts of the Javelin, and Plymouth decided to push the Barracuda.

The Mustang II started with a stock body shell intended for the first of the '64 1/2 models, but then this was exaggerated, with a jutting grille and nary a hint of bumper protection, hidden headlamps that would have been illegal, simulated knock-off wheels, no bumpers in the rear, and a lift-off hardtop. The taillights were three individual units per side, also originally planned for the 1965 Mustang, but later changed to one taillight per side. The interior was two-toned, blue and white, with the blue on the inserts of the seats, white around the outside and outer bolsters. The dashboard had a more integrated console than was used in the production Mustangs.

The prototype was touted as the "Two-Plus-Two," a car built for two adults up front with the addition of the small rear seat, making room for four, ideal for a young family with space for only toddler-sized children to ride in the rear (though a press picture does show Lee Iacocca driving it with full-size British race driver Graham Hill riding in the back seat). Ford tipped off their growing passion for motorsports by having the Mustang II make its debut at the Watkins Glen track in the spring of 1963.

Earlier, Dan Gurney, a Shelby Cobra driver at times, toodled around the same track in the mid-engined prototype Mustang I. So this new four-seater was confirmation that, while the Mustang I had been totally impractical for mass production, having been built with racecar layout in mind, the next generation concept—i.e. the car the public would get—would be totally practical, well... once they added bumpers and headlights that met the sadly antique lighting laws of the USA.

Back in the early Sixties it usually took 3 to 4 years to get a new car from first drawing to the first pilot models rolling out of the assembly plant; however, partly because the Mustang was based on the already existent Falcon, it had a gestation period of only 18 months from the time funding had begun, to the first production cars rolling out the factory door.

To say it was an instant success would be understating its reception. It sold 22,000 cars on the first day! Why was it so popular? Well in a way, it was sportier than the Falcon could ever be, plus it had hints of Euro-car bling (maybe it was that mesh in the grille). Some called it the "Poor-man's Thunderbird." The $2,500 price tag was very welcome too, in addition to the soon-to-be-available plethora of optional V8 engines.

Now on to the specifications of the Mustang II: It was basically the same car as the stock 1965 (OK, '64 1/2) Mustang, except for the extended nose and different tail. It also had a lift-off hardtop, which customers assumed would be available when the Mustang came out (they didn't know they would have to wait several generations for that option).

It had a 289-cubic-inch high performance engine, though the first Mustangs would only have a 260-incher if you opted for a V8. The engine was already "Cobra-modified" and mated to a four-speed manual transmission.

Will it ever be sold? Well, Detroit is a beleaguered city, and the car is owned by the Detroit Historical Museum. It's conceivable that the museum may someday need to sell a car or two in order to keep its doors open. If it does reach the auction block, we predict this will be the most valuable Mustang ever sold (Unless of course, Ford ever decides to sell the Mustang I mid-engined two seater). Look at it this way: since its maker never sold it per se, it's still a *one-owner car...*

Chapter 17
Pretender to the Throne (Bugatti Royale Type 41 Kellner Coupe)

You can never tell who wants a refrigerator.

Briggs Cunningham, who is discussed elsewhere in this book in the context of the sports cars bearing his name, was an American patrician. He was not just born with a silver spoon in his mouth but a platinum one. His middle name was "Swift" and the Swifts were the owners of a large meat packing firm.

He was one of those heirs in the pre-war era who didn't have to be at the offices of the family's business site, just collect dividends and maybe attend the annual board meeting. He called himself a "sportsman" which was kind of a '50s euphemism for "nothing else to do in life but play." And play he did, like competing in the America Cup yacht races in yachts he commissioned from scratch.

And he also ran his own cars, bearing his name, at the 24 Hours of Le Mans before he switched to marques like Jaguar, Maserati and Corvette. (He also ran Cadillacs which showed a deep faith in GM). Far from being arrogant as one would expect a man to be with his fortune, he was quite the personable chap. He must have been, because in the world of barn-finders, he hit a home run when he talked the Bugatti family out of what would become one of the most valuable cars in the world, the second to the last Royale, the Kellner-bodied coupe chassis, serial number 41.141.

The Type 41 Royale is said to have come about because Ettore Bugatti, known as *Le Patron,* took exception to the comments of an English lady who once compared his cars unfavorably with those of Rolls-Royce. This critic inferred that *true* Royals such as the Royal family of England would never leave the brand they loved (not to mention drive a foreign car—the horror!).

So, maybe to spite that Royalist, he built a huge car, hoping to sell it to Royal families all over Europe. Some say it was because he hoped to get a contract from the French government to make V-16 aircraft engines, and his plan was then to cut the prototype airplane engine in half, so he would also have the engine for a huge car fit for royalty. Bugatti engines apparently never made it to airplanes but ironically the extra engines for Royales did make it to railroad locomotives powered by either two or four of the eight-cylinder units.

The prototype for the road car was nearly 15 liters, a true monster. In "production" form, it was reduced to a mere 12.8 liters; each cylinder still displacing more than a modern economy car engine, yet with a claimed modest output of 275 horsepower.

A REFERIGERATOR? WHO WOULDA THOUGHT?

How did Cunningham wrest the car from its builders? Here's a story that is a good example in the visit-the-automaker strategy. On a visit to France in 1950, a friend introduced him to Bugatti's daughter L'Ebe. She had the three unsold Royales bricked up in the family home at Ermenonville. They had been hidden there for the duration of the war, and the way you discouraged those wily Germans from looting them, presumably, was to brick up a building so they wouldn't know what was there (hey, there's no door so there must be nothing in that building…how dumb are we?). Well, the occupiers might have had an inkling, but were more concerned with the machine tools that they could use for the war effort than they were what old cars the family had stashed away. Or maybe their Germanic pride convinced them nothing Bugatti had in the way of car design could touch a Mercedes.

She agreed to sell Cunningham the Berline de Voyage and the Kellner, two of the six Royales made, but felt that the Coupe Napoleon—the most dramatic of them all—should stay in France. The cars were exchanged for a small but undisclosed sum of money, plus a couple of new General Electric refrigerators, then unavailable in France.

On their arrival in the States, the Berline de Voyage found its way into the Harrah Collection, a car collection owned by casino magnate William Harrah, a collection that eventually grew to 1,000 cars. The whole collection eventually came to be sold when Harrah died and he had failed to establish a trust to operate the museum on its own so some cars had to be sold to save the rest.

The Kellner car then went to Cunningham who still had the other Royale he had bought. Cunningham had never embarked on a restoration of the Kellner during his 37-year ownership, even leaving the interior original. Unlike the American luxury car of the prewar period, the Duesenberg, the Bugatti Type 41 lacked a speedometer, rev counter or even a fuel gauge, but there are a few minor instruments clustered in the center of the basic-looking dash. Like all French luxury cars before the Second World War, the Royale is right-hand drive (and he was aiming it at the Royal market).

Cunningham enjoyed his car for decades, keeping it in a museum in Costa Mesa, California, until he suddenly decided in 1986 to close his museum and sell all the cars. Some say the reason for his cashing out quickly was due to the government changing its rules regarding the ability to write a car collection off by having a museum dedicated to them. Others point a finger at the new Mrs. Cunningham (When the wife speaks, good cars go).

At any rate, In 1987 the whole collection went to a man named Collier, who was a car racer himself (and whose father and brothers had raced with Cunningham before the war, when the Collier brothers had their own private racetrack built at their estate overlooking the Hudson River). So it was an "emotional" sell, selling the cars he loved to someone he knew. Plus, Mr. Collier had the money. However, Mr. Collier's taste was more in postwar cars, particularly Porsches. He didn't have need for a monster car, so the car was consigned to Christie's auction at the Royal Albert Hall in London, where it went for £5.5 million ($9.7 million USD) to Swedish property tycoon Hans Thulin.

Sometime later, Thulin offered it through Kruse Brothers in 1989 in Las Vegas, where Ed Weaver bid the car to $11.5 million, which was declined by Thulin, whose reserve was $15 million. On the collapse of his empire, Thulin sold the car in 1990 for a reported $15.7 million to the new kings of the car collecting world: the Japanese. In this case it was the Japanese conglomerate, Meitec Corporation, who kept it in their modern building basement until 2001, when Bonhams sold it by private treaty (means "undisclosed deal") through Bonhams & Brooks. More recently it has been offered by Swiss broker Lukas Huni.

The originality of the Kellner-bodied car ishows how little use the car has had in many decades since it was built. When a British journalist flew to Japan to drive the car (when it was priced at $10 million) he noted the windscreen's primitive brown tint was turning blotchy with age. And this on a car with only 15,000 miles!

Lesson for barn-finders? Try, before you have your first meet-up with the owner, to make every effort to find out what the car owner needs. Americans who hear this story are dumbfounded, I mean even in 1950, how hard was it in France to get a refrigerator? Apparently hard enough in Molsheim, France, to swing the deal with the Bugatti family. Anyway, in a nutshell, the trick is to find out what they need and to satisfy that need…and drive away in your prize.

Chapter 18
The Junkyard Bug (Bugatti Type 41 Royale)

Yes, found in a Bronx junkyard.

It is a damn good thing that Charlie Chayne, a top engineer at Buick (where he was chief engineer from 1936 to 1951) went to the horse racing track now and then, because in 1937, while at a track called Roosevelt Racetrack, he saw a magnificent open car, a huge car, bigger than a V-16 Cadillac, bigger than a Duesenberg. It had a custom body made in Germany. He just had to have that car.

He did some investigation into who owned this car, called a Bugatti, but didn't make an offer. However, he did let it be known far and wide among car enthusiasts that he wanted that car should it ever come up for sale. It was a Bugatti Royale.

The Type 41 Royale was no ordinary Bugatti, not that you could ever say any Bugatti was "ordinary." Bugattis are to European luxury cars what the Duesenberg SJ was in the U.S. before the war, the crème de la crème. This Bugatti Type 41 Royale was the brainchild of Ettore Bugatti, and also a hugely expensive misstep in the history of his firm.

In the 1920s, Bugatti was expecting to get a contract from the French military to build 16-cylinder aircraft engines. The contract never materialized, but Bugatti felt he could use half that engine, a straight eight, to form one of the most amazing luxury cars in history. The Type 41 Royale engine had massive displacement: 12.7 liters, or over 700 cubic inches, roughly twice the size of most of the largest production V8s that would be built by Detroit four decades later. This is still the largest engine of any car to be sold privately.

Equally massive was the 15-foot wheelbase which, when bodied, stood about five feet tall at the hood alone. The car was incredibly imposing, whether in limousine or coupe form. Unfortunately, Ettore's timing was terrible—the world was about to enter into the period of economic malaise known as The Great Depression. He might have even had an inkling that he was building what would become four-wheeled white elephants, because one of the interesting things about the car is the radiator cap, a replica of a Rembrandt Bugatti elephant sculpture. (Rembrandt was Ettore's brother, the sculptor in the very artistic Bugatti family.)

This particular Bugatti Type 41, SN 41 121, was the sole subject of a book called *The Complete Car Modeller 2* by Gerald Wingrove, published in 1991 and again in 1994. This body style is more accurately known as a "Drophead" Coupe—a fabric top that goes down is the "head" and the "drop" meaning you could drop it. Chayne found that it was made to the order of Dr. A. Joseph Fuchs, a German orthopedic surgeon and successful amateur racing driver.

The good doctor reportedly paid $41,000 for just the bodywork by Ludwig Weinberger of Cologne, who was known for doing custom body jobs on BMW 328s before the war. The whole Bugatti, body and chassis, would be more like a million dollars today. The finished car was delivered to him in 1932 but he didn't get to enjoy it for long.

Shortly after Adolph Hitler came to power in Germany in 1933, Dr. Fuchs slipped away to Switzerland and from there to Trieste, Italy. Eventually he discovered that there was a place for fugitive Jews in Shanghai. He had his massive Bugatti shipped to him there, but by 1937, the advance of Japanese troops into the south of China put the Doctor and his Royale on the move yet again. He emigrated to Canada, and eventually ended up in New York state, where Chayne providentially saw his car while the Doctor was at the racetrack.

There were no more sightings of the car after the war started because at some point the block froze and cracked in the New

York winter and it sat out back of the Doctor's house under a tarp where it was immovable. Needless to say, there was no place at the time that you could order a spare engine block, the Bugatti factory having been occupied by the Nazis (and they weren't taking orders from Americans, thank you).

Even if you could order an engine and get on a ship, freighters were being torpedoed on the North Atlantic in frightening numbers, some being sunk within sight of New York City!

Yet Chayne did not give up. The book *Le pur-sang des automobile* by H. G. Conway has extensive coverage of this car, and the story of how it was discovered in a junkyard in the Bronx area of New York City in 1943. The Doctor had tried to sell it with the broken block but there were no takers, hence the junkyard route. Then Charles Chayne's widespread enthusiasm for the car paid off. A friend called up and told him he better move fast because it was seen in a junkyard in the Bronx. Though based in Detroit, Chayne sent funds for his friend to buy the car for him and the deal was done in 1943 reportedly for $400 plus $12 tax, making it one of the all-time great finds in barn-find annals. He began to repair the engine and restore the car after peace returned in 1946.

Being an engineer, he couldn't help but modify the car a bit but all for drivability reasons. He had a custom manifold built toting four Stromberg carburetors in place of the original single carburetor and converted the original mechanical brakes to hydraulics. He also replaced the aluminum wheels, having new ones made to the same design.

During its restoration, the exterior color was changed from the original black (some say the car was black and yellow originally) to oyster white, with dark green trim. Chayne also replaced the interior, modifying it to make it more adaptive to his 6-foot, 3-inch frame. In 1958, he and his wife, Ester, donated it to the Henry Ford Museum. The Museum has no plans to sell it (but, shame on us, we didn't ask).

David Lillywhite, an editor at Britain's *Octane* magazine wrote, "...the Royale Cabrio by Ludwig Weinberger, 41121, is the only fully convertible cabriolet, and for this it is arguably the most valuable."

Lesson to be learned? From the moment Chayne saw the car parked at a racetrack, he began a dossier and began taking notes tracking it. He let every car friend know that he wanted to hear about it if the car showed up. Of course, when it did, being a high ranking engineer at GM, he had the research facilities to make repairs—maybe more than any hobbyist could hope to have access to. But the key was first in finding the car, and, secondly, being ready to buy when it hove into view.

Ultimate lesson to be learned? Don't ever scoff when someone says, "Say, I heard there's an unusual car in that junkyard...."

Chapter 19
Smokey's Last Revenge (1964 Corvette XP-819)

GM fights to wrest back a prototype, but loses.

If you went to the 2012 Amelia Island's Concours d'Elegance you might have noted an unusual chassis on display called the Corvette XP-819. This is yet another story of impassioned engineers and designers creating what they thought would be a great car, only to have it tossed in the ash heap of history. Well, sorta. It really comes down to a battle between "Mr. Corvette" as the Belgian-born, German-educated engineer Zora Arkus-Duntov was known (though the Corvette already existed when he was hired at GM in 1955) and his nemesis, Frank Winchell, who was in charge of R&D out at the GM Proving Grounds. Each man had his own fiefdom.

Zora, who had raced a mid-engined Porsche at Le Mans in '55, was considered by one and all (or the press anyway) to be GM's No. 1 expert on racing and all things sports car. Winchell was less in the limelight, due to the fact that the projects he was working on were secret. They only got publicized when the car was a show car or announced as set for production.

In a nutshell, the battle over the XP-819 can be summed up as which was better for a sports car—rear-engine, mid-engined or front engine? While Zora liked the idea of making mid-engined Corvettes and had already engineered the CERV II, a mid-engined 4WD prototype that was on the cover of *Motor Trend*, R&D's Frank Winchell believed that you didn't need to go mid-engined. He thought a rear engine was not so bad as the nay-sayers said. After all, hadn't Porsche succeeded for several decades with the rear-engined, not mid-engined, 911?

So Winchell's group mounted an aluminum block V8 over the rear wheels of a prototype with a sort of spine frame similar in shape to the front-engined Lotus Elan. No problem in making the engine—GM had been making aluminum V8s for racing for years. Once they had the mechanical layout, Winchell called up Larry Shinoda, the Japanese American designer who was Bill Mitchell's "pet designer" (with his own private studio in a basement of the design center) and had him design a body, which to be charitable, was not much more than a series of Corvette clichés stitched together.

The body was paired with a marine-spec reverse-rotation small-block V8 mated to a two-speed transaxle. Ah, but wouldn't a sports car be better with a manual transmission? Yes, it would (in those days before automatics became so versatile as they are today) but GM wasn't about to pony up millions to have a transaxle designed for it.

Even after decades, the car remains controversial because it is a symbol of the battle between Zora and Winchell. Jerry Burton, who wrote a biography of Duntov (Bentley Publishers, 2002) was quoted in the *NY Times* saying, "Winchell was introverted and quiet. Zora was a showman who resented not being more involved. He felt that anything to do with Corvettes should be under his control." The design did have one idea that would have saved it, running the gas tank through the central backbone in a flexible urethane bag. That helped make up for the car's 69% rear weight bias. It also previewed other technology like the adjustable pedals, a one-piece removable roof and urethane foam bumpers.

Then came the testing. Though Winchell probably turned red with embarrassment, the car proved to be "tail-happy." That's a racer's expression for "wants to over-steer." Shinoda had predicted it would pull 1g lateral force on the skid-pad, but the trouble came in getting there—the rear end would come around on you when you least expected it. Paul van Vaulkenburgh, an engineer at GM at the time who later became known as a journalist/tech editor on *Sports Car Graphic,* was a test driver who managed to crash it. It turned out it required larger tires on the rear than the front just to hang onto the road. If you tried running the same size tires all around, it would spin out. But GM, back at that time, wasn't too keen on providing different-sized tires on the same car, owing to the problem of what did you do when you had a flat tire?

SMOKEY THE BANDIT

Now comes the intrigue, involving an infamous racecar preparer, the late "Smokey" Yunick, who ran a racecar garage in Daytona Beach, Florida, that bore this slogan over its doors: "The Best Damn Garage in Town." It turned out that Yunick was best friends forever with Semon "Bunkie" Knudsen, a high flying GM executive (even a second generation executive at GM). Knudsen was forever grateful to Yunick for "tuning" Pontiacs back when GM was sponsoring Pontiacs in NASCAR.

"Tuning" is a word I put in quotation because Yunick was in point of fact, one of the all-time great cheaters in racing, subscribing to the theory that "If you ain't cheatin', you ain't winning." GM, as per the protocol of the time, had ordered the prototype to be destroyed and sold for scrap. That was done but, they should have figured, the car going to Smokey, that there would be some blowback later on. It was reportedly cut into two pieces and Smokey thought he would use a part here and there.

Reportedly it was stored in an old paint booth in Smokey's Daytona Beach shop, until it was sold to a Chevrolet dealer in the late 1970s. According to an article in the *New York Times,* the dealer was Steve Tate who "recognized the unique XP serial number in the parts pile and promptly bought the car from Yunick, eventually reassembling it. Once the frame was together, pictures of the car when it was at GM were obtained and a new mold made to make a new body, the two mated, and viola! A collector's item!"

Smokey, who has since died, was getting revenge by putting

94

it back together, maybe for Winchell who didn't like his project being deep-sixed.

Ironically when it was put up for auction, a new controversy erupted. Before the gavel could fall, GM's phalanx of lawyers descended upon the auction huffing and puffing, saying in effect, "That car was never supposed to be sold!" But the judge, maybe a guy who once owned a GM lemon, ruled that GM couldn't have it both ways: they had already written off their expenses by destroying the car. Now that a later owner stood to profit from the car resurrected, they couldn't come back and claim it, or forbid that owner from selling it.

Of course, GM could have bought it back to put an end to the problem, but the last thing they wanted was a cobbled-together prototype that reminded the public of the ill-fated Corvair, a rear-engined car that brought them a lot of grief in 1965 after safety crusader Ralph Nader brought out a book that highlighted its peculiar handling at the limit.

The XP-819 prototype went through a few more owners and ended up in the hands of someone positioned to display it properly, Mike Yager, founder of Mid-America Motorworks, a Corvette and VW parts and accessories supplier based in Effingham, Illinois. He bought the XP-819 at a Monterey, California, auction in August 2002.

When Yager bought it, according to Stuart Schwartzapfel's story in the *New York Times,* a lot of work had to be done. "We discovered the car was put together very crudely, after taking delivery." He took it to a shop called Corvette Repair in Valley Stream, New York, owned by Kevin Mackay, who, before this car, restored significant Corvettes like the Briggs Cunningham team racecar that won its class at Le Mans in 1960 and the 1963 Corvette Coupe Speciale Rondine, a one-off Pininfarina-designed show car.

Kevin Mackay told the *Times* about the X-819: "It was a diamond in the rough. The entire center section of the frame was missing. We rebuilt the chassis and reskinned the car by grinding the body down and adding layers and layers of fiberglass."

When it wasn't done in time for the Amelia Island Concours, the Concours management was enlightened enough to allow a display of the drivable chassis—sans body, but with functional brakes, steering column and two seats—and Yager plans to have the complete XP-819 shown at the same show in 2014. *The Times* quoted Yager as saying: "When I think about 819, I know that I will be able to confidently tell people who visit my museum, 'You have definitely never seen one of these before.'"

Amelia Island Concours founder Bill Warner told the press: "So many valuable prototypes disappear or end up in the junkyard once their usefulness ends. I'm glad this one made it back to tell its story. It's a unique piece of GM heritage and a design that might have worked if it had more development and testing time; just look at the Porsche 911."

Barn-finder's lesson? Don't believe people who tell you, yeah, that car has been "destroyed" or "cut up." Maybe they *were* cut up but, if so, all you need is a welding torch to make it live again.

Chapter 20
From World's Fair to Woodward
(1964 Corvette Coupe)

Wherein a Concept Car "falls" into executive hands.

Flashback to the mid-to-late '60s. I am in my hometown Detroit (actually I grew up in Berkley, which is most known among hot rodders for the Vinsetta Garage at 12 1/2 mile and Woodward) late one night doing the Woodward Ave. cruise thing, driving that four-laner in endless loops from Teds in Royal Oak, up to the Totem Pole near 14 Mile.

One cold night I am sitting in the Pole when a red Corvette cruises through. Not just any Corvette. I can see it is candy apple red, and has these humongous side pipes. The light bulb should have flashed on in my head that it was the 1964 New York World's Fair Corvette styling car. I was in fact at the fair, but I digress… Anyway, from my 10-second glance I knew this custom-painted car was something pretty damn special.

Flash forward 40 years or so. I am at Pebble Beach for the concours, and while crossing the lawn on the way to the con-cours grounds, I pass the Blackhawk Collection display. Same car. It had many unique features, not the least of which was the unique fuel-injection housing protruding through a hole in the hood, similar to the top-of-the-line Corvette in 2012. In a way, this car is close kin to the special Corvettes built for the wives of GM exec Bunkie Knudsen and Harley Earl.

Officially, this car was built expressly for display at the 1964 New York World's Fair. When that show folded, the car went to a warehouse where reportedly the unique instrument cluster was removed. After that, fearing the car's safety in NYC, GM returned it to Detroit where a modified '63 production car instrument cluster was installed.

Enter Alex Maier, another top exec for GM, a VP no less. He thought this little bolide would be a nice toy for his 16-year-old son, Steve. He didn't have to worry about his son burning himself, or his friends on the exhaust (like you did on 427 Cobras). They were plastic, with no real side exhaust. Maier ordered the mechanics in the Engineering garage to put a production exhaust under the car.

Steve Maier must have been an exemplary teenager. Except for maybe cruising Woodward, he treated the car well, even refusing to wear shoes in the car. He kept it all the way to the late '80s when he realized hey, he owned a piece of history.

The first buyers to successfully glom onto it were a quartet of Texan businessmen who bought it as an investment. The car ended up in Texas. Werner Meier, a Corvette restorer in Detroit, knew more about what the car was than most, and flew there to try to buy it. But his hopes were dashed when Werner realized that he would have to sell five of his own cars to get it, so he ultimately passed on it. Some deals involve too much sacrifice, but on the other hand, sometimes it's worth dumping everything you have to get that one great car.

The car had a 375-horsepower, 327-cubic-inch fuel-injection system with a taller doghouse than standard, which is why the hole was cut in the hood. The engine was painted black and complemented with a ton of chrome accessories. One major change to the drivetrain was the addition of disc brakes, not available in 1964. The car went instead to famed Corvette dealer, Corvette Mike in Tustin, California; and from there to the famous Blackhawk Collection where your author saw it in their display at Pebble.

In 2001, another famous Corvette collector by the name of Mike Yager, bought the '64 at a car auction held during the weekend of the Pebble Beach Concours d'Elegance. Who did he choose to restore it? None other than Werner Meier, the specialist in Detroit who not only craves Corvettes, but former GM special Corvettes that were built for car show displays and/or executives.

Now this was the case of a "barn find" where the car never had been "let go" to descend deep into a state of shabbiness. To the contrary, it arrived clean and showable; but to an expert like Meier the adjectives "clean" and "correct" are not always the same thing. The car needed mechanical fettling in the brakes, new rubber bushings, and the knock-off wheels were wrong. And finally, all those involved agreed that it was important for this particular car to have the side exhausts functional. Meier made the whole system.

This car enjoys a special status compared to the "executive's wives cars" like the Knudsen and Earl roadsters, because it was made as a show car for the World's Fair and was seen by millions. Any changes on the car are understandable, made after its show career when, as a daily driver, young Maier would take the car to the Tech Center garage to fix what broke, so naturally they'd replace the '64 parts with parts from later Corvettes if they fit.

The repair crew there weren't thinking "originality," they were thinking "let's get this car back on the road quick." For example, as noted by barn finder expert Jerry Heasley, the clock is '65 vintage and the brake master cylinder is '67. The presence of metal grates on the floor take some explaining. GM VP in charge of styling, William L. Mitchell, liked those grates and had them installed on half a dozen GM show cars.

What are they for? Suffice to say, Michigan is a muddy, slushy place in winter, and the grates allow you to clean the crud off your shoes. The holes on top of the body at the rear also take some explaining. They look like exhaust ports on a Chris Craft speedboat, but they were simulated brake exhaust vents.

Another Bill Mitchellism of the Sixties was going to six taillights on show Corvettes, though the original production cars from '63 to '67 had four in all. Actually, the clay models of the Stingray series of Corvettes had six tail lamps, so that was the original intention, though at the last minute, they reverted to four. Also, if you look real close, they aren't original Corvette taillights, but are much wider with a larger-diameter.

The Corvette emblems in the back and on the glove box door were special, also non-production. Neither is the grille. It's an egg-crate design, but hand-fabricated from aluminum plates. The door panels were outfitted with lights that flashed sequentially when opened, and also the panel itself had a metal-like surface for a very clean look.

The Corvette had high-back bucket seats that featured special leather trim that were re-upholstered inside to regain their plumpness that was lost during years of road use. The car has cut-pile carpeting instead of the original loop. The weather-stripping is red, whereas in production cars it was black. The interior was completed with a re-holstered console. They decided not to repaint it, but were able to repair the tiny cracks from show car paint. The result of all this effort? A car that has to be worth a million at least.

Lessons to be learned? First: flog me with a cat-o-nine-tails for being flat-out lazy. If I was the car enthusiast I say I am (and back then I was a much younger man to boot), I should have leapt from my car, ran up to the Corvette before it went out onto Woodward again, found out who was driving it, and periodically pestered young Maier with calls for the next few years in the familiar but effective wear-them-down-to-the-nubs technique.

Specific lesson for readers: If you have read of a show car, or concept car, that went to a private owner employed by an auto-maker or automaker supplier after its show career, best check those executive rosters closely, as one of the former show cars might still be in their family garage, just as this one was for decades. Anybody who asked might have got it.

Including me.

Chapter 21
The Burning Woman (1964 Cobra Daytona Coupe)

Lost, then found...with no small amount of tragedy inbetween.

Back when I was writing one of my Shelby books, in the '70s, George Stauffer, a prominent Cobra collector, told me there were six Daytona coupes built, but although the whereabouts of five were known, there was a sixth one that "belonged to a crazy old lady" who refused to sell.

He was talking, of course, about CSX2287, the one car out of the six made that was bodied in the U.S, and the very first coupe made to Pete Brock's immortal design. It is a very historic car: the first coupe built, the first to win a race, and immortalized by its fire in the pits at Daytona in February of 1964 which, fortunately, did not destroy it.

The car was rebuilt and raced and helped build the Shelby-American legend by getting the Cobra past the 165-mph barrier the roadster had hit in aerodynamics. Then it disappeared. Only a few people knew it still existed and among them was Donna O'Hara, who it turns out wasn't that old by the time the car emerged into the sunlight, but she definitely qualifies by most definitions of "crazy." She was a former Sears employee who was in a dispute with her boss at the time of her death, and had been fired.

The Cobra didn't come to light until the year 2000, some weeks after she was found by police at the edge of death in the wee early hours of the morning on a horse trail in Fullerton,

California, with burns over 90% of her body. She died soon after. She had a father who was once a bodyguard for famed rock and roll producer Phil Spector. Spector was the connection to the car. First a little background into rock and roll in the Sixties. Back then, it was perfectly legal to buy a racecar right off the Le Mans track and drive it around. Sonny and Cher had a Ferrari 250LM, Dean Paul Martin had a Ferrari P3/4 and Spector had the Daytona Cobra. Spector finally got too many tickets in it and told his bodyguard to "get rid of it."

Was it disposed of in some far-off country? No, it spent the next 30-plus years in storage where Mrs. O'Hara had put it after she drove it to high school every day. As the price of Cobras increased, the wheelers and dealers of the Cobra world like Lynn Park, Stauffer, and even Shelby himself, were hot on the trail.

But only a few, including Park and Shelby, found the lady and tracked her to her door in Anaheim. She wouldn't budge. Even Shelby, a notorious lady charmer who had dated at least one Miss Universe, failed.

Despite the number of people that talked to her, only a couple got to see the car, so it was known that it still existed. When I was told it existed, no one would tell me the city where the owner was, otherwise I could have run an ad and hey, maybe smoked it out. Everyone involved in the hunt was being greedy, not wanting to share what they knew and, as a result, the barn finders were coming up cold.

First, let's go back and examine the car's pedigree: completed at AC Cars as a chassis-only and air-freighted to Shelby American in Venice in November of 1963, it was then hurriedly readied for the Daytona Continental, a 2000km FIA-sanctioned endurance race only three months away. The chassis was immediately modified and Brock constructed a plywood body buck to use as a pattern for the body panels which were hand-formed at Cal Metal Shaping, a specialty shop in Los Angeles. The individual body sections were then brought back to Shelby-American where they were welded into a seamless body. Once the car was completed it was tested at Riverside by Ken Miles, and despite all the jabs Brock took before it ran, it smoked the roadster's best times and Brock's Folly was vindicated. The kid had done good!

It was painted Viking Blue and made Daytona, the first FIA race of the 1964 season. Cobra team drivers Bob Holbert and Dave MacDonald were holding first place after 7 hours when a freak fire during a pit stop occurred, caused when gasoline being poured into an already full tank splashed onto the overheated rear end and hot brake rotors, and that put the car out of the race. Surviving crew members say now that they could have had it running again in less than an hour but Shelby withdrew the car and all discussion ended.

A month later, at Sebring, the car vindicated itself by finishing 1st in class and 4th overall. It was then posted overseas where it ran as part of a team of Cobra FIA competition roadsters at Spa, Le Mans, Rheims, Goodwood and in the Tour de France. In '65 it was painted the 1965 team colors, Guardsman Blue with a pair of wider white stripes, but only ran one race that season—Le Mans—where it failed to finish. The car was returned to the States, refurbished, and put on display at various car shows. By then it was obsolete, so Shelby didn't mind loaning it to a group that wanted to take it to Bonneville, where it set 23 national and international speed records.

The car looked so rough after days on the salt, that Shelby was willing to part with it. It just looked too rough. Jim Russell, the owner of American Russkit, a Los Angeles company that made plastic-bodied scale model kits and slot cars, bought CSX2287 for $4,500. For that price Shelby-American even went through the car. The engine and transmission were removed while the chassis, running gear, brake calipers and wheels were sandblasted to try to get rid of the corrosive salt. The chassis and running gear were repainted black, the headers sandblasted and repainted white and brakes rebuilt.

A fresh stock 289 Hi-Po engine with Webers was installed along with the original transmission. The ducting, the original seats and interior were cleaned and refitted, while Russell specified that a tamer GT350 street clutch be installed. The car was thoroughly tested to insure that it was running smoothly before it left Shelby-American.

The next time the car popped up was when the owner advertised it in December 1966 in *Competition Press*, a racing newspaper, for $12,500.

The coupe was purchased (the actual sale price is not known but is now being reported as $7,500) by Phil Spector, a record producer famous at the time for his "wall of sound" concept as well as producing hit groups like the Ronettes and the Beatles. Spector had an extremely onerous personality, and was wont to take out a pistol and shoot it in the general direction of anyone who disagreed with him. After getting one too many speeding tickets, he had offered the car to his bodyguard, George Brand, who had come to work for him in 1968.

When Brand took the car, according to him he purchased it for roughly $1,000. He had divorced his wife Dorothy around the time he began working for Spector. Why he thought his daughter needed a 180-mph car to drive to high school one can only guess at. Maybe he felt guilty leaving the home. Whatever—it improved her popularity among the gear-heads at high school.

At any rate, his daughter Donna married and changed her last name to "O'Hara" and lived a quiet life until decades later when the 54-year-old up and committed suicide by pouring gasoline on herself and setting herself alit one night in Fullerton park.

The police in point of fact found her still alive but with burns over 90% of her body. She died en route to the hospital. At first the police didn't know who she was. She had neglected to go to the horse trail in the dead of night with any i.d. so at first the police had no clue who she was and there wasn't the usual nearby abandoned car to trace her.

It took them seven weeks to connect a missing persons report with the deceased, and that's only after a fellow Sears employee and former boyfriend of Mrs. O'Hara reported she was missing, which he only discovered when she failed to make a house payment on a rental property they owned together.

Her mother, who was in her '80s, in processing her daughter's papers, subsequently found a letter from a British car dealer based in Montecito, near Santa Barbara, offering her daughter millions for the car. The Brit, on the trail of the car for some time, had shamed the legion of American barn finders paltry efforts by simply hiring a private detective and giving him the last owner's name which had been printed in the SAAC Cobra registry.

She wasn't, it turned out, that hard to find.

She was a homeowner in Orange County, and a recently employed person—which makes it duck soup for a detective to find someone. The dealer, on finding Donna O'Hara's address, had written her a letter which went unanswered. That was the letter the mother of the deceased found. The mother then called the dealer and arranged for a $3 million sale. (A good price, she must have researched it and found it was one of the most valuable of 998 Cobras made.)

She went to the storage yard where the car was only to find the yard owner had changed locks on the lockup for non-payment of the bill. She had the lock broken, removed the car, and it was trucked up to Montecito in the dead of night, reportedly the tow truck operator not even being given a destination, only a rendezvous point. Why? Because the ownership of the car could still be contested, as everyone involved soon found out. There's an old rule in the law called "possession is nine points of the law" that means, in effect, you operate from a position of strength if you have the object of dispute in your possession (so tow first, ask questions later).

Lynn Park, incidentally, was hot on the trail of the car, but filed his injunction to stop the car from being sold too late, the car already having been whisked northward.

The British buyer had notified potential bidders of the car's emergence while the car was still en route to Santa Barbara. The first bidder was Steve Volk, a Cobra collector in Colorado, who said he would come to buy it but he didn't want to come to California on a holiday, so he put off his trip for a day.

Mistake.

A Pennsylvania surgeon didn't tarry, paid a reported $4 million for it and now owns the car, which is the pride of his museum.

Did everyone live happy ever after? Not quite. The former high school boyfriend of Mrs. O'Hara, a man named Kurt Goss, showed up to claim the car and, in a court proceeding, said Mrs. O'Hara had given him several cars weeks before her death, most of which could be classified as junk, but on the paper bearing her signature it listed the Cobra among the other cars. He had, it turned out, driven the car way back when Donna had driven it to high school and no doubt lusted after it ever since.

He laid claim to the money paid to Mrs. O'Hara's mother, who unfortunately had donated most of the money to the church. The judge accepted his claim. This writer does not know if Mrs. O'Hara's mother had to "make good" out of her own funds but her lawyer said the judge's decision "was a grave miscarriage of justice."

At any rate, the story took on a life of its own. (Hey Hollywood—you want a story with all the elements of classic noir?)

What's the lesson for barn finders? I have to laugh when I think of the guys who told me they were on the trail but the fact of the matter is that only one barn finder opened his wallet far enough to hire a detective to nail down its owner's location. His letter got him the car. Sure he only owned it for one day but since he made between $850,000 and a million dollars in one day flipping it, I'd say any money he spent on the P.I. was money well spent, wouldn't you?

Chapter 22
A Four-Cylinder Ferrari (857 Sport)

Yes, they made them and this one took decades to unite with its engine.

Ferraris are famous for having twelve cylinders, but it so happens that one of the biggest sellers among the prancing horses at the 2012 collector car auctions in Monterey was a four-cylinder Ferrari, a car that had a checkered career that all ended happily. The car is the little known 857 Sport, a two-seater that at first glance, looks like a full-fendered Testa Rossa, or some would say a 121LM.

The four-cylinder engine was designed by Aurelio Lampredi for the '52 world championship in just a few weeks. It had twin overhead cams, both gear driven, two spark plugs per cylinder, dry sump and twin carbs. Ascari won the F2 and '53 World Championships driving a 500 F2 powered by a four-cylinder engine so Ferrari knew the same design could be used in sports cars.

There were several four-cylinder sports cars preceding this particular car including the 625TF, two 735 Sports and the 500 Mondial. In '55 four 857 Sports were made, of which this is the last one off the assembly line. The "857" name is per Ferrari practice which refers to the volume of a single cylinder. The power was 270 horsepower at 5700 rpm but later it got to 285 horses at 6000 rpm.

The car made its debut in the Tourist Trophy race at Dundrod in Ireland. Three works cars were entered by Ferrari but Gendebien crashed one of the cars on practice before the race so only two ran. Of course the Mercedes 300SLR "steamroller" (a much more expensive car with greater speed, supported by a vast factory presence) won.

In an article by Keith Bluemel in *CAVALLINO* he says that Gendebien test drove three of the factory Monza models before they were sent to races, liked two of them and hated the car shown here, saying it was almost uncontrollable. Still, he was assigned to race it, and being a factory driver, he sucked it up and went out there and crashed, but lived to tell about it.

At this point, Ferrari indulged in a little smoke-and-mirrors to offload the car. Or maybe I could be generous and classify the subterfuge as "stuff-you-don't-tell-the-buyer." It so happens he had a customer for a new Ferrari, John Edgar, an American high roller (whose family owned a firm that made scales for supermarkets) who, once he switched from hydroplane racing to car racing, liked to have the newest cars and to hire the best up-and-coming drivers and Edgar had ordered a new Ferrari, thinking he was getting an 860 Monza. Instead he got the crashed-and-rebuilt 857S.

SWITCHEROO

Well the 857S had been stuffed but expertly repaired at the factory and though Bluemel doesn't tell if they redesigned the suspension, they must have corrected its nasty penchant to understeer because once Edgar got it, it began to run well, taking two wins. The usual driver was Jack McAfee but Edgar had added another driver to his scuderia, the amiable and ever adaptable Carroll Shelby (yes, *that* Carroll Shelby, the Cobra guy). Shelby was better in a bigger engined car, but adapted well to the four-cylinder Ferrari. (In his career he raced more than 50 different marques.)

The 857 Sport as shipped to Edgar also had an elegant tailfin rising out of the headrest fairing. Very few Ferraris had this. Distinctive were the two hood lumps to clear the carburetors. Ritchie Ginther also piloted it at one race, Ginther later not only being a factory team driver and development engineer but also figuring significantly in the future of Shelby-American, being a development driver on the GT40 during its gestation.

The 857 then went to a Stanley Sugarman of Arizona who had Jim Connor, McAfee and Ginther pilot it for him at various Stateside races. Why did Edgar sell it? According to a picture caption in the book *American Sports Car Racing in the '50s*, co-authored by Edgar's son, "Although the 857 won two races for Edgar, it was a maintenance nightmare and was instrumental in Edgar switching to Maserati in 1957."

It's difficult to recall now that Ferrari has been so dominant for decades but back then Maserati was still a strong force in sports car racing, offering a viable alternative to Ferrari if Enzo and his Machiavellian tendencies got to be too much to stomach. Briggs Cunningham, "Gentleman Jim" Kimberly, and others did the marque switch as well.

CHEVY IS HEAVY

Then comes the name of a famous wheeler dealer—Oscar Koveleski—who besides running a famous scale model company, at the time bought and sold interesting cars (having the models, he knew which cars were significant). He bought the 857 through Jim Hall, perhaps even through the dealership called Carroll Shelby Sports Cars where Shelby was partnered with Hall's brother Dick.

Kovelski didn't like the way it ran and did what a lot of Ferrari owners of well-worn Ferraris did in those days—dropped in a Chevy. The car was run with the bow-tie brand engine all the way through 1965. Bluemel says Ferrari owners were so scandalized that they wanted to buy it from him to restore it to the prancing horse clan. Only a few knowledgeable collectors were collecting Ferraris in those days but by the mid-'60s it was already thought sacrilege to pollute a purebred Ferrari with a cast-iron lump of pushrod Detroit V8.

ANDY IS DANDY

Then the car went to a really strange owner—one that this writer was unanle to ascertain could even drive—Andy Warhol.

Yes, that Andy Warhol, co-inventor of what is now called "Pop art." He had it painted yellow with black painted wheels. This author hasn't found a painting of it yet by Andy but Andy not only depicted cars on canvas on occasion, he sometimes painted real cars (most notably the BMW M1 "art car") which have become fine art themselves.

Finally it went to another owner where the car got a Ferrari engine again. Not a four (those engines were hard to find) but a V-12. The next owner of note was Chris Renwick, a British car salesman, who for a time worked out of a dealership near San Diego. He sold it to Sir Anthony Bamford, a British collector and, oh, yes, a billionaire (owns JCB Excavations) who has owned many significant racing Ferraris including a 206SP Dino, a P3/4, etc. Then it went to an Italian Count until being sold to a Frenchman.

All this time the original engine was traveling its separate route through the Ferrari world. It turns out it's a lot harder to find a Ferrari chassis for a four-cylinder engine than it is to find a Ferrari engine for a Ferrari chassis. The car's original engine was in Australia for awhile but, perhaps realizing they couldn't get the car the engine belonged in, the Aussies asked famed attorney and Ferrari collector Ed Niles to broker the engine. Ed offered it to David Cottingham, a British scientist who had become bored with science and decided to leap from the safety of a good job into the unknown morass of restoring racecars. He loved Ferraris. At the time Cottingham didn't have a chassis to put the engine and tranny in but lived in hope the chassis would come to him. His reasoning was only logical if bordering a tad on wishful thinking: if he was the owner of the engine and the engine was not for sale, the owner of the car—whoever it was at the time—would forever have a non-original car. It was a battle of wills. He who stood firm would win.

And, in the end, Cottingham was right.

Twenty-nine years later his patience was rewarded when the French owner of the car offered him the car. Cottingham took it to his shop, DK Engineering, which by now had grown to a multi-million dollar enterprise, and temporarily put in a 250GT V-12. Then he restored the car. Fortunately, the son of John Edgar had a huge photo file on the car as it was in the Fifties and with that as reference, they were able to get the car back to its original configuration, dispensing of the remodeled rear fenders that had been put there during its time in the wilderness as a Chevy-powered hybrid.

The car not only made its debut with its proper four-cylinder engine at the Goodwood Revival vintage race in September 2011 but James Cottingham, one of David's sons—who was probably just a toddler back when his father had bought the engine—was the pilot. He started in pole position and ran strong through most of the race but withdrew with falling oil pressure near the end.

In August 2012 the car made it back across the Atlantic to Carmel, California, where it was put in the tent of Gooding & Co., one of the premier auction companies. When the gavel came down at the auction, the car fetched $6.27 million. Lesson learned: He who owns the engine might eventually get the car…but take it from me, you got a lot more clout when you own the chassis instead of the engine.

Chapter 23
The Car with Four Bodies
(Ferrari 400 Superamerica)

Hey, can we help it if the coachbuilder keeps changing their mind?

This is a story of a car that was more than what you saw at first glance. A car that may turn out to be one of the most valuable Ferrari Superamericas ever made. And I turned it down.

Here's the story. Several decades ago I dropped by Gary Bobileff's place in San Diego. He said he had a Ferrari Superamerica for sale. Now to differentiate between Ferraris of the '60s a tad, the 250 series consisted of either street cars or raucous racers but together, they were the bread and butter of the factory in the late 1950s; the street cars paying for the racecars which were noisy, fast and raceable with a few modifications.

But Europe's most glamorous performance carmaker also built limited editions of cars for the high and the mighty (such as royalty or CEOs) who wanted their Ferrari to be special, one they would not be likely to see coming their way on Rodeo Drive, or while driving through Monte Carlo. Such a car was the Ferrari 400 Superamerica.

Just the name is interesting. Likely not that many Italians had been to America at that time (except for Sergio Pininfarina who had come to America as a guest of Nash when he designed the Nash-Healey sports car). I think while they were working on the car, the Italians envisioned America as a land with arrow straight roads stretching to the horizon toward the mountains or the sea, roads you could go flat to the floor on, to 170 mph and beyond.

The Ferrari 400 Superamerica was changed in numerous ways from its 410 Superamerica predecessor. The chassis was shortened to 95.2 inches (2420mm) versus 102.3 inches (2600mm), and it had a narrower track front and rear. Most important, it had a new engine from a different designer. While the earlier generation 410 used a Lampredi-designed V-12 with roots in Ferrari's 375 Formula 1 car, the 400's V-12 adopted the general architecture of the first Ferrari V-12, the engine designed back at the firm's beginning by Gioachino Colombo. The bore was increased, the stroke lengthened, and updates included those found in the Ferrari 250 GT engine, such as coil valve springs instead of the so-called "hairpin valve springs."

The new engine displaced 3,967cc. Rounded to four liters, this model marked Ferrari's change in nomenclature, this being the first time a Ferrari's model designation indicated the overall displacement of the engine, rather than an individual cylinder's cubic centimeters multiplied by the number of cylinders. Horsepower was quoted at 340 at 7000 rpm. Pininfarina did the styling for the first Ferrari 400 Superamerica (chassis 1517 SA), which made its debut at 1959's Turin show.

That first 400 was not at all like the later production cars. It had some really odd styling features for a Ferrari. A one-off destined for Fiat's Gianni Agnelli, it had nearly flat sides, a vertical rounded corner grille cavity and American-style quad headlamps. At least they made up for that one with a much more attractive cabriolet (convertible) by Pininfarina, which made its debut at the Brussels Motor Show. Pininfarina built 10 cabriolets in all. Scaglietti—Ferrari's in-house coachbuilder, produced a Spyder and a berlinetta coupe; but the car that gave its general shape to all the subsequent 400 Superamerica coupes was the prototype unveiled at the 1960 Turin Auto Show. It was an elegant but restrained shape built on chassis 2207 SA, the car that I almost bought.

It was first labeled "Superfast II." Aldo Brovarone, the Pininfarina stylist who designed the car, told reporters at the time that his inspiration was the Vanwall F1 car. All the Ferrari 400

Superamericas that followed, including those from 1961 on, had a wheelbase extended to 102.3 inches (2600mm).

While at a distance most 400 Superamerica coupes other than the first one look the same, the closer you get, you can see small differences, making each a "custom" in that the high and mighty buyers were permitted to request individualized touches to suit their whim, say a chronometric stopwatch set in a holder below the dash so the owner could demonstrate to a passenger the acceleration or custom-fitted luggage matching the upholstery.

Now what was unusual about the car Gary had, which was light green when I saw it, was that it had a roofline of a 400 Superamerica but some touches that made it seem like an earlier car or a speciale (special car with features dictated by the buyer). Gary said it was "a bit of a truck" to drive and had it fairly priced at $35,000.

That was more than I could stretch to at the time so I demurred but at least I wrote down the chassis number—2207. It was easy to remember early Ferrari chassis numbers because, up until that time they had built that car, they had built so few cars!

In those days, before the internet, I could find little information. You either had the books or old *Ferrari Market Letters* or knew somebody that did and pleaded with them to xerox what they had and send it.

A cursory search in the books yielded the information that 2207 was a very special car because at different times it was one car and other times another car. I found that, in short, it was Pininfarina's development "hack," used by them to try out different designs which they exhibited at auto shows, to see if it generated any orders. Some were so experimental (like being able to cover up the grille) that the ideas never reached production.

If you find what is a very special car, the prudent thing to do would be to find a world-class expert and pay them what they ought to be paid to "vet" the car. Such an expert in the Ferrari field is Marcel Massini, a Swiss living in Berne. I did not, alas, know of his existence then or of his remarkable and widely-praised record keeping. To show to what extent an expert can vet a car, I quote a letter he posted on to a Ferrari forum. This is only a preview sample of what buyers and/or owners would ask from him—in the form of a dossier of known facts—before they plunk down major money on a rare car. And this quote is from 2008, so no doubt, now that it's several years later, a dossier ordered by someone interested in the car would stretch to book-size and would require the price such a custom-made report deserves.

To quote his forum posting back in 2008 on this car:
• 3-13-October 1960 Shown at the XLII Torino show as Superfast II, painted white (Bianco MM 12435) with black interior.
• Thereafter: Modified with air scoop on the hood, rear wheel arch skirts removed, no-draft vents, small air intakes on the fenders.
• 13 May 1961: Certificate of origin issued.
• 19 May 1961: Sold by Ferrari to Pininfarina SpA, who paid 4,500,000 Italian Lire.
• 19 May 1961: Registered on Italian plates of Torino "TO 381641."
• Thereafter: REBODIED by Pininfarina into Superfast III with radical body changes.
• 15 September 1961: Chassis at Pininfarina SpA.
• 28 November 1961: Solex carbs replaced by Weber carbs.
• 21 March 1962: Chassis frame completed.
• 15-25 March 1962: Shown at the XXXII Geneva motor show in Switzerland, now painted metallic green with full red leather interior.
• April 1962: REBODIED again by Pininfarina, now into Superfast IV, with four headlights (330 GT 2+2 prototype/design!), repainted darkblue (Blu Notte).
• 2 August 1962: Sold by Pininfarina to De Nora.

Yes, you read that right. The car, during its time in Italy, had three, maybe four different bodies. Rather facetiously, I would have to say that, in order to show this car properly at a concours like Pebble Beach or Amelia Island, you would have to have all the different bodies standing by and a crane to lift one body off and lower another on the chassis, repeating this procedure every couple hours. They would be:

· Superfast II in white
· Superfast III in green
· Superfast IV in blue

And there may have even been a fourth body with a different nose, and a gold metallic body. It is understandable that one of the earlier noses was changed because the car had a means of blocking off the air intake on cold days and maybe that feature didn't actually work, as things on concept cars often don't. Or the hidden headlights might not have been functional. Or they just wanted to change the car's looks so it wouldn't seem an old design.

At any rate, at some point it was fitted with the standard open headlight nose of the production series; but that concours suggestion isn't the end of it, for even when you switched the body, another judge might come along and decide it's incorrect. Like the broken clock that tells the correct time twice a day, the body on the car would only be correct as to shape and color and interior trim one third or one fourth of the time if you kept the same body on the car. (Racers have the same problem with a racecar that raced at different events for different teams. Do you restore your racecar as per how it looked at Le Mans in '61 or how the same car looked at Sebring in '62?)

As an aside, I estimate SN2207 is now worth roughly $1-2 million. Lesson learned: Even with the rudimentary information Bobileff provided, I should have realized at the time that any Ferrari Superamerica was worth buying. After all it was a car that, from its very conception, was meant to be a step up from the "garden variety" Ferraris like the 250PF coupe. It could only go up in time.

Another lesson learned: There were experts in Ferrari and/or

Pininfarina who could have educated me further, but, on the excuse this was 40 some years ago (and I really didn't have 35K in my pocket), I can beg off my *faux pax*. And will admit now that I didn't know any better. The lesson is, when presented with a rare car like this, do your homework fast and you can buy it right.

I didn't.

Finders keepers, losers weepers.

Chapter 24
The Ferrari in the Field
(Ferrari 750 Monza Spyder)

*Proof that one man's weed
is another man's flower.*

Let's say you are a car guy,
but not the world's leading
authority on any one brand.

Let's say, further, for one reason or another, you
are on a private ranch in Texas, invited there. You are hired to
wash some horses, and in doing so, you happen to look over the
fence and see what looks like a racing Ferrari. Let's add to this
fantasy. You spit out your tobacco juice, push your Stetson back
on your head, and ask the horse owner (a lady) a question, trying to be as casual as you can be:

"Say, what kinda car is that over yonder?"

She says, something to the effect of, "Oh that? That's just
some old Ferrari raced by Count dePortago or something or
other."

All this actually happened to one car-sharp cowpoke in Texas,
a man whose name was Rick Grape. One story says Mr. Grape
was invited to wash horses; but one of his offspring wrote the
author and says he was a professional, so suffice to say that however he got there he was on the property legally.

Which is a lesson learned right there. You can't get too far
trespassing.

Another version of the story is that Grape heard there was
an old Ferrari at the ranch, but this doesn't mean he didn't vol-
unteer to wash horses in order to gain access to a viewpoint
wherein he could have the objective in sight.

Hey, whatever it takes.

To appreciate the caliber of his find, a little background is in order. Although Ferraris are traditionally known for their V-12 engines, which won most of the victories for Ferraris in the '50s and '60s, they were also producers of six-cylinder and even four-cylinder cars. Ferrari had dominated open wheel single-seater Formula 2 racing in 1949, but Gioacchino Colombo's diminutive 1497cc supercharged V-12 used in the Tipo 125 GP car had been an embarrassing failure for the Scuderia in the first two years of the new F1 World Championship, with archrival Italians Alfa Romeo winning the title in 1950 and 1951.

With the World Championship adopting the naturally-aspirated 2.0-liter or 500cc supercharged Formula 2 rules for 1952-3, Enzo Ferrari knew that a major change in engine strategy was called for and he looked to England for inspiration. The four-cylinder engines developed by Alta, a British racecar builder, used less fuel, and were much lighter in a class where there was no minimum limit and also had a broader torque band that better suited the four- and five-speed gearboxes of the era.

In the early '50s Ferrari instructed his favorite engine designer, Aurelio Lampredi, to design a new four-cylinder engine and in 1952 a Lampredi-developed 2.0-liter alloy engine was introduced in a Ferrari 500 F2. Driving this car, Alberto Ascari captured the World Championship in both 1952 and 1953. However, Ferrari's focus was not just F1. He knew he could build cars that could win the new World Sports car Championship, introduced in 1953, and subsequently sell a lot of racecars and road versions of those racecars.

Initially he concentrated on building V-12 powered cars such as the 250 MM and 340 MM to fly his flag in road racing events such as the Le Mans 24-Hour race and Sicily's Targa Florio. But since he had the racing four-cylinder engine he also decided to introduce four-cylinder cars.

There were a couple models before the 750 Monza, which this car is but I would get you lost in Ferrari technicalities to go through their gestation. Suffice to say, the model eventually evolved into the 750 Monza.

The way Ferrari cars got their nickname back then was to be named after the event in which they made their debut. Which explains why the new four got the name "750 Monza." Sitting on a 2.2-meter length wheelbase with the usual welded tubular steel chassis, it had the advantage over a V-12 of a lighter engine, which gave it more balanced handling.

The suspension was independent, with Ferrari's usual unequal-length A-arms and transverse leaf springs in front, and his usual de Dion axle-beam, transverse leaf and parallel trailing-arms in the rear. A sore spot with some drivers was still the presence of drum brakes at a time when the English were switching to discs. And it had slow steering, four turns lock-to-lock. Then again, the lighter weight over the V-12 paid off in better fuel economy. If you could leave out a couple pit stops for fuel you could win a race.

The 750 Monza went into limited production in 1954, with coachwork designed by Pinin Farina (the firm's name then still being two separate words) but wrought of aluminum by Sergio Scaglietti, at first an outside repairman of crashed Ferraris who had a shop near the factory. In fact, after this car, Ferrari liked his work so much that he appointed Scaglietti the de facto "in house" coachbuilder for racing Ferraris, a job he kept all the way until his retirement.

All this is just background to what, in this writer's estimation, remains one of the most classically interesting barn finds in the Ferrari world—the car I call the "Rick Grape 750 Monza" not only because I like saying the name "Rick Grape" but because it was a true barnyard find, or to be technically correct, "open field" find. It could be summarized as "visitor discovers prancing horse abandoned in field."

The Houston-based Grape apparently had come across the car, chassis 0498M, at a Texas ranch in the early 1990s. It had apparently originally been stored in a barn, but in later years room was needed in the barn so the poor old Ferrari had been unceremoniously dragged out and left under a tree, exactly where he found it. He bought the car even before he quite knew its historical significance. The seller had said it had been driven by "de Portago" but Grape had no idea who that was. He just wanted a Ferrari because he thought they were neat looking cars.

He later found out the claim was true, that it was indeed an early ex-factory team car that was piloted by Britain's Mike Hawthorn and the Spanish nobleman Count Alfonso de Portago in the Goodwood Trophy Nine-Hour race in 1954 in England, but they had failed to finish.

Alfonso later died in a fiery crash in a Ferrari, but not this one. He lived life to the fullest, and died at the wheel.

The 750 Monza was later sold to American George Tilp who hired Santa Monica native son Phil Hill to drive the car in five races in the U.S. during 1955. (Hill would later win the Grand Prix Championship and oh, yeah, Le Mans, for Ferrari.) Then, as far as drivers, the car went "amateur" with a lot of races recorded by amateur drivers in small events at forgotten tracks like Mansfield, Louisiana.

At some point apparently something went wrong with the original engine and it was fitted with a replacement four-cylinder Ferrari engine from another rare 857S. Finally in 1958, the owner at that time, a Mr. E.D. Martin, advertised it for $8,000 (which was a lot of money back then, as in some parts of the U.S. you could still buy a house for that). Still, the car moved on down the road but not before suffering the indignity of—in 1960—having a cast-iron block pushrod Chevy V8 engine installed.

Before you recoil in horror at the thought, you have to reckon with the fact that such a conversion was the fate of many a Ferrari and Maserati back then, where someone liked the looks but either couldn't find a replacement for the real engine or thought, what the hell, Detroit power would make the car better (it didn't). In 1963 someone named Jim Hinson in Texas bought it, and parked it near Houston.

Flash forward 32 years to 1995 and there's Grape—the man who knew too much—looking over the fence at a car that looked to him suspiciously like an old racing Ferrari.

Abandoned. In a field. Prancing horses danced in his head and he reached for his wallet.

His "prize" had no engine or transaxle when he bought it. Plus, no oil tank and incorrect brakes. All he was buying, basically, was a good frame, a front suspension, a fuel tank and original but pummeled body work—sufficient to guide a future restorer. The body was covered with dents, but the aluminum body hadn't oxidized that much.

At first he had visions of returning this rare four-cylinder Ferrari to the racetrack in a vintage race. But over the next four years, as he costed out finding the correct engine (if it still existed) and then finding the proper transaxle, and then doing the gauges, the brakes, the fuel system, the interior and, oh, yes, the paint plus wheels and tires, well, the total was astronomical.

He gradually came to the sad but inevitable conclusion that—while he bought his treasure at a bargain price—it was going to cost an arm and a leg to get the parts needed to make it authentic (Jerry Heasley, who also profiled the car in his book *RARE FINDS* says the cost Grape was quoted for the correct serial number engine for the car—found in the UK—was $750,000).

Eventually discouraged, he sold it to an enthusiast in Brisbane, Australia, who already had a fine collection of British and European sports and racing cars and was financially equipped to deal with the sky high prices of correct in-period parts. After the car went to Australia the new owner found the chassis still in good shape though he had to replace some of the alloy bodywork. Victorian restoration specialist Graham Smith at Bellbrae Paint & Panel near Torquay worked on the chassis and body while a worldwide hunt was put on for the mechanical bits.

Fortunately a transaxle was found with UK historic racing specialist Rick Hall. The car was painted Rosso Corsa (racing red), dispensing with the white paint it had worn while an "American" racecar (back in those days, cars were painted colors "assigned" to each country, for instance Ferraris were red, British cars green, American cars white and blue, etc.). Now the car just needed a heart—a four-cylinder 750 Monza engine, not exactly common.

At first the Aussies couldn't find one so it was temporarily fitted with a 3.0-liter V-12 engine from a Ferrari 250 GT, a temporary expedient which had already been done on Monzas elsewhere (even in-period), in the 1950s. With that engine the car was raced, and became a star of shows like the Suncoast Classic Rally.

Then a Ferrari four became available, from Tom Wheatcroft in the UK, who came up with not only a correct four-cylinder engine, but one with a unique Australian connection. While racing in F1 and F2 in the UK in the early-'50s, ex-WWII Spitfire Squadron leader Tony Gaze made a practice of bringing back European racing cars to his native Australia and to New Zealand to campaign and then sell—something Aussie and New Zealand racers did a lot in the Fifties. One of the cars he brought back was an ex-works 1952 Ferrari 500 Formula 2 car that he had upgraded to F1 specification with a 750 Monza 3.0-liter engine acquired from the Ferrari factory.

Many years later the engine was removed when that Ferrari was restored back to its original 2.0-liter F2 beginnings and the 750 Monza engine became available to the Aussie owners of 0498M 750 Monza. Auto Restorations in New Zealand rebuilt the engine to its original factory specifications and it was installed in the Monza to make the car complete.

Lesson learned? You can luck out as a barn-hunter even if you don't know quite what you are looking at. This car was a Holy Grail to Ferrari folk. A Ferrari racecar is a Ferrari racecar, no matter how far down the ladder it has fallen. Of all brands and types of cars, this author would venture to say a Ferrari works racecar is worth saving if it hasn't been squashed flat by a steamroller.... And Jerry Heasley says that Mr. Grape, who has since passed on, was proud of his role in rescuing this car.

Chapter 25
The eBay Ferrari (Ferrari 340 America Spyder)

If you know more than the other bidders, you can score big-time.

Okay, it's 2009 and you are a Ferrari guy *par excellence* and a buddy calls you up and says something to the effect of "Hey, turn on your computer and take a look at an ad on eBay. There's a goddamn vintage Ferrari on there for under $30,000."

That was the case with a San Diego man, Tom Shaughnessy, who had a pal call him up about a car he had seen on eBay. Now Tom Shaughnessy is not your ordinary casual reader of ads. A longtime collector and car restorer, he maintains files on rare cars, principally Ferraris, and spends every waking hour either working on them, or searching for them. It was with high hopes he looked up the ad. But when he saw the car advertised in an eBay ad out of a Frankfort, Illinois, garage sale by Mike Sanflippo, he no doubt was chagrined, because it didn't say "Ferrari."

However, Shaughnessy's contact had been following the car long enough to know this could be the real thing. How would he know? Well, you could call it instinct or you could call it having an inkling. Like, say, maybe years before, he had heard "Oh, yeah and, last I heard, that car went to Chicago and wouldn't you know someone put a goddamn kit car body put on it."

Still, if it was the real thing, the price was right; just a shade over $26,000. Shaughnessy got the same inkling. He was one of the few on earth that realized, even without all the information he would need to authenticate it, this could be The Big One.

Remember that moment in the movie *JAWS* when the three men in the boat first see the big fin in the water? Same thing.

Shaughnessy bought it for less than one percent of the car's estimated value if ever restored. But it wasn't all roses. The car did not have an engine. That alone is a major problem as a correct V-12 engine would run about $200,000 or more. And it did not have the right body. Instead it had a fiberglass Devin body installed almost 46 years before. Now the Devin, taken by itself, ain't a bad lookin' car, Devin being one of the first manufacturers of kit cars back in the Fifties, and deliberately making bodywork that looked vaguely European, Ferrari-ish or Maserati-ish.

It also had no Ferrari transmission, which considering the rarity of such a piece, would have alone cost at least $75,000. The car had fallen so far from its Ferrari identity that it had been bought originally by the seller—a retired drag racer—with the sole idea of making a dragster out of it. This, in another marque context, would be like taking a hand-made James Young-built Rolls Phantom V and making a funeral hearse out of it (don't laugh, it's been done).

Amazingly, once Tom contacted the seller with a real cash offer, the man stuck to his price and did not raise it even though the number of responses should have tipped him off that there was interest in the car as a Ferrari instead of some old half-finished kit car. His attitude was, hey, I'm making a tremendous profit—after all, he had paid only $200 for it 15 years before, so if he could sell it for $26,000, he would still make more than a 13,500% return on his investment. Automotive archeologist Tom Cotter (author of *The Cobra in the Barn*) rates this find as one of the all-time great barn finds, saying: "It's up there with the Delahaye 135M that was discovered in Czechoslovakia and won Pebble Beach."

The seller, to his credit, had gone way beyond what he had to, even dismantling the car and photographing the frame and parts, sending this info far and wide via the internet. Once he saw pictures of the frame, Shaughnessy had no more doubt. He knew

Ferrari chassis—he had several in his workshop. They had oval tubes where most other tube-framed cars had round-section tubing. Once he got the chassis number, it was just a hop, skip and a jump to linking it with a long-missing Ferrari car. But since eBay is looked at by everybody and his brother, he was now beset with worry that some other prospect out there in the internet world would make the same discovery. But even if they did, apparently, the world of eBay is a lot of guys and gals bidding on stuff, always trying to underbid and you can count on one hand the number that will actually jump in a plane and cross the country to look at a car in person. Shaughnessy did. With the money.

One account of the transaction says after his bid was accepted Shaughnessy consulted Ferrari authority Hilary Rabb. (A note about consulting experts: They don't come more honest than Rabb. See final chapter where there is a warning about who you choose to consult with to check a car's authenticity.) Rabb confirmed that chassis number 0202 A was indeed a chassis number that corresponded to a long-missing factory racecar, not one bought by an amateur in America who won some local event. No, if it was that number, the same as a long-missing real factory (called in Europe a "works") racecar.

One story about the find said that Shaughnessy then immediately doubled the finder's fee to the fellow who had pointed out the ad to him (more about that later). What's the big deal with the serial number? Because Ferrari had a weird way of numbering cars, and this one had an even-number chassis, meant it was a factory competition car, one of only roughly 475 made between 1948 and 1974, almost every one of which is accounted for. And most every one of which is worth a million or more.

Shaughnessy now almost had all his ducks in a row. He lived in modest circumstances, and is not one of your gold chain Rolex-wearing diamond-encrusted pinkie ring crowd. He husbands his resources so to speak in the event he will hit paydirt so he can strike when the iron is hot when he makes a good find. After winning the eBay auction, he later told Ferrari collectors that he had been prepared to go as high as $262,000 had somebody else recognized 0202 A and started a damn bidding war.

Afterwards, with the car on the trailer and signed off title in hand, he checked with Swiss Ferrari expert Marcel Massini who claimed that 0202 A, once restored, with the right engine, right transmission, etc., could be worth $3 million.

Only twenty-five 340 Americas were built. Nine were bodied by Touring, eleven by Vignale (this is one) and five by Ghia. Fortunately there are two sister cars: 0196 A, and 0204, so the reference material to guide a restoration exists in the flesh (tin). At this writing, it is said a full restoration is planned.

Massini, the Swiss expert, published the history of 0202 A. The car was a veteran of the 1952 24 Hours of Le Mans with Maurice Trintignant/Louis Rosier sharing driving tasks, but they didn't finish. It then was loaned to Italian Piero Scotti, who ran some key races and took first in three hillclimbs. It had a few other events in Europe until U.S. Ferrari importer Luigi Chinetti brought it to the3 U.S. in 1953.

Next it went to racer Ernie McAfee in Los Angeles who owned it until 1958, when it went to a Paul Owens of Houston, Texas, who committed the frequent sin (in America) of install-ing a Chevrolet V8 (yeah, I know the guys who do this always intone a Carroll Shelby-like accent when they say: "there ain't no substitute for cubic inches").

A dark shadow is the fact that a crash came, and a passenger was killed. The chassis was then fitted with a Devin kit car body and next time the car surfaced there was an ad run in *Sports Car* magazine offering to sell the whole kit and caboodle for $4,250. It then went to Utah, a State where few would think to look for a factory racing Ferrari (If there was a sports car track there in the Fifties, nobody outside Utah knew about it) so that was as good as hiding it six feet under. That was in 1963. By 1990 it showed up in Chicago where Sanfilippo bought it, mostly for the svelte body which, if you squinted real hard, looked Ferrari-ish. Sorta. Kinda.

On the surface, the deal looked great but the truth is that few people in the U.S. would have the courage or experience to tackle a car needing this degree of restoration. Even the chassis was incomplete with the front spring missing; the center section, and rear were modified with the rear leaf spring mounts cut off. At least the brakes were complete, as were the axles and wheels. Back when he bought it, Shaughnessy pegged the restoration costs between $500,000 and $600,000. At the time of purchase, his estimated rough costs were at $200,000 for a 340 motor, $25,000 for a transmission, $20,000 for a differential, and oh, another 100 grand for chassis preparation and repair. And a new body? Metal benders were available—but, where back in 1953 the body would have cost $2,000, today you can multiply that by 50 times.

Because he had collected Ferrari bits and pieces in anticipation of someday finding a really rare Ferrari, Shaughnessy already had a running engine (though not the one the car came with), a rear end, a transmission, a pedal box, a radiator, and an oil cooler. He was not halfway home, but a good bit of the way. He also had a line on where the original engine was. There once again crops up the eternal problem with old Ferraris: one bloke has the chassis, while another far far away is hoarding the engine that car was built around. Eventually the two could meet but you have to wonder at what cost cometh this cosmic re-union?

To his credit, Shaughnessy was said to be worried how Sanfilippo would react to carping comments that, if he had such a winner, why didn't he hold out for more? Amazingly Sanfilippo wrote to Shaughnessy and said that he neither had the knowledge, the resources, nor the contacts to restore the car properly. He considered his role done in saving the car from a worse fate.

Lesson learned? No. 1 in this case: have the records to check against when you hear of a rare car so that you can move fast. No. 2: Be bankable. It might mean selling off one or more of the cars you already have, but you have to be ready to move (financiers call this "being liquid"). No. 3, and key, Shaughnessy handsomely rewarded the person who gave him the tip. Shaughnessy's generosity meant that his pal may call again.

Chapter 26
The Italian Corvette (1963 Corvette Rondine)

Where Italy tried to out-do Detroit with an American designer.

The Corvette is as American as apple pie, or a Louisville slugger. So to some Corvette buffs, it's almost sacrilegious to think about some Euro poof redesigning it. From the beginning GM's attitude was something to the effect of, "You Europeans do what you want with your cars, but this is our car and we don't need your input." It's been that way ever since, though every year the new Corvette looks a little more Ferrari-ish, and every year some Ferraris look a little more Corvette-ish.

But I digress. Mid-year Corvette fans think the 1963 Stingray "aero" coupe is the cat's pajamas, the ultimate in Corvette designs. But, we have to be honest here, to a functional purist, it has a few flaws, like fake vents on the hood, fake vents on the side and fake knock offs on the hubcaps (though there were real knock-offs available for a while). Hardcore car people hate fake things. If you're going to have a scoop, it should scoop. A vent should vent. Yadda-yadda.

Italians, thankfully, are not about fakery. So when the famous design house of Pininfarina sought a GM contract (they had enjoyed such a contract years earlier doing some production Cadillac Eldorado broughams) they did a purer design for the Corvette. A clean, modern design with no fakery, and it was beautiful. The irony is that the designer was Tom Tjaarda, a tall handsome young man from Birmingham, Michigan, whose father had been an important engineer in Detroit. Tjaarda earned a degree in architecture from U-M, but left Michigan in 1959 for Italy where he worked for Pininfarina and then Ghia (and later Ghia again where he did the design for the production Panteras).

After a number difficult years, the Chevrolet Corvette slowly but steadily grew in popularity throughout the 1950s. In 1960, the production reached the planned 10,000 units for the first time. Although the overall design of the "C2" second generation Corvette was completely new, in actuality the rear end design (called "duck's ass" by the irreverent) had been "previewed" on the C1 in 1961, and was carried over. But of course the big trick item up front on the '63s was hidden headlamps in the leading edge of the nose, actually reverse rotational flip-ups, which would remain a Corvette feature until 1967. An oddball theme on the coupe in 1963, stolen from a Bertone design for a one-off Alfa, was a split rear window which Bill Mitchell, the VP in charge of design, fought for, but was allowed to keep only one year for fears of anticipated complaints from customers about poor visibility.

Technically, the new series had some features in common with the previous one, such as a steel ladder chassis and a fiberglass body, but at least they had taken the big step of replacing the live rear axle with a double wishbone and transverse leaf spring.

Following the time-honored principle of "don't make every-thing new at once," the 1963 engines were carried over from 1962 and all displaced 327 cubic inches and produced 250 to 360 horsepower. For 1963 Chevrolet also changed the optional package codes, which now consisted of one or two letters combined with two or one numbers. From then onwards until modern days, specific models are referred to by enthusiasts for their optional package code, like ZL1, Z06 and L88. Naturally, they only do this when it's a high performance option.

Because it still had a separate chassis, and the body could be unbolted and lifted off, the Corvette became a subject of interest to Europe's coachbuilders, all hoping their design would entrance Detroit and they would get that fat contract. Pininfarina was one of the would-be suitors and, at the 1963 Paris Motor show, they launched the Rondine Coupe. Its design wasn't all new, because there's a one-off Alfa 2600 roadster designed by Pininfarina as a one-off that is a near identical twin, but it was a new shape for the Corvette. Even though Pininfarina didn't score a contract with GM for the Rondine, many of the same elements appeared on the mass-produced Fiat 124 Spyder. When still owned by Pininfarina, the car was shown at the 2005 Concorso d'Eleganza Villa d'Este where the Italian coachbuilder's 75th anniversary was celebrated.

The Rondine was a damn good example of how different a Detroit chassis could be if only Detroit would allow in a little Euro design influence. After Detroit switched to unitized chassis the chance that a European coachbuilder could score a body design or body building contract was reduced dramatically. The exception of course is when Cadillac did come to Pininfarina for the design and coachbuilding of their two-seater Allante, a car that this writer suspects was unduly influenced by GM design even though half the reason for going to Italy for bodywork was to get that European influence. GM hyped that Italian coachbuilder connection but maybe not sufficiently and the Allante died off fairly quickly compared to the still alive Corvette.

The Rondine had a roof change while it was still a current show car. At first it had a chopped off slanted inward rear window like the 1957 Mercury Turnpike Cruiser but then it was changed to a fastback, similar to the Iso Grifo coupe. That is rare for a coachbuilder to change a design on a concept because, to them, once a concept is a year or two old, it is already history.

The Rondine Concept went on the block in January 2008 at the annual Barrett-Jackson auction in Scottsdale, selling for $1.6 million before commission and taxes. It was a wise move, because now some private owner will show it at his own expense and when they do that, Pininfarina will still get the applause and ink in car magazines. So how could I possibly consider this car a "barn-find" when it never saw a barn and was bought at such a high price (full list at the time)? It qualifies, in this writer's view, as a barn-find in that it was still in the original maker's "barn," demonstrating that the first place to find a rare one-off car is at the home of the coachbuilder. And hey, since it was sold by the people that built it, it's even better than a one-owner, being a "no owner" until it was bought at the auction.

Chapter 27
Executive Perqs (Chevrolet Corvette SR2)

Wherein three GM executives exercised their power.

"Hot damn! A factory racecar built by the biggest automaker in the world! Why, that sucker oughta smoke the foreign tin." That's what American sports car fans probably said in '56. Well, it would be nice if we could say that prediction came true. But, in truth, the Chevrolet Corvette SR2 was an exercise in naïveté—showing exactly how much the world's biggest automaker didn't know about car racing.

How did these three cars come about? The whole thing started with a father trying to please his son. What happened was that Harley Earl, the VP in charge of Styling for GM, had a son, Jerry, who wanted to race a Ferrari he had bought. The old man didn't want him to race but, if he was insisting on it, then Earl Sr. at least wanted him not to race a Ferrari. What sort of message would that send American enthusiasts—that the Corvette wasn't good enough? That you had to go to a damned foreign car to go fast?

Well, that just wouldn't do. No siree. But first a word about the 1956 Corvette factory racecars, called SR cars. The Corvette racing initiative started out when Zora developed some Corvette test cars with stock cars that he modified and brought to the Daytona Speedweeks in February of 1956. All the flying mile events were still run on the sand since the racetrack wasn't built yet. Zora had tuned the engines to 240 horsepower. And that would carry the car just past 150 mph. Among the drivers on the sand were John Fitch, Duntov himself (who prided himself on being a Le Mans veteran, having raced a Porsche there in '53) and aviatrix Betty Skelton. Later Zora upped the horsepower to 255.

The speed wasn't enough to beat most Ferrari V-12s but it certainly put the two-seat Thunderbirds on the trailer and after 1957, Ford, with their tail between their legs, withdrew from helping any T-bird racing efforts and made their '58 and later Thunderbirds four-seaters aimed at the luxury market. The name "SR" referred to Sebring Racer.

The ingredients of the six SR racers made in '56, according to Corvette expert Jim Gessner are: Chevy made six 1956 SR-1's with the "Sebring Racing" package, one every color and with every option plus the 581 special HD Suspension and braking system, and; RPO 449 engines (240 horsepower), standard shift, and RPO SR options. Most had the following:
- Halibrand magnesium knock off wheels
- HD front and rear suspension
- Lyeth Engineering (Hi-Tork) 4:11 limited slip differential
- HD front and rear springs
- Finned brake drums
- Cerametallic brake shoes
- Vented backing plates
- HD front stabilizer
- Low restriction exhaust system
- HD radiator
- HD shock absorbers
- Dual fan belt drive
- Shortened steering column with fast steering ratio
- Special ignition wiring
- HD clutch
- HD racing air cleaners
- Firestone 6.70-15 Super Sports—170 tires
- Side scoops to cool rear brakes

Chevrolet did indeed field four of these SR Corvettes in the '56 Sebring 12 hour, though surreptitiously entering them under the name of various dealers. Three ran the stock size 365-incher and one, running in a modified class, had a larger 307-cubic-inch V8. The one with the larger engine also had Rochester mechanical fuel injection which would become an option in '57, and a gearbox made by ZF in Germany that never would be offered on a Corvette. The highest any of the Corvettes at Sebring finished was 15th, that one driven by famed American war hero (one who had piloted a P51 Mustang shot down over Germany) and race driver John Fitch.

The Corvette SS, the purpose-built car with magnesium body on a handbuilt chassis, dropped out after only 23 laps when its rubber suspension bushings crumbled. When that happened, some wondered how much of a racing expert this Duntov guy was, but maybe Earl had insisted on those so he could drive the SS around on the street.

One of the features of the Sebring racecars then offered on the street cars sold in any showroom was the Cerametallix brake linings (they were drum brakes). These worked to stop the heavy car but only if they were properly warmed up first, something many Corvette owners learned the hard way out on the street.

There's also a report that Smokey Yunick, a famous racing mechanic who had a shop in Daytona Beach, stroked and bored the original 283 engine in one of the SR racers out to 336 cubic inches. That car also ran Nassau and was even expected to run at the 24 Hours of Le Mans until GM suddenly pulled the plug from the racing budget in 1957.

Why did GM pull out of sports car racing? Because highway safety was getting a lot of publicity then, *LIFE* magazine printing pictures of blood-covered bodies of high schoolers killed playing "chicken" and so forth week after week, and GM wanted to look socially responsible; so all their racing support went "underground."

Funding factory-supported racecars was suddenly deemed politically incorrect in Detroit. Never mind entertaining the thought that if they would have won any of these races it would be a different story!

Then came the project for Harley Earl's son, the trio of cars called the SR2. The first one was supposed to be pure racecar. So reluctantly Earl ordered a Corvette in-house, had it fitted with the finned drum racing brakes and suspension used at Sebring (in the Corvette racecars with the RPO582 special suspension), and then sent it over to Styling.

Two designers—Bob Cumberford and Tony Lapine (the latter of whom eventually became design director of Porsche)—were assigned to make it look more, well, Ferrari-ish. So they extended the nose, and put a humongous fairing behind the driver's bucket seat and a big ol' tailfin coming out the rear deck. Actually the first one had a low fin on the back deck, flush with the top of the seats, but it was later moved to a place of higher prominence atop the fairing behind the driver's seat, a la Jaguar D-type. The car had the inset coves of all '56 Corvettes but true to ol' man Earl's design chops the inserts were filled with brushed stainless steel.

Now you would think that GM at the time could build a sophisticated racecar; after all, GM had annual sales of about 13 billion then, and was twice as large as Standard Oil. They could have, by consulting the right people and tying in with the right subcontractors, built a car that would have run circles around Ferrari. But no, they pussyfooted around and lost a lot of time and money making the car a styling statement, a sort of PR car for the Corvette brand and subsequently it wasn't that fast. Then, too, maybe Zora Arkus-Duntov, a snow-haired chain-smoking sophisticate called by the press "the father of the Corvette" (though in truth he was hired after the Corvette was already in production) didn't want too much development spent on it because he was working on an all-out, from the ground up racecar, the Corvette SS; a magnesium bodied beast that set GM back $2 million!

Duntov supposedly tuned the street SR2, using some of the racecar parts that had been developed for Sebring. It was also dolled up in the dashboard area with a wood steering wheel, more gauges than the normal Corvette, which were set into a stainless steel panel, and even a radio. The nose was extended to resemble the all-out Corvette SS racecar, but extending that nose must have added 200 pounds! The regular windshield was taken off and little wrap-around racecar plexiglass windscreens installed. All three had unique parking lamps that had screens in them for cool air to enter the screened backing plates of the front brakes. They looked like fog lamp nacelles from a distance but had a real purpose.

Was the car fast? Uh, no. On June 23-24, 1956, according to a website called Yenko.net, "the car was entered in the June Sprints at Road America in Elkhart Lake, Wisconsin. Jerry Earl drove the car in practice and not being familiar with its handling, spun it out fortunately incurring no damage." Dr. Dick Thompson, a Washington D.C. dentist who moonlighted as a pro racer, took over the controls and completed the six-hour race in a respectable position. He told the GM folk that the car was overweight and needed more horsepower.

Jerry Earl continued to race it in the Central Region SCCA through 1956 and '57. He did heed the call for more power and at some point the new special 331-cubic-inch fuel injection V8 was installed along with the new-for-'57 optional four-speed transmission. The taller fin was also installed over the winter with a special gas tank filler cap. However, the car didn't become a serious racer until Jim Jeffords, National B/P SCCA Champion in 1958 and '59, bought the car in January 1958 and began to develop it. Jeffords got Nickey Chevrolet to sponsor it, whereupon it was painted purple and got the silly moniker "Purple People Eater" (after a popular song about invading aliens). Jefford's later sold it to racer Bud Gates who was also an Indianapolis Chevrolet dealer. Gates raced the car at Sebring in '59, sold it to Vernon Kispert, and the car went into a second racing career as a drag racer with the moniker, "The Terror of Terre Haute."

He sold the car to a recycling yard and it went through a few owners who never got around to titling it until Rich and Char Mason of Carson City Nevada bought it and brought it back to its former glory, returning it to the racetrack at the Monterey Historic Races.

Bill Mitchell's red SR2, SN E56F1002532, followed a different route. It was to become more of a serious mechanical prototype, though it too was dolled up as much as Earl's car. According to the RegistryofCorvetteRaceCars.com, it was actually entered in Sebring in '57 by Lindley Hopkins of Miami. It was later sold to Ebb Rose, a sometime Indy racer, after Sebring. Rose actually had Carroll Shelby drive it in one race. Yes, that Carroll Shelby, who would later become world famous for developing the Cobra. It was then sold to another Texan, John Mecom, an oil man who bought one of everything. (In the Cobra era, he would field Chevy-powered cars against the Ford-powered cars fellow Texan Shelby was running).

This car had the 366-cubic-inch V8 rated at 325 horsepower with two four-barrels; when first built in February '57, it was fuel injected. It had the three-speed manual, the Sebring suspension, Cerametallic brake shoes, and Halibrand mag wheels of the type that appeared later on racing Cobras. It was restored by a Florida man named Bill Tower in 1986 to the way it looked at Daytona in '57. Bill Tower is a legend of his own in the Corvette world. His background includes racing the Top Fuel "Rat Trap" digger in the late 1960s, working on the Space Shuttle launch program, and working for GM from 1965 through the mid 1980s sometimes for the man whose job at GM was to secretly supply racecars to racers, Vince Piggins.

Mitchell's SR2 was used to test the Rochester Fuel Injection system and for a driving session on the packed beach sands of Daytona where it was piloted by full-time race driver Buck Baker, who set a class record of 152 mph. That one had brake ducts to cool the front brakes and side scoops to cool the rear brakes. Two-inch offset air ducts rammed air to the engine.

The Mitchell car was trimmed to 2,300 pounds from the stock Corvette's 3,000 pounds (plus), and had a giant 48-gallon gas tank. Mitchell made sure his had a taller fin over the driver headrest than Earl's did. His car was faster and lighter, but didn't race. Mitchell was a die-hard, pedal-to-the-metal guy, and he wanted whatever he owned to be as flamboyant as he was. In creating such cars, he was also showing Earl he was a worthy successor for when Earl retired. It worked out just ducky—he got the job!

FOR LOOKS ONLY

There was one last SR2 built, one which barely deserves the name "SR2" because it didn't get the mechanical upgrades. This was built for GM president Harlow Curtice, a man who was reportedly dead-set against racing! It may have been constructed as a gift (a bribe to sway him to like racing more). If that was the reason, it didn't work. He still voted down GM sponsorship of racing efforts. The car had most of the styling features of the first two with the added additions of a bolt-on removable stainless steel-covered hardtop. There were Dayton wire wheels as well. That car is shown in this book, recognizable by its hardtop. Ironically some lucky neighbor of Curtis bought the car when he grew bored with it.

Eventually it ended up on a used car lot in Northern Michigan. Werner Meier, a Corvette restorer, heard of it and drove all the way up there, rescuing from what would probably have been a dreary life of street races in small UP towns, because the Upper Peninsula of Michigan is an area populated by copper miners or lumbermen who favor four-wheel drive pickups.

The reason it might have sat on the car lot was no doubt because it was probably priced too high. Meier went up there, bought it and restored it. It became a superstar at various auctions later.

Lesson learned? Buy a one-off car in a town where nobody recognizes it. You could say 'whoop-de-do'—the SR2s didn't bring that much to the table of world sports cars, because they were too heavy and Earl had his minions waste far too much time trying to make them beautiful instead of making them fast. Point well taken; but on the other hand, even with the racing ban, the mere existence of the Sebring racing cars (touted in Chevrolet magazine ads and the buff books) and the subsequent SR2 cars seen at the major auto shows paved the way for a more sporting Corvette to be built to sell in the showrooms. GM was soon offering the race-like options like 4-speed manuals and fuel injection by 1957. Disc brakes would come almost a decade later.

MYSTERY CARS

There was also a white SR2 look-alike called the SS, which had two stripes down the middle, the brushed alloy side coves, and twin plexiglass racing windscreens. The author is still tracking that car which has been hidden for nearly half a century. No doubt when it emerges it will have a tale to tell, and it will be interesting to see if it is accepted by the followers of the True Faith as an SR2 or merely some kissin' cousin.

Lessons to be learned for barn-finders here? Racecars, of all collector cars, have a finite life or short shelf life when they are still competitive. Sometimes they go from a factory team to a private team and keep getting kicked downhill to less-funded forms of racing until they are pirated for parts. From the very moment the sponsors of the car exit the building (such as the moment GM announced they were quitting support of racing) they often are pushed out the door to the first guy with cash in hand.

Since GM hangs onto most of its concept cars (think what the original Corvette Shark or Mako Shark would fetch at an auction), that makes the ones that got away—like the three SR2s—so much more valuable.

And the owners of the cars have a plus over those who own concept cars made by companies no longer in existence. Every once in a while, GM has the introduction of a new car and then feel they need some of the glory of the past to spice up the intro. At that point, the red carpet is rolled out for owners of cars like the SR2, to bring their cars home to Mama...for a fee of course.

Chapter 28
"Le Monstre" (Maserati 151)

Sometimes ugly is damn beautiful.

OK imagine a pure-bred sports car, a factory prototype that actually raced at Le Mans for Chrissake, a car designed by Giulio Alfieri himself (the most famous Maserati engineer), ending up at one point in the famous Oakland roadster show with a button-tufted interior, where it wins the "People's Choice" award. Hey, weirder things have happened.

The Maserati 151 was a very limited edition racecar, a very dramatic looking car for the times but one plagued by more than its share of sheer bad luck. However, hope springs eternal, as you can see by the time you reach the end of this story—as the lone survivor of the four originally made races again, at Goodwood and other venues.

First the history of how the model came about. The type 151 came about in the 1962 season when Maserati decided to develop some fairly radical front engine cars using their new V8. Years earlier they had a similar car, the 450S coupe bodied by Zagato which showed promise and this was sort of a reprise of that car but with a more aerodynamic body.

Fortunately there was a new experimental class so they could develop some without having to plunge into making 100 units for homologation as a GT sports car. Both Aston Martin and Ferrari got into competition with Maserati to make prototypes for this class where the displacement limit was four liters.

It is ironic that Maserati chose a front engine design when they had already made the mid-engined birdcages so you might say the 151 coupes were the swan song of the front engine Maserati racecars.

The chief engineer was Giulio Alfieri who surprisingly did not use the small tubes space frame of the "birdcage" design but went back to the old standard of a ladder frame with two large tubular members running end to end. The engine was previously used in racecars and in the 5000 GT car. It was a 4.2-liter four cam, but by decreasing the bore, they got it under the 4-liter limit. Carburetion was through four twin-choke Webers. It was dry-sumped with a claimed output of 360 bhp.

The car's Achille's heel (which they didn't find out 'til later) was the rear suspension, an articulated DeDion type designed by GianPaolo Dallara (later to design the Pantera chassis), complete with extra struts on both sides, which allowed for additional lateral movement. This was chosen to lower the unsprung weight.

The transmission was a five-speed Colotti gearbox mounted in the rear with the differential. The proportions of the car were so unusual that a one-time owner, Chuck Jones, said: "As the driver, you were sitting next to the differential."

The body design was very controversial. Working with professors at Milan University, they chose to have a straight roof with a chopped off "Kamm effect" rear end on some of them (similar to the Ferrari "breadvan") though this one has a fastback plus a chopped tail below that.

Headlights on all four were faired in.

Three cars were completed just in time for entering in the 1962 24 Hours of Le Mans; two were allocated to the American sportsman millionaire Briggs Cunningham, who was loved in France for previously coming to race there with cars bearing his own name (as well as Cadillacs).

Another 151 went to Colonel Simone's (despite the French sounding name he had been a U.S. Air Force pilot) Maserati France team.

All three coupes bombed out at Le Mans. Thompson, the "flying dentist" crashed Cunningham's first 151 in the 5th hour when his brakes failed. But his second car, piloted by McLaren/ Hansgen made it to the 13th hour when they blew their car's engine. The French team's 151 only made it into the 10th hour before it dropped out.

According to a story in the authoritative Maserati club magazine *Il Tridente*, Cunningham sold a 151 to Bev Spencer, a San Francisco Buick dealer who liked to race. The price tag was $7,950. Spencer sponsored it in a local California race at Vacaville.

Meanwhile, one of Cunningham's other 151 coupes, SN 004, was having its own adventure by having a big block Ford engine (a 427) jammed into it, in a way presaging by one year the Cobra Daytona big block that Shelby tried to build in '64 (but Shelby changed the order half way through building and it was brought back to 289 specifications). Cunningham hired Alfred Momo to do it, and the driver selected for a short race at Daytona was NASCAR veteran Marvin Panch. Unfortunately, it got away from him and flipped over, catching on fire. Since the doors went partway into the roof, you couldn't get the doors open, but four other drivers, led by "Tiny" Lund, beat the rescue crew to the burning car and used muscle power to flip it upright and got Panch out alive. Since Panch couldn't make his ride for the Daytona 500 after that, he asked Lund to drive and wouldn't you know it, he won!

The Maserati France car remained in Europe and was prepared for the 1963 Le Mans event. Fortunately, the displacement limit of four liters was lifted and Alfieri replaced the original V8 with a Lucas fuel-injected five-liter, rated at around 430 bhp. Renamed the 151/2 and driven by Andre Simon and an American airline pilot who moonlighted as a racer—Lloyd 'Lucky' Casner—the car made no impression on the more advanced mid-engined prototype Ferraris in the race and went out after just a few hours with gearbox problems.

But Alfieri was not convinced it was a loser. He stretched the chassis by 10 cm for additional high-speed stability and the body was replaced by a more elegant and efficient design. The engine was made larger and now cranked out an impressive 450 bhp.

At the 1964 Le Mans Maurice Trintignant was forced to start from the pits after the accelerator cable snapped, but once in the race, he shot by 38 cars in the first hour. Though it soldiered on for 99 laps and hung in there almost nine hours, it went out with electrical problems.

Then came a fatal blow. Entered in the 1965 Le Mans test session, which is held in April prior to the June race, Lloyd "Lucky" Casner left the track at speed on a wet surface and crashed fatally. That was the end of the 151 in Europe.

THE STATESIDE 151

Which brings us back to chassis 006, the intact Cunningham car. Once the cars were back in the States Cunningham had briefly chosen to run the intact car but entered it in only two events with beer manufacturing scion Augie Pabst behind the wheel. But Pabst was forced to retire from the Bridgehampton 400 km with a seized piston after running as high as third. At Riverside, he finished seventh.

Disappointed, Cunningham offered the car for sale and car dealer Bev Spoencer bought both the smashed one and the intact one, plus four engines and a lot of parts. Now why did he want the smashed one? We asked him. "Because you had to take apart the frame to get at the differential so it was just as easy to buy the whole car to get that differential," said Jones in a 2013 phone interview.

Jones had made the friendship of Skip Hudson, an up and coming driver, and they had a race team called Meridian Racing. They prepared it for racing at the smaller tracks in California. Jones also put in some soundproofing and upholstery and used the car on the street, where it made a startling appearance. "It would do about 175 and I remember for a brief time it was the fastest road car in the U.S.," he recalls. "At the time you had no smog inspection and it only cost $12 to register it. I used to get up early and drive the 12-mile road that circled a lake called Lake Matthews, using that as my own little race track."

He did make a few changes. He didn't like the two sidesaddle gas tanks so replaced them with one tank at the rear. He lowered the nose and put on a clamshell hood that could be lifted en masse with the fenders a la Jaguar E-type. He also put a hump in the roof. "I looked around for something aluminum and went to Sears and bought a $1 frying pan and put that on the roof and had my welder weld it on to give Skip some helmet room. That was the kind of thing we did back then," he told the author.

At one time he had the car finish third at Cotati, a small little California track used for regional races. What a come-down for a car that had raced at 24 Heures du Mans!

Jones, from a pioneering family that owned considerable acreage in Orange County in a cattle ranch, at one point found himself under water and offered the car for sale. A controversial Frenchman came down from San Francisco and bought the car, trading it for a new Lincoln Continental plus $4,000 cash.

What about the other 151—the smashed car? "I threw it in a landfill that is now the University of California Irvine," says Jones. "Back in those days racecars were considered to have a short life and nobody wanted to unwrinkle a car that had been hit hard when you could buy used racing Ferraris in Italy for peanuts," he told the author. (Jones, when he got on top financially again, remembers buying five racing Ferraris from Crepaldi, the official dealer in Milano, for $11,000 total).

The Frenchman was tagged "controversial" because he seemed to trade on the fact that he was related to the last Prime Minister of France before the Vichy government took over in 1940 after the Nazi invasion. Jones remembers the young man having a lady friend who was quite old and quite rich and rumors at the time were that there may have been a problem with who signed her checks. At any rate, the Frenchman went to jail for fraud.

At some point (the author hasn't found anyone who will own up to it) the Maserati was shown at the Oakland Roadster show, a show mostly populated by little Deuce roadsters, where it reportedly won a prize for "crowd favorite."

It sat on the West Coast from 1965 all the way to 1983, at which time it was bought by a German collector Peter Kaus, who displayed it in his Rosso Bianco Museum, dedicated to Italian sports cars.

But eventually Kaus sold the entire contents of his museum in 2006, and that 151 coupe was run through the Bonhams' sale at Gstaad, fetching CHF 1.85 Million, and coming out as the top seller of the auction.

It was bought by an American collector of Italian cars and motorcycles, and shown at a few events before being treated to a full restoration.

By 2011 the car was finally set up right for racing and finished 3rd in a controversial race—the RAC TT Celebration race of the Goodwood Revival. Sharing driving tasks were Joe Colasacco and Derek Hill (son of 1961 World Champion Phil).

The new owners were gracious enough to invite Jones, by then an octogenarian but still of sound memory, to inspect the car to see how it squared with his memories of more than half a century ago. "I am glad they did not customize it to be their vision of how it should look but instead stuck to how it looked originally," says Jones.

Lesson learned? The absolute best time to buy a racecar is right after it's time in the sun—when its original racing career is over and it has no good venues left to run in. Remember—when that Frenchman bought it from Chuck Jones, vintage racing didn't exist yet in America, at least not to the caliber of the Monterey Historics founded by Steve Earle. And the fact was that, being developed for long circuits like Le Mans, it was too much car for the small regional tracks of rural California. Lesson No. 2: It's OK to buy a car that's been customized by the owner—if you can change it back to its original form. Now that there is vintage racing, like the events run at Goodwood and Le Mans, the car can live again and show its original promise—hey, watch out, Ferrari 250GTOs!

This writer predicts it will no longer have to go to the Oakland Roadster show to be appreciated.

Chapter 29
Ferrucio's Surprise (Lamborghini Miura Spyder Targa Roadster)

Hey, he was only the maker of the car…why tell him?

Pity the poor auto parts suppliers to Detroit. When they want to poke their head up and get recognized by the public, how do they do it? Do you really think anyone going to an International Auto show is going to come over and look at your step-by-step process for making chrome? Good luck on that. But there's another way: staff your booth with sexy long-stemmed models dressed in clinging dresses. That works. But how about being more novel, buying a beautiful rare one-off car from Italy and customizing it with your products as if your stuff was OEM (original equipment manufacturing)?

That is exactly the story of the one-off Lamborghini Miura Spyder which first existed in 1968 as a show car to tout the services of Carrozzeria Bertone, whose designer Marcello Gandini did the design for which they built the coachwork. Reportedly the car was done without the knowledge of the founder of Lamborghini, Ferrucio Lamborghini, who probably wouldn't have thought the foundation of the car was strong enough to have an open roof. It started life as a coupe, but since it was commissioned by Carrozzeria Bertone, coachbuilder of Lamborghini at the time, in this case saying it's a "factory car" means the factory was the coachbuilder's factory, not the car factory. But who would know better how to design an open version than the coachbuilder who built the coupe?

Originally the "Lamborghini Bertone Miura Roadster," as it was officially christened (though "roadster" usually refers to a car without roll-up windows), was finished in a light metallic blue with an off-white leather interior with red carpeting. The dashboard and steering remained black, and the steering wheel itself was the original avant-garde, almost art-deco styled unit that was also used on the Marzal one-off Lamborghini show car by Bertone. This Miura carried chassis number 3498 (which, in accordance with its one-off prototype status, is not even listed in the factory's original production chassis number register), and P400 engine number 1642 was fitted.

When the Miura Spyder was unveiled in 1968 at the Brussels auto salon, it was a sensation. Ferrucio Lamborghini, the firm's founder, later on reportedly rained on Bertone's parade by telling the press he never thought of the car as an open car because the chassis and windscreen were not built in anticipation of the additional stress. Hey, what a way to cement relations with your coachbuilder!

He may have been right. The car was brought back to Sant'Agata where Lamborghini's own people, in consultation with Bertone, and perhaps taking Ferrucio's words to heart, deemed it impossible to put into production.

It was some time after that (and no doubt because Ferrucio didn't talk about buying the design) that the car was sold by Lamborghini to the International Lead and Zinc Research Organization office, based in Detroit, who decided it made a perfect platform to display their techniques of using zinc alloys in their coating and plating systems. They painted it a dark metalflake green and added bits of chrome trim here and there along with horrendous hubcaps to show the glory of chrome (hey, GM was BUILT on chrome). In its new guise as the Zn75, it appeared in car shows such as Detroit, Montreal, Anaheim, London, Tokyo, Sydney and Paris.

What happens to a show car when its career is finished? Well, what better fate than to go to a Museum where more people could see it? So in 1981 it was donated to a Museum in exchange for a $200,000 tax receipt (which in this writer's view was an over-estimate of its value back then). The car then disappeared largely into obscurity for 25 years...well, not obscure to the visitors to the museum, but it wasn't seen out and about at Pebble Beach and such.

Although the museum invested what must have been considerable time and energy into refurbishing the Miura Spyder, a Museum restoration isn't always a full restoration, at least not in the "Pebble Beach" sense. There is "pretty" and then there is "correct" and a world of difference between the two.

Somehow In 1989, it was purchased by the Portman group, and spent a period shuttling from auction house to temporary owner, likely because its full history and significance was unknown by most of these temporary owners. It even spent some time in a Japanese collection. In 2002 it returned to the USA for a brief sojourn, before finding another home with a Ferrari collector in France.

In December 2006, the Miura Roadster was finally purchased by a New York property developer, Adam Gordon, who at a huge cost, had the car returned to its original 1968 Salon de L'Automobile Bruxelles light blue livery and trim. The returning of the car to its original condition was completed in late August 2008. The shop chosen to do it was the Bobileff Motorcar Company run by Gary Bobileff in San Diego who had specialized in Lamborghinis for decades.

The car was reportedly later offered at a Bonhams auction in Gstaad, Switzerland, for an undisclosed amount (possibly to keep the tax man at bay). Whoever owns it now has an original carrozzeria-designed, one-off car in its original look, surely worth much more than when it would be when it was the temporary captive of a Detroit auto parts maker.

Lesson learned? Sometimes you can find a race horse hidden under a donkey's disguise. (Wasn't there a movie made about some race horse that looked wonky as all hell but still took first in the Derby?) Well this car was the same damn thing—in its Zn-75 guise, it looked a bit Kalifornia Kustom, especially with those horrid wheels, but it was still a one-off purebred under-neath, if you knew your Miuras.

So listen up, barn finders: do your homework so that when you first spot a car which has a purebred pedigree like this one disguised as something else, you can make your move.

Chapter 30
The Hotel Lamborghini (Miura Coupe)

Some guys park a car and (almost) never come back.

Elsewhere in this tome I use my favorite line about hanging out with rich people; "A crumb off their table is a whole meal to me." Well, Greek singer Stamatis Kokotas, a sort of Greek version of Elvis (with even thicker mutton chop sideburns) was already doing well in the '60s when he met Aristotle Onassis, a famous shipping magnate (famous also for marrying the widow of John F. Kennedy).

At one point Onassis took a liking to Kokotas and gifted him with a very special Lamborghini Miura that he had ordered for himself. It was a dark brown car with a full leather interior, unusual in Miuras which had previously either come with cloth interiors or vinyl. This car was built November 14, 1969, as a model "S," with 20 more horsepower than the plain Miura P400 and some reports say it had the SV upgrades which would mean separating the engine oil from the transmission oil.

At any rate, it had a lot of special custom order things like engraved alloy switchgear, a special leather steering wheel and the aforementioned upholstery. Kokotas was the right guy to appreciate the car as he was an accomplished rally driver and already had a car collection.

One report is that he might have put as many as 50,000 miles on it but eventually it suffered an engine problem and he found that the recommendation of everyone who knew Lambos was the only place to really fix it right was at the factory. So the car was parked in the underground garage of the Athens Hilton and the engine sent off.

Thirty years passed, with the car a-molderin' away in the hotel underground lot.

The car was endangered when the hotel got a major renovation in 2003 in preparation for the 2004 Summer Olympic Games, so it had to be moved from its original parking place to another parking place in another building where it was parked next to a gullwing that had seen better days. Finally Dimiotrios Spyropoulos, Managing Director of Veloce Classic & Sports, a London-area car dealer, convinced his old friend Kokotas to bring the car out into the sunlight and to send it to Coys "True Greats" December 4th auction in London.

Ah, but what about the engine? Amazingly Lamborghini gave it back. Amazing because Lamborghini had changed hands as an automaker at least three times since they had been sent the engine. It had been sitting in their museum for decades. It seemed there was some problem over the payment of the bill. But now that the car was worth oodles that was taken care of.

The motor was reunited with the car but not installed for the auction. The auction catalog hyped the fact that, of the 140 S models made (before the factory went to the SV spec version) it was built with "luxury items available from the factory, like air conditioning, but the individual touches went well beyond that. Inside the air vents, passenger grab handle, gearshift, electric window switches, ignition switch surrounds, and horn all have unique engraved alloy elements. Outside the eyelashes surrounding the headlights have the alloy touch as well as a unique lower front clip with four extra driving lights mounted centrally below the grille."

But they were a little overoptimistic about what it could fetch, thinking "it would break its top estimate of £370,000 (currently about $593k) when it crosses the block." it was a no-sale at over $400,000 but they managed to sell it later to a private party and as we go to press, we are told by Davide DeGiorgi, also of Veloce Classics, that it will be running soon.

It's also a good illustration of what you can find if you hang with the rich. Lesson learned? Start a dossier on celebrities who like cars. You can never tell what they have in their basement. Odds are, anytime during those decades when the Lambo was collecting dust "in the dungeon" it could have been bought for a song.

Chapter 31
The Most Beautiful Car in the World
(Bizzarrini Spyder)

And how I missed getting this one three times!

This is a tale of unbridled lust, the story of the world's sexiest sports car, and one man's obsession for over 2/3rds of his life to keep the one he lucked into.

Actually it's about two Bizzarrinis (pronounced BITZ-R-EEN-E). That was a little known Italian marque that was built new with Corvette power in the mid-to-late Sixties.

I discovered the marque quite by accident. Back in the mid-'60s I was in a library at Wayne State University looking for books on poetry when I saw a British magazine, *Autosport*, and was transfixed by a report on driving the Iso Grifo A3/C, the two-seater sports car that became the Bizzarrini after the owner of the Iso factory, Renzo Rivolta, had a parting of the ways with Ing. Giotto Bizzarrini, the famous engineer whose previous claim to fame was with the Ferrari 250GTO, went off to his native Livorno and set up a small shop to continue making the A3/L (street car) and A3/C (racecar) under his own name while Iso continued on making a tamer looking steel-bodied Chevy powered Iso Grifo.

The designer of the Bizzarrini and its predecessor, the Iso Grifo A3C, was Giorgetto Giugiaro, then a little known designer at Carrozzeria Bertone, now the world's most famous car designer.

When I read the article (which changed me from a poet to a raging car aficionado) I thought I would never be so lucky to see an Iso 3C (the Bizzarrini didn't exist yet) but then, as luck would have it, I came across my first Bizzarrini in the metal only a few short years later when a colleague in the ad agency I worked in told me, if I went over to a nearby Corvette shop,

I would see what he described as "an odd foreign car with a Corvette engine." I went over there and saw, jammed among the Corvettes, a T-topped Bizzarrini coupe. But it was so different from the Iso Grifo A3/C I saw in the magazine that I didn't immediately make the connection with the car I had seen labeled an Iso Grifo A3/C. I tried to ask if it was for sale and they said, "no, it's only here for service." Years later I met Mark Sassak, the owner of the car, who filled me in on how he came to own this sensationally sexy car.

First, an explanation of the unique top: according to Sassak, the red car I saw in Detroit that became his was originally built as a Spyder but it had a three-way top which could be configured as:

1.) no top, as open Spyder

2.) roof roll over hoop only

3.) roof roll over hoop with center bar and removable t-top sections

His red car was originally painted a dark blue. When shipped to the U.S., the U.S. buyer, Mr. Harold Sarko, an Detroit industrialist, requested to have it re-finished in Ferrari red. The three-way roof configuration was used again but this time allowing the steel roll bar to be removed with wrenches.

The car was turned over to Mr. Bizzarrini's new production manager, Salvatore Diomante, to finish the details before being shipped. Among the mods was a two-piece rear window attached to the bottom of the roll bar to allow the window to be opened and closed by sliding in tracks. The roll bar had two mushroom head bolts on each side that dropped into a slotted chrome track mounted to the top side of the body, locking the roll bar in place; but just before they shipped it they began to worry about chassis flex and put in a T-bar connecting the roll bar to the windshield. This design became nicknamed "the T-top."

Two half tops were added, built of aluminum but covered in black composite twill fabric. They secured with pins that insert into the center support much as in a '68 Corvette. A T-bar tool is used to unlock and remove them for storage in the trunk.

At one point, after Sassak had moved to Las Vegas, he had some paint work being done and had the rear roof and T-bar unbolted. When his painter left Vegas leaving the car unfinished, Sassak asked around about who was the best paint and body-man for such a car and was advised to go to Bill DeCarr in Bellflower. When DeCarr put together the car, he made the top bolts visible so it was easier to detach the top.

But first, a chronology of the red T-Top's history in America. At the time the car appeared in the Corvette shop in Detroit it was still owned by its first owner, Harold Sarko, a Detroit industrialist who had made some investment in Bizzarrini's firm and received the car as a result.

Sarko's love affair with the car had started when Sarko was traveling in Italy and saw the car on display. To him it looked like it was ready to take off. He found out who built the car, and went to Livorno to see the factory. There he met Bizzarrini and invested in the company, receiving the first and only production Spyder in the color of his choosing and with an interior tailored to fit him.

Once it got to Detroit, he couldn't get the heater to work, and since it had a Corvette drivetrain, he took it to the 'Vette Shop to solve the problem. It was a few months later that John Sassak, Mark's father, bought the car. Sassak Sr. was a business associate of Sarko and had been ready to buy a Ferrari until Sarko convinced him the Bizzarrini was more practical because of the Corvette engine.

It was a memorable day in Mark Sassak's life. He recalled it for the author.

"I'll never forget the first time I ever saw the red Bizzarrini," Mark recalled for the author. "I was 14 years old the day my dad drove the Spyder S.I. home in the summer of 1969. When I saw the Spyder drive by for the first time heading towards my house I could not believe my eyes. Then once I found out it was my dad's new car I cannot explain the feeling that came over me. To see something that beautiful, the lines were just pure sexy and it looked like it was doing 200 mph just standing still. I knew right then I would own this car one day it and it became a passion from that point on. I did not know it would take another four years but I waited. I started saving money to buy that car that very day. I would have to wait another four years as my parents separated and my mom moved us to Las Vegas. I would go back to visit my dad in the summers. In the summer of 1971 I returned to work with my dad at his tool and die business in Livonia, Michigan, along with my older brother John Jr. At the end of the summer my dad offered the Red Bizz to either of us as an enticement to join the family business full time. My brother John Jr. agreed to stay on and buy the red Bizz and with great disappointment I headed back to Vegas."

"A few years goes by and out of the blue my dad comes calling to recruit me back to Livonia to work with him in a new computer game business venture. I agreed to go back to Detroit and jumped in my $450 1964 Dodge Dart to head back. I spent the next year living at the factory working seven days a week saving money. My brother was still driving the Red Bizz Spyder as an everyday car. It was sad to see how the car was falling into disrepair from years of neglect. It started when he had to cut the pricey hand-bent headers and take flex tubing to connect to new Thrush side pipes in place of rusted-out mufflers and tail pipes. One of the Campagnolo magnesium caliper disc brakes had locked up so John Jr. unbolted the brake caliper, bent the copper brake line and tied it off to the inner frame. The nail in the coffin was while when my brother John Jr. was driving down Haggerty road and the independent rear end mounts broke loose from one too many hole-shots, dropping the rear end, half shafts and U-joints to the frame grinding to a halt. The Spyder sat outside in the rain with the T-Tops leaking, damaging the leather interior."

"Short on cash my brother came to me to see if I wanted to buy the red Bizz so he could buy a new Chevy Vega. I calmly agreed and gave him the cash. Four years of patiently waiting paid off and my dream came true, I own the car! I couldn't get the title transferred fast enough. I patched up the abused car and drove back to Vegas. For the next ten years I drove the car hard and often. At 21 I was a black jack dealer and driving a rare one-off Italian sports car, I did my share of terrorizing the Las Vegas strip, taking bets from late-night street racers and unsuspecting Corvette owner who thought they were up against a 246 Dino Ferrari or some kit car like a Fiberfab. Oh yeah and the poor show girls whose legs were branded from the Thrush side pipes as they were getting in and out of the car for a ride. Lots of fun before a well-deserved restoration. I had been in Vegas for five years when the wheel bearing went out. I parked it at a Shell station on the Las Vegas strip."

On a personal note, who should go drive by on the Strip at that point and see the Bizzarrini sitting in a gas station on a jack with one wheel off but your author? I left a note. It was not answered.

Now, to continue Mark's story: "It is a miracle of interaction but who should go by and see the car but Max Balchowsky, the famed mechanic that built the Buick-powered Ol'Yeller cars for sports car racing out of junk parts, cars that would beat Ferraris with drivers like Carroll Shelby at the wheel. Max contacted me because he serviced stunt man Carey Loftin's three Bizzarrinis (the ones that had appeared in the *Love Bug* movies, as Max did movie work) and he knew where to get the parts. Max told me that Carey had one time ordered a Spyder but never was able to take delivery. Max invited me to his shop in Hollywood and it was a thrill to be there to see another Bizzarrini—they only made a shade over 140 of them so I would go years without seeing another one. Later I got to meet Carey himself. When that meeting between us happened, it was at Max's shop, and he was excited to see that there actually was a production Spyder. My car was a Spyder but with a T-top roof attached that could be detached."

Sassak remembers: "When I met Carey Loftin, he pulled out a catalog sheet advertising the car and said he got the catalogue sheet back when he put a large deposit down on the car. He opined that he thought there were seven Spyders built. I had done a lot of research and concluded only three were built."

Sassak's visit to Los Angeles was not without peril to the car.

"The car narrowly escaped destruction a few weeks later," he recalls, "when I was staying with my sister in Malibu and had it parked on Pacific Coast Highway. I woke up after a big crashing sound and went outside and found six cars had all smashed together but all of the wreckage was just ahead of the Bizzarrini."

As another personal ancedote, wouldn't you know—your author, minding his own business, was driving through Malibu during Mark's visit, and sees his red T-top Bizzarrini in front of a house near the Pacific Coast Highway. I leave a note. The note is not answered. I ask myself—just how big is the friggin' U.S. that I now have come across the same car three times in three different States? I could say that finding it again meant I was fated to own this car but it hasn't happened yet.

Why didn't he answer? The upshot is that Mark was not then or now interested in selling the car. As the years went on he became the world's single most intensive Bizzarrini fan; which led him ultimately to the search for the fabled third Spyder. This was a Spyder only, without the T-top roof that could be attached. *Road and Track* had published a picture of it in 1966 but in their caption said "it was not finished." That would have dampened most fans' ardor but not Mark Sassak.

He realized that it was also the Geneva Auto Salon show car. He recalls, "I felt that the prototype still had to exist and I needed to find this car. I knew that the *Road & Track* picture caption gave the impression it was just a "pushmobile," that is the Detroit phrase for a non-running car with just enough equipment like wheels and steering to push up on a stage. But I knew from my research that it had an all-aluminum body, not just a fiberglass mockup body, and a real numbered chassis with a full interior, working gauges, hubs, steering gear, brakes, a Borg Warner trans, working lights, and all it needed to be a running car was the engine."

Mark knew that a 327 Chevy small block was a rare hard-to-get thing in Italy, but within a mile of his house he could have bought one thousand 327-cubic-inch Chevrolet V8s and had them delivered to his door. Sassak wasn't the only one searching for the third Spyder. "There were journalists who had an inkling of where it was but either they didn't tell me because they wanted to find it first or because they wanted a finder's fee to tell me where it was. That just made me more determined to find it myself," he recalls.

Meanwhile there was the blue Spyder, the second one built. Sassak found out about this car's existence in America when an author/barn finder came to Las Vegas to visit him and look at his car which was then stripped down to the bare metal. This same barn hunter had helped a man in Oakland Hills, California, named Howard Turnley find the blue Spyder in Italy.

"But that car had been repaired incorrectly in the nose so he wanted to measure mine," recalls Sassak. "Also the taillights in the blue car had been changed because of prior rear end damage. That car had been through 4-5 owners and had a lot of changes. Later that car was donated by the Turnleys to the Blackhawk Museum in Northern California."

Of course it was meant not to be resold but car museums usually have—deep down in the contract—the right to de-accession cars, i.e. that's a fancy Museum-ese synonym for "sell." This could be because of a changing mission, such as a need to show cars more relating to the reason the museum was set up, or just because the museum needs money to keep the doors open or they have an opportunity to buy another car with the money that they want more.

"So," continues Sassak, "I am back in Michigan and I hear the car is coming up for auction. I told the auction company I wanted to buy it before the car rolled across the block but it was too late—it was scheduled. I would have to take my chances against other bidders. I flew to the auction in time but saw the California collector who likes Bizzarrinis most sitting in the front row right alongside the same fellow who had found the car originally in Italy for Turnley. I could see the barn finder was no doubt trying to collect a second finder's fee by having clued in the Bizzarrrini collector of this car's sale. Well, I was out-bid. I called my wife to express my disappointment but she buoyed my spirits by saying 'Don't worry, there's better things coming.'"

"My wife was right. About a year later, in 1999, a friend named Ed calls me up and queries me, asking me if I was sure only two Spyders had been built? I affirmed that and he tells me, well, hold on to your hat because there is a third Spyder in Italy being offered through a private individual. No ad, this was strictly a word-of-mouth deal. He sends me a color photo and I knew immediately that there was only one Spyder like that—the *Road & Track* car; that one had a different nose than my red one or the blue one. My brain went into overdrive. I got the name of the owner, a lawyer, named Dr. Luciano Mancini, in Pisa, Italy. At first I was worried it would be hard to find him because there were lots of Mancinis but fortunately I knew he was a lawyer so I found him. But before calling Mancini directly I felt I needed a proper introduction to buy such an important car so I called an American friend in Detroit, Bob, who speaks fluent Italian and, when we got together, he called Sig. Ing. Giotto Bizzarrini for me and translated, saying I was the owner of the red Bizzarrini spider and needed to ask questions about the silver car. Ing. Bizzarrini said he knew Mancini well and that Dr. Mancini was his lawyer back when he had been an automaker. And he confirmed that, yes, indeed, Dr. Mancini had the car and he had been by his home many times always urging him to get it running. Bizzarrini even thought it would be a waste of time for me to come to Italy to try to buy it but I told him I was willing to take the chance. We made an appointment and Bob said he would get his brother from Italy to be the go-between over there and meet us at the airport in Italy."

Sassak's full story continues: "I checked with my banker wife who was standing by to wire transfer the amount to the bank in Italy. I was maxed out by sending that but I made sure to bid enough to still cover customs duty and shipping. So when I arrived at the airport in Italy there was my friend Ed from Detroit and his friend Franco, who knew Dr. Mancini. Franco was a 'car finder' who went around and found cars for Ed. Both of them would find buyers for car owners who wanted to sell and then collect commissions when the cars sold. I knew Ed from the Meadowbrook concours where he was the emcee and Ed had announced my red car winning awards. When Franco told Ed about the Spyder in Italy, the first person Ed called was me. There had been a worrisome moment just before I left when another collector called me out of the blue and asked about the existence of a third Spyder but I didn't spill the beans. I don't know how the 'leak' got out but at that point I was confident that I was ahead of any competitors, already being in Italy with the money."

"We scheduled a meeting at an inn used by vacationers. Ing. Bizzarrini arrived with his wife, who I had met in the early 1980s at Pebble Beach in California. It was a three hour meeting. During the meeting we found out that Giotto himself had owned the car since 1969 when he loaned it out to the coachbuilder Stile Italia (SI) for promotional use and, in turn, they had made it operational, painting it blue, making the headlights work, adding a back window that was recessed into the body of the car. The rear window would roll up and seal into the roll bar with the roll bar removed the window was used as a windscreen. This is the design used today. The wiring harness for 12 volt was already in place. The car didn't get an engine until it went back to Mancini. Bizzarrini himself installed the engine to pay a legal bill stemming back from Bizzarrini firm's bankruptcy. At the time Bizzarrini had asked Dr. Mancini if he wanted to sell the car but he said Dr. Mancini liked owning such a rare work of art and didn't want to sell."

"But, despite Ing. Bizzarrini's misgivings, we were undeterred. We went to meet Dr. Mancini the next day. And he took us below his villa to his garage and he had about eight cars in there, most of them apart with parts like windshields, engines and the like scattered about. There was even a big block right-hand drive aluminum bodied GT5300 coupe there, one that had been disqualified at Le Mans (later identified as BA4-106) that had a cracked frame from the engine putting out too much torque. The blue prototype Spyder was complete but I could see it had a primered front end and rain-damaged interior and sat under an inch of dust. I checked the VIN and other numbers and every number corresponded to Bizzarrini's descriptions. Dr. Mancini pulled out a magazine showing the red Spyder from the U.S. and it took him a minute to realize that the car in the magazine was not only a match to his but that it was my car. I assured him that not only was I dead serious about buying his car but that I was the best qualified person on earth to restore the car as I owned the only true original sample of the spider."

"But of course this was Italy, not the U.S. where everything is slam, bam, thank you Ma'am. You have to sit down and enjoy a meal with whomever you are doing business with and have some grappa and establish your bona fides so to speak. So we spent the whole afternoon there at his home, enjoying a ten course meal his wife and daughters and son prepared for us, and drinking wine, and even some vintage whiskey he had. The only trouble was the negotiations were not going that well, and finally my friend, Tony, jumps up and calls Dr. Mancini to a side room and it seemed like when they came back two minutes later Dr. Mancini is all smiles and shakes my hand and says to me 'You own the car.' It turns out that Tony had gone beyond the sticking point—as is often the case in Italy—that car owners of old cars are liable for a huge fine if they don't register a car every year whether it's running or not, a fine extending all the way back to the original date of purchase. Of course this car had not been running for many years. Well, hell, I happened to be a little adept at import/export myself so I saw that as no problem. We all jumped in Tony's car and drove to a government customs office where we convinced them the car was not part of the original bankruptcy. It turned out that the Customs official was kind of an aficionado and he said, 'As long as the chassis number is in accordance with the Bizzarrinis we shipped out of here 30 years ago, it's OK.' And of course the numbers on the documents matched the numbers of the car. It was hunky dory but we weren't clear of Italy yet. Next I had to find a freight forwarder. We hired a tow truck driver to pick it up the next morning at 8 am."

"We all showed up the next morning, drank a little of that strong Italian coffee, and Dr. Mancini was a little teary eyed as he steered it up onto the tow truck so it could be transported to the container yard at the port of Livorno. Ten days later I was unloading the container in Canton, Michigan."

There's a whole lot of lessons to be learned here. I would have to call it the ultimate barn-finder story as far as tenaciousness. If you could get an Oscar for finding your dream car, Mark Sassak would have one on his mantle.

The first lesson is an excellent example of don't-believe-what-you-read-in-magazines as Mark Sassak, in his heart, never believed the car was destroyed despite what *Road & Track* had implied in their cavalierly written caption. The third Spyder case is also an excellent example of go-to-the-original-builder strategy, as it turned out Ing. Bizzarrini knew exactly where the car was for 30 years but just didn't bother to tell previous Spyder hunters. Finally there's the lesson entitled "Employ a Local Contact." In this case, Bob's brother Tony, was an invaluable part of the negotiating team.

Would Dr. Mancini have sold the car if Mark Sassak did not happen to be the world's leading expert on Bizzarrini Spyders? Maybe not, but that is a real-life demonstration of the unwritten rule that some owners don't want to sell their long-hoarded treasure unless you—the buyer—can assure them it's going to go to a good home where it will be treated right. In this case it was and is.

Mark Sassak spent a fortune to get the car running and into concours condition and has since shown his pair of Bizzarrini Spyders at several major shows.

Lesson learned? Mark Sassak lucked into that first Bizzarrini by happenstance. But you have to admire his tenacity in hanging onto it, and resisting the temptation to sell it through all those years even when it was an unknown marque in America; scorned by the Ferraristis and others for being a "hybrid" with a cast iron lump of Chevy under the hood. He educated himself on the marque until he became one of the world's leading experts and in the process educated many more in the history of an obscure but significant marque.

He deserves that car. I don't.

Chapter 32
An "Exotic" from Detroit's "Little Fourth" (AMX/3)

The mouse that (almost) roared.

Allow me, dear reader, to paint the scene such as it was on the field of battle in Detroit in 1970. Ford had announced they were building a mid-engined GT car. Actually they had played with the already-in-production DeTomaso Mangusta first, but decided the way it was built was not up to their standards. As beautiful as the Mangusta was, they rejected it and chose to order up the Pantera, an all-new car from the same builder. This car would be built in unitized form, much as most cars in Detroit were at the time.

This decision, ironically, was made when the Pantera was still just a wood model 1/5th in size and no real cars had been built or tested yet. However, Henry Ford II, chairman of the board, had stated in no uncertain terms that what he wanted to put into Ford showrooms was an Italian car, and damn it, his underlings better find one fast if they wanted to keep their jobs.

Over at GM, John Z. DeLorean, a key executive and one of the few in Detroit steeped in exotic cars (he drove a Maserati Ghibli on the street), was not about to let Ford get all the ink. He had the XP-882 mid-engined Corvette prototype dolled up for the auto show circuit and for one brief moment in time, the press was entranced that GM would have a mid-engined car to rival the Pantera. (When they saw the dirt on the engine, they thought, "Hey, this is no pushmobile, this is a running driving test car. Golly!")

But DeLorean's showmanship effort was all for naught. For one thing, GM was wary of any car whose engine was not in front. That's because a few years earlier safety crusader Ralph Nader had written a book on the Corvair called *Unsafe at any Speed* which implied that its handling quirks were due to the fact that the Corvair had the engine in the rear. That and the tooling costs scared off GM on mid-engines. GM knew that sports cars traditionally had manual shift transmissions, and since no transaxle was readily available, they hardly wanted to spend several million tooling up for one (today, automakers like Ferrari don't even bother offering a manual shift on some models, the automatics have progressed that much).

Chrysler did not have a two-seater, and no plans for a mid-engined car, but the third competitor in this would-be race was the unlikely "little fourth" company that was always in the shadow of the so-called "Big Three." The real story is that America once had hundreds of automakers; but along the way they died, or merged with more completive companies. Some are remembered; like Duesenberg and Packard, but most of the pre-World War II marques are forgotten like Moon and Dort (I was in the Army with Dallas Dort, a descendent of the people that founded Dort and he kept asking me when Dorts will be revered classic cars. I broke his heart when I told him "never").

American Motors was the last of the once hundreds of little automakers to try to fight GM, Ford and Chrysler. AMC came from the 1954 merger between Nash and Hudson and their first successful car was the Rambler, a distinct family sedan that sold well and had a reputation for reliability (and the teenagers liked those seats that folded down into beds). AMC dropped the Hudson nameplate though; in the past it had performance models. AMC dallied with performance cars at times in the Sixties. The author fondly remembers the car called The Machine, a white car (with red, white and blue trim) that was a hot number. The author drove it while it was a *Motor Trend* test car. Nobody else on the staff wanted to drive it because it came from AMC (more about that car later).

The sportiest car the firm built in the Sixties was the AMX, really just a short wheelbase Javelin, but considered sporty because it had two seats. Dick Teague, their VP in charge of styling was a former Packard designer before the war, and a sophisticated designer who knew everything they were doing in Europe. His problem was he had a miniscule budget. He astounded the car magazine journalists when he unveiled the AMX prototypes, the first of which involved using Vignale, an Italian coachbuilder, to build the body.

That first car, which survives, was front-engined, but then things got more exciting involving the name AMX. Just as the news about Ford making a mid-engined car hit in the car magazines (at first by the way it was just called the DeTomaso 351 before being named Pantera), AMC unveiled the AMX/2, completed in 1969, a mid-engined design. The first one was completed in-house and was little more than a fiberglass ornament, having no engine or interior. Ironically, the famous designer Giorgetto Giugiaro, founder of the design house Ital Design, had been awarded a contract to make a full-size AMX pushmobile (non-running car) to AMC's drawings but he chose foam to make it in and when it arrived, it looked amateurish and was blown away by the in-house AMC design. Later, of course, Giugiaro would learn how to make flashier finished prototypes and go on to create many famous and respected designs.

Then came the AMX/3. This is what whetted the car magazine editors' appetites further. The fact it was a running, driving car was like dangling meat over a cage of hungry pit bulls. Teague had AMC hire Giotto Bizzarrini, of ex-Ferrari fame, to make a production-worthy AMX/3 out of the non-running show queen AMX/2. This was no big deal for the guy who had built over 100 cars bearing his own name; all Corvette-powered front-engined cars, plus a handful of mid-engined prototypes.

Bizzarrini planned to use the AMC V8 engine, which unfortunately was a lump of iron with no record of accomplishment like the small block Chevy; but at least he solved the gearbox problem, going to the Italian firm Oto Melara which used a similar gearbox on mid-engined military vehicles. Its only flaw was that it was a 4-speed, not a 5-speed like the Pantera's ZF gearbox.

From a design standpoint, the AMX/3 was a step ahead of the Pantera, in that it incorporated a soft "safety bumper" where the Pantera had separate "bumperettes" (two separate mini bumpers) fore and aft. The AMX/3 was also more modern in having flat black paint in the engine lid area.

Making the press absolutely ecstatic was the news that BMW was testing the car on a test track. This was beyond what Ford had done (where are the test track pictures of the Pantera?) and beyond GM who had only built the XP-882 is a proving grounds project with no real plans for production.

Then, suddenly, the air went out of AMC's balloon. Ford announced that the Pantera would be $10,000—a heady amount at the time when only one American car had such a high price, the Lincoln Continental Mk. III, but that was still a retail price that was too low for AMC to match with the AMX/3. They would have had to charge $11,000 or $12,000 just to break even. They scrapped the project. This writer feels they were never really serious about it—that the whole program from start to finish was all a cosmic joke at the behest of Teague who, being styling chief of "the little fourth" decided to jerk the chains of his brethren at The Big Three by making them think he was going to give them some competition.

Bizzarrini was thenceforth issued orders to destroy all six prototypes. Fat chance. That would be like telling Michelangelo to destroy his six latest sculptures, even if they were commissioned by private clients. He didn't, and the six were, in the words of one writer, "lost, found, sold and lost again." Some have been restored.

The interesting part is that each of the six is slightly different as new ideas occurred to Teague. They don't quite get the respect that, say the Corvette XP-882 does when shown but you have to reckon with the reality that AMC itself went bust and was swallowed up by Chrysler so there is no AMC Museum or PR entity to encourage the restoration and display of prototypes bearing their name like GM does with the Corvette (except for the ones that got away, see Two Rotor Corvette and XP-819 chapters).

The owners of the six AMX/3 prototypes are forced to go it alone with no factory support, Chrysler having absorbed AMC but making no signs they ever heard of it; but AMC enthusiasts are a hardy bunch, and if you comb the internet and see their sites, you see they have done a good job of documenting and resurrecting cars that were supposed to have been put through the band saw.

HOW THEY WERE SAVED

Now you would expect Dick Teague, being a good soldier, would not interfere with the order from his employers to destroy the cars; but hey, you are talking world-class car enthusiast here. He did the opposite, going to Italy and buying two of them with his own money. When his first steel-bodied AMX/3 arrived in Michigan from Bizzarrini in Italy, he was reportedly miffed because pieces had been taken off the car, maybe by souvenir hunters; plus the car did not run, and was even off the specified proportions because of inept conversions from metric to English standard measurements.

The car did eventually run and at last report was up to 30,000 miles. Scotty Dawkins, a friend of Teague, bought the car in the early 1970s and it has been displayed at the Gilmore museum in Hickory Corners, Michigan. Dick Teague had received the car painted green but then painted it yellow. This was a great find for Mr. Dawkins as the car would cost over one million to make from scratch today. Back then, in 1970 AMC paid only three million to produce all five AMX/3s.

A second AMX/3, which came in aqua metal flake, was driven by its buyer to a girlfriend's house where it was stored it in her garage that had a dirt floor where it sat for many years. Unfortunately the soil under the car produced a mold throughout the interior that turned it from white to black. This is why some refer to this car as the "chicken coop" car. The car is now undergoing a complete restoration.

Another of the original six is called "The Monza High Speed Test Car," and was photographed on the racetrack in Monza, iconically very close to Ferrari's factory. The initial report was that the car had nose lift, so it was only run up to 145 mph, though a chin spoiler could have solved that. BMW wrote a report praising the stiffness of the chassis.

Bill Demichieli, a restaurant owner in Indianapolis, Indiana, reportedly bought one of the AMX/3 cars for $6,500 while it was still in Italy. His contact was Tom Meade in Livorno, Italy, an American who had gone to Italy and lived there for several years buying and modifying exotic cars when used Ferraris were only about $3,000-$4,000. He ran ads in *Road & Track*, volunteering to be the go-between as he had on many other exotics sold to Americans by Italians. Meade shipped the car to Baltimore, Maryland. When Demichieli went to pick it up, the amount owed was more than he had thought but the cruel reality was, if he wanted the car, he had to pay it.

He had the unique experience of driving a car that was supposed-to-be for some years, but a divorce in 1976 forced him to sell it. Mr. Jack Cohen, who also lived in Indianapolis, Indiana, became the new owner. Jack was an aircraft mechanic with US Airways who stood 6 feet, 7 inches and reportedly wanted the car because he had been a close friend of Teague's and owning the car was a tribute to the dream of his friend.

In the 1980s Jack sold the car to Mr. Kirtland of Baton Rouge, Louisiana. It helped the car's original appearance a lot when he was able to take off the American Racing wheels and mount Italian-made Campagnolo wheels, including a full size spare. The last time Mr. Kirtland took the car to Pebble Beach he put 400 miles on the car driving around.

Another of the Teague-owned cars that Dick bought from AMC in 1978 was sold to George Doughtie Jr., who sold it to Pat Ryan's Prisma Collection. During this time the car was advertised in *Hemming's* for $225,000, which by today's standards is still a bargain for a hand-built prototype. It later went to Bernie Carl, the investment banker. Bernie added a front spoiler which really helped the car at high speed. This car varied from the others by having a scoop and gas filler doors on both sides. The AMX/3 was restored at Autosport Designs Inc. in Huntington Station, New York, and showed Europeans what could have been when it made an appearance at the 2008 Goodwood Festival in England.

THE CAR ON THE POLE

Now in racing, to say "the car is on the pole" is a good thing. It means your car did so well in practice, it's earned the right to be on the front of the start grid for when the race starts; but in the case of the AMX/2 pushmobile, a non-running fiber-glass life-size model used by AMC to study the car before going to a running prototype, it was not so good to be the car on the pole. Some clown bought the pushmobile and put it on a pole to advertise his used car lot in Ephrata, Pennsylvania (we really shouldn't call him a clown because he saved it from being thrown away and now it lives again).

When this "pole car" came up for sale in a newspaper classi-fied in California, a collector named Tom Dulaney jumped on it right away and became just the third owner of the pushmo-bile (other than AMC) since Teague donated it to a museum in 1973. Of course, any replicas built were only replicas and prob-ably not be allowed to park near the real ones at toney concours like Pebble Beach, but still it's a tribute to the AMC design that somebody wants to spend the money to make an AMX/3 by using a mold made from the AMC original; it's a little closer to the real thing than one made up of whole cloth.

Going back to the AMC Machine test car I was driving while at *Motor Trend*, after several months, I felt guilty driving it and not writing about it so I tried to call up American Motors to return it. Nobody answered. A Great American car company had gone down the tubes. Disappeared. Been swallowed up. It took me a couple more months to find out who was taking their property and I deliv-ered it to an anonymous office in Orange County (I should have kept it, though there would have been problems registering it).

Chapter 33
The Second Most Beautiful Sports Car (Iso Grifo Spyder A3/L)

The most beautiful after the Bizzarrini 5300GT Spyder.

What if I told you that the most beautiful postwar convertible in the world is sitting in a junkyard in Los Angeles? I speak of the Iso Grifo A3/L, SN 002. Iso S.p.A. in Bresso was a firm back in the Sixties known for producing the family sedan Iso Rivolta IR300, a 2+2 coupe based on a Chevrolet Corvette power train. This car had come about after a British company had hired Bertone to design a fiberglass bodied four-seater with Corvette power. A few were made but when Renzo Rivolta, owner of Iso, drove one, he thought he could do them one better. He had Bertone design a similar steel bodied car, the Rivolta. His chief engineer was one of the engineers who left Ferrari in 1961 during the famous "palace revolt," Giotto Bizzarrini.

Bizzarrini set up his own consultancy where he had clients like ATS, Lamborghini and Iso. In 1963 he engineered the Iso Grifo A3/L (L for Lusso, Italian for Luxury) for Renzo Rivolta, who was looking for a follow-up to his Iso Rivolta GT. The body was designed by Giorgetto Giugiaro at Bertone, while Bizzarrini confined his expertise to the mechanicals. This is the car that became the Bizzarrini, partly as a result of Bizzarrini's zeal to go racing. He also designed a full race version of the Grifo called the A3/C (C for Corsa) with a dramatic modified alloy body.

His credentials? Oh, did I mention he designed the 250 GTO when he had worked for Ferrari (only the most famous and most expensive collector car in the world)? To make his sports car for Iso sleek, he moved the engine so far back that you had to adjust the valves through a hole in the dash! But after a few were made Rivolta let it be known that he wasn't about to sanction a racing program. In response, Bizzarrini left Iso and retired to Livorno to market the A3/L and A3/C under the Bizzarrini name. Rivolta now needed another design for what would be a road car only, so he went back to Bertone who asked his designer Giugiaro to come up with something tamer, and that was the steel-bodied car that became the production Iso Grifo.

Just over 400 Iso Grifos were made, most with Corvette power, though the last few had Ford 351 V8s. The first coupe prototype came to America and a barn finder found it and it subsequently went to a Museum in Northern California.

Lesser known and seldom seen is the companion to that A3/L prototype, a one-off Spyder companion car, also a design by Giugiaro, with many of the same unique design features (different from the production Grifo). That too, came to America. The author ran across it decades after its short show career in a car dealership in Culver City, California, where it was for sale at a price of $22,000. This was a price hard to justify at the time, me not realizing what its significance was. The next I heard it was in a junkyard in Los Angeles. The serial number is 002 which makes it a prototype for sure. The time to buy it cheap was in 1970.

For those who comb old magazines for ads, in the July 1970 issue of *Road & Track* there is a classified ad for this same one-of-a-kind Iso A3/L (Grifo) Spider for sale in New York for $12,500. Writer Marty Schorr, who owned an Iso Grifo coupe for many years, told the author that he used to see the car parked on New York City streets covered with snow. The rust was showing through even then.

Why didn't I buy it? Well, my first excuse is that I didn't see that ad when it was that price until the year 2013, over 30 years later. Fully restored, at the right auction, this writer predicts it is today worth 100 times more. Oddly in the ad picture from when it was a mere $12,500, it has some vertical bars on the front, maybe to defend it against poor parallel parkers in New York. The really stunning part of the design is the side pipes, coming out of the body side with horizontal louvers to protect you from touching the hot pipes.

The author's interest in this car's continued existence was piqued by recent pictures found on the internet of a dark green Spyder at a car show in Germany; but on checking I found out that several coupes were converted to Spyders after the year 2000. Oddly enough, the ones I have seen don't have the correct nose. At the time of this writing, neither does the oneoriginal in Los Angeles, obviously the victim of a nose crunch.

But the operative question now: is 002 for sale? Well, I haven't been by that junkyard lately. Suffice to say they have rather large dogs. I could go back, maybe with a bigger dog, but the yard operators are infamous for stockpiling cars like 300SL gullwings, and 904 Porsches, and they even have a prewar Mercedes that is reportedly worth $11,000,000 so they know the value of everything. Cars worth a million dollars have come out of that junkyard. The time to get it was when it was in Culver City and the salespeople there didn't have a clue.

Lesson learned? When you see a prototype car, beg, borrow or steal what you need to buy it because when it comes to future value, you can't beat the first one ever made. In this case the Iso Grifo Spyder was the last one ever made as well. Estimated value when restored? Two million…

Chapter 34
A French Jaguar (1966 Jaguar Loewy One-off E-type)

From the same guy who designed the Lucky Strike logo.

Imagine you are at a car show and up rolls a prototype one-off special car. All your instincts tell you that this car is something special. But nobody around seems to notice. Maybe because it is not show condition as all the other cars in the show are. And because mostly it looks like a customized Jaguar E-type which is what it is. It was who designed it that is significant. There is one name that is golden (in most circles) of mid-century American industrial designers and that was Frenchman Raymond Loewy. He designed such iconic works as the Greyhound bus, spectacular bodies to cover old coal-burning Pennsylvania Railroad locomotives, the Coke bottle, the Lucky Strike cigarette box, and a series of Studebakers, from the Starliner to the Avanti.

He lived, when not in Detroit, in a modern house in Palm Springs that had a swimming pool that was half in the house and half outside! As self promotion, he would re-design cars that other people already thought were pretty svelte, cars like the Lancia Flaminia, BMW 507, and a 1966 Jaguar XKE Coupe, Chassis no. 1E30635, shown here. You might not care for his designs but Loewy was the man who dared to call the other creations coming out of Detroit "jukeboxes on wheels." (Some feel that his criticism failed to acknowledge his own output of gold-painted custom road cars that were pretty "flash" in their own way.)

173

Going back to the car I saw in Beverly Hills at the annual Concours on Rodeo, it had some bizarre features. I didn't mind the tunneled-in taillights, but the roof spoiler looked like a tiny windshield to shield people riding in the rumble seat, if there was a rumble seat, which there wasn't.

The '66 Jaguar E-Type coupé came out of long-term storage to be auctioned at Bonham's in Monterey, California. Apparently, if you piece together its history a man named Jerry Coffey bought it from Loewy in Paris and sold it to Mr. James Murry Hunt who wanted it because he was an architect and designer who had once studied under Mr. Loewy. So in this particular case, the buy was more of an emotional buy than from a guy who liked Jaguars (file this under "cars owned by famous people").

Actually this was Loewy's second Jaguar re-design, modified by a French coachbuilder. The E-Type was modified by Pinchon-Parat of Sens, France. The first one, a 1955 XK140, was re-bodied by Boano in Italy, and had a lot more chrome used in interesting ways following the body curves, in the manner of Figoni et Falaschi, French coachbulders, before the war. That car burned out, so it may not have been re-built (the author hesitates to say "destroyed" as too many cars in this book were once described as "destroyed," yet you can get in and drive them today).

James Coffey bought the car after an ad appeared in the Paris edition of the *International Herald Tribune* in the late '60s or 1970. The ad told prospects to call at Raymond Loewy's office. He only kept the car a year and sold it to Murry Hunt, who was so anxious to buy it he bought the car sight unseen, imported it to California and kept if for the rest of his life. The car was long lost by Jaguar enthusiasts, as it spent almost 40 years in Mr. Hunt's garage.

Finally it came up for auction at Bonhams. The auction catalog gave it quite a bit of space, saying, "The startling E-Type coupe on offer is one of only two Jaguars restyled and customized by world-renowned industrial and automotive designer

Raymond Loewy (it is the only one of them remaining; the other was created from a 1955 XK-140, and was demolished in a fire in 1957). Pinchon-Parat of Sens, France, accomplished the substantial redesign coachwork on this E-Type and the car was owned and driven by Mr. Loewy while he lived in France and Monaco. Mr. Loewy's accomplishments are many and varied—he designed everything from office equipment to locomotives; his portfolio includes the uniquely tapered Coke bottle, and among his well-known logo designs are that of British Petroleum (BP), the Shell Oil Company, and the United States Postal service. His best known automotive design work was for Studebaker, including his assembly and spearheading of the team that designed the Studebaker Avanti of the early 1960s."

"Mr. Loewy's E-Type was left mechanically stock; his redesign work restricted to the body panels, and side window openings and glass. The car was shortened fore (25cm) and aft (12cm); the new nose encompassing a dual headlight treatment, with the quad lights mounted behind plastic covers. The car's original radiator opening was also dispensed with in favor of a large oval shaped metal grille, which likely improved the E-Type's marginal cooling capacity. The factory taillights were replaced with Chevrolet Corvair units frenched into the quarter panels, and the dual exhaust pipes, which normally exit just below the rear license plate, are splayed outward, exiting the tail of the car at approximately 45 degree angles. A unique glass 'spoiler' was mounted at the trailing edge of the roof."

"Mr. Loewy anticipated today's Center High-Mounted Stoplight regulations by placing a large, red taillight in the aft cabin, visible through the 25% larger than stock rear window, activated by the brake pedal. The interior remains otherwise stock. The car is original and exactly as designed by Mr. Loewy and constructed by Pinchon-Pirat. It is reported to run well, and be in solid mechanical condition."

"Given a thorough detail and mechanical service, the Raymond Loewy E-Type will represent a certain invitation to many of the world's great concours, and with 2011 being the 50th anniversary of the original E-Type's debut, one could hope for no more a unique and historic example of such an iconic model than this."

The car was sold for $128,000 USD including premium.

Now I can hear you asking: "How does this rate as a barn-find when good money, i.e. fair market value, was paid at an auction?" Good question. Here's the answer: it all has to do with rarity. It was a one-of-one E-type Jag designed by Loewy; and it was bodied by a French coachbuilder.

Where an ordinary E-type coupe might be too common to be accepted at Pebble Beach or Amelia Island (unless you hit a year when Jaguar is a featured marque), this is a car with a story—one that offers a captivating glimpse at the lifestyle of one of America's greatest industrial designers. Of course you have to ask what would a full restoration cost? Ah, that's the joy of the "preservation class" being instituted at most major concours—with that option, there's a chance such a car could be displayed unrestored…as found….

Lesson to be learned? What you have here is a car designed by a world famous designer known to have created a series of one-off cars as rolling advertisements for himself. If you were following logic, and were a fan of Mr. Loewy, you could have found this car decades earlier among those who revere Loewy (see last chapter for recommended search strategies). In this case, if you found it, you could have hit pay dirt before it ever rolled across the Bonham's block.

Chapter 35
Sprint Speciales (Alfa SS)

Wherein the Author buys the right model but the wrong car.

In the world of Alfa Romeos, the SS (Sprint Speciale)occupies a rather odd place. Before I bought my first one and had only seen them in pictures, I thought, hey, these are great looking cars. They were designed reportedly at Bertone by Franco Scaglione, a mercurial designer who came and went, doing great cars and then disappearing for decades (the last decade of his life he lived out of the car field and finally died of cancer). Among his achievements were the experimental cars, the Giulietta Sprint and Sprint Speciale and other cars for other makers. In 1959 he left Bertone and became an independent, doing the Porsche 356 B Abarth Carrera GTL, a very collectable Porsche.

First a little history in the SS: The first prototype of the Giulietta SS appeared from Bertone Carrozzeria in 1957 at the Turin Motor Show. After two more prototypes were presented in successive shows, the production version was unveiled to the press in June 1959 on the Monza race track. Only the first few produced had the "low nose," and were aluminum bodied. They would have needed to make 100 to have it homologated as a production sports car but all the rest of the production cars with the high nose and bumpers were steel bodied with aluminum used only for the trunk, hood and doors.

Also, the first cars were equipped with Weber 40 DCO3 carburetors, later changed to 40 DCO2.

The engine in the first Giulietta series was a 1,290cc Alfa Romeo Twin Cam four, a design with hemispheric combustion chambers and twin overhead camshafts.

The Sprint Speciale was comparable in performance to a Porsche 356. Then came the 101.20 series cars, still at 1300cc. Small changes included steel doors, Weber 40 DCO2 carburetors, a higher front nose, and a change from plexiglass side windows to glass. Plus, bumpers were added front and rear, and minimal sound-proofing. With the 1,290cc engine maximum speed was around 200 km/h (120 mph). All Giulietta SS models had 3-shoe drum brakes at the front and drums at the rear. Export versions had 101.17 designation. Side badges had "Giulietta Sprint Speciale" script.

The third version was the tamest one, first shown in March 1963 at the Autosalon Geneva. The 1,570cc engine with Weber 40 DCOE2 carburetors was taken from Giulia Sprint Veloce. Most Giulia SS models had disc brakes on the front wheels. Side badges had "Giulia SS" script. Production ended in 1966.

Some sources say 1,366 Giulietta Sprint Speciales and 1,400 Giulia Sprint Speciales were produced, but in the Alfa world there's always someone who has the "inside info," and different production numbers.

MY CARS

The first shot I had at buying one was when I met a trans design student at the famous Art Center College of Design, the school that trains most of the world's car designers. His was a "low nose" one but I can't remember now if it was all aluminum or just some parts were aluminum. At the time he was just taking a job in France and putting it in storage. That would have been the one to get, especially in all aluminum. I think he claimed only the first 20 were all alloy.

A South African Alfa expert wrote me on the Alfa forum: "There were only 5 low nose SS's made in alloy, thereafter the rest in steel, they were The 'Spinta' show car, then chassis 00004, 00005, 00007 & 00009—they are kinda very valuable now, at I'd hazard a guess of 30 to 50% over a steel bodied car. There is one other alloy bodied SS, chassis 00061—there were some questions over this car at the time as it's after the run of the alloy cars. If you accept its provenance, that makes 6 Low Nose Alloy SS."

But I passed up the chance to buy his car. Instead I chased some others. I think I paid like $20,000 for my first one, a steel bodied Giulietta SS with the 1300 engine. I can't remember how I caught wind of it but the owner was a car artist who had spent a lot rebuilding the engine, which was a jewel, a work of art that you would want to mount on a pedestal in your palatial beachside mansion and just stare at. The pity was he didn't have enough to finish out the rest of the car or even to install the engine, which I had to pick up separately.

I didn't realize until after I sold it that, between the small engine and the large engine, the 1300cc is more prized than the 1600cc because it was a more race-tuned engine.

These models are so little known that you can't even peg the horsepower of the Giulietta version; one source says the power output was 110, 112, 116 or 120 horsepower, take your pick.

I sold that first one because I was never going to get around to restoring it and I was dismayed when I went to an Alfa parts shop in Long Beach and they had no body parts, and no trim parts for an SS. Welcome to the world of rare cars! It might be the same brand but lots of luck finding parts.

Then what really infuriated me was when I went to the Monterey Historics during the time I owned it and saw a Giulia 1600cc version already entered in the race, with one small dent, sitting in the pits with a sign "For Sale" and the price something like $12,000. So if I had only gone to Monterey with a checkbook I could have bought a running driving car for far less than I bought a car with the engine out of the car. I had not properly surveyed the market!

After the first one sold I still had the Alfa disease—I bought a second SS. I can't even remember where, but this one was also apart. It was after I bought it I found from the Alfa fraternity that the larger-engined Giulia versions were considered turkeys between the two, because they were not as highly tuned as the Giuliettas. And they weren't popular in vintage racing because they were heavy in the nose and didn't handle well. If you want a good handling Alfa of that era, think GTA.

So here I had bought one of my dream cars thinking that I could get rid of it any time at a profit because all Alfa owners covet it and will, from the moment I advertise it, inundate me with offers. Not so—when I advertised it, the phone was mute. On that second car, I lost thousands just to get it out of my garage. Here's the irony. After both my bad experiences with the steel-bodied cars, neither car ever reaching running status, the guy who went to Europe to work returned stateside, called me up and said he was ready to sell the all-alloy low nose car. But at that time, I was in no position to buy. If I would have kept his contact info, I could have periodically kept in touch with him in Europe and had a check waiting for him when he got off the plane.

Now it's a couple of decades later, maybe three decades (hey, who keeps track?). You hear about Alfa Sprint Speciales going for anywhere from $85,000 to $154,000.

That low-nose all alloy car? Those in the year 2013 run, oh, $200,000. And so it goes. Don't mention Alfa 'round my house. It hurts too much.

Lessons learned? Do your research on your favorite models. You may find that, although famous names are attached (Scaglione, Bertone) that they are not as prized within that marque's models as you think they are. Then, too, I found a curious thing about the Alfa fraternity (yeah, I know—I'll get letters for saying this). There is a vast gulf between the financial resources of owners of the ordinary Alfas and those of collector Alfas, a veritable chasm. So if you have one for sale, the low-buck cognoscenti will refuse your car for all sorts of reasons but the truth is they don't have the money, where if you had one of the really super collectable ones (say a 1900SSZ or any '50s one with a racing connection to the Targa Florio or Mille Miglia) you are dealing with an entirely different class of Alfa aficionado who can sit down and write out a check for several hundred thousand USD. It's a marque where the low-buckers have superb knowledge of the marque but can't afford beyond what they have and the high-buck enthusiasts can pick and choose among the best. I should have hung with one of the *cognoscenti,* the educated experts, and I would have bought the low-nose.

So my short foray into the Alfa world was a bruising one. I survived with all my fingers and toes intact but still bear bruises you can't see. I suspect there's other marques where the same thing is true, say look at the price difference between a Mercedes 300SL of the Fifties and a Mercedes 190SL of the same time period. One is a car worth more than a three bedroom two level house in the 'burbs and the other is a car you might still find for $20,000.

Chapter 36
A Dutchmen Builds a Dream Car
(Lotus Etna Concept Car)

A Lotus fan goes over the edge.

Let's say you like mid-engined cars; and let's say you like Giorgetto Giugiaro, the most famous Italian car designer of the late 20th century. Now ordinarily you would think, "Well, I'd have to look in Italy for something he designed." He did lots of Maseratis for instance. But would you think to look in Britain? Somebody did. A Lotus specialist from England discovered a few years ago that Lotus was storing a lot of old prototypes. Lotus had changed owners, had its ups and downs, and they just didn't need the car anymore.

The 1984 Etna concept, if produced at the time, could have put Lotus in the superstar class. Instead, it nearly disappeared, only to be saved by an enthusiast in Holland. The car was the hit of the 1984 NEC Birmingham Motor Show as the star of the Lotus stand: the Italdesign-styled, V8-powered Etna concept. It basically used an Esprit chassis and had a new body designed with a splendid drag coefficient of only 0.29. It was penned by Giorgetto Giugiaro, who did the original Esprit. The engine was an experimental Lotus V8 and everyone who saw it thought, "hey that's the new Lotus in 1988!"

It was only logical that Lotus, builders of winning grand prix cars, would harbor ambitions to progress to being builders of the fast road cars, much as Ferrari did. More important to the auto industry as a whole at that point in time though was a mysterious feature called "active ride," which used a computer to make for adjustable height settings and self-leveling that promised to make the drive consistent in all conditions. One person said as you drive it, it samples the road surface and anticipates what's coming and adjusts the suspension accordingly. Lotus had already built that into a F1 car, piloted by Nigel Mansell.

The engine also held much promise. The engine's evolution started in 1978 with the assignment by Colin Chapman to Lotus engineer Tony Rudd, of making an all-new V8 that could crank out about 320 horsepower with 300 lb-ft of torque. And, oh, by the way, use as many existing parts as possible from the 16-valve slant-four already used in the Esprit, Elite and Eclat models; and incidentally, be able to meet U.S. emissions regulations. Rudd was starting with a good engine, the type 907, and quickly designed two of them into a V8 block, though he had to design new DOHC heads.

The power output was quoted as 335 horsepower at a modest 6500rpm, although a maximum torque figure of 295 lb-ft at 5500rpm hinted at a power delivery slanted toward the high rev end. The new engine was called the Lotus DV8 engine, aka Type 909. Its further development dropped due to problems in the production of the Esprit and Excel; the Lotus firm was struggling to stay alive.

Then came Chapman's death in 1982, along with the 1979 Iran-Iraq war's role in rising fuel prices. Together they hurt Lotus, whose sales fell to a trickle.

Who should come along as the savior of Lotus? That colossus of the West, General Motors. They bought Lotus in 1986 but the truth was they didn't give a fig about the Etna. They were more entranced with the Active Suspension, and even fitted it to their own prototype. The problem was it worked great in the lab and on the test track, but producing a car with it confounded them. (Their Corvette prototype with this suspension was later offered at auction.) Lotus went back to a more conventional design that became the production 1989 front-wheel-drive Elan. The Esprit was redone in '87, but didn't have the Active Suspension, and the new Lotus V8 didn't see the light of day until 1996, as an engine that was totally unrelated to the Type 909.

The Etna show car went to dead storage until 2001, when Coys had an auction of Lotus leftovers and the Etna reappeared after being hidden for nearly 20 years. A Lotus specialist named Paul Matty bought it and then it went on to Olav Glasius, the chairman of Club Lotus Holland, who at the time was building what has been called the world's most important collection of Lotus racing cars. The Etna was in shabby shape when picked up, and ironically much of the roof blew away while the car was being transported on an open trailer. The car then went to Ken and Neil Myers, who run a restoration firm in Northampton, UK. They took on the project of making it run again.

Originally, the idea had been to only make it a static non-runner pushmobile, but once Ken and Neil began poking about, they saw it had an engine and gearbox. They were inspired to make it run, though it was still missing a few vitals like a fuel system, ignition components, and induction system. Rebuilding a prototype engine was a challenge because the idea of sharing parts with the existing slant-four was a pipe dream. That, and there was only one other engine in existence; so basically the engine restorer had to do a redevelopment job on the engine. The finished car eventually appeared at the Goodwood Festival of Speed, showing all the Brits what could have been.

The car was eventually put up for sale as part of Olav Glasius's collection, which included 24 Lotus cars that covered a huge span of Lotus innovation and achievement from 1953 to the present day. The racecars were the plums of the collection, ranging from Mark VI through Marks VIII and IX, and including the Team Lotus works Le Mans veteran Type 11s. Not to mention such delectables as an original and unspoiled Formula Junior Lotus 27, and an ex-Formula 1/InterContinental Lotus Type 18. Glasius, the collector's collector, surprised some by putting his collection on sale. He was a collector with a strong ambition to preserve history.

He told a Lotus website, LotusBuzz.com, "The story is very sad. I have built up the biggest Lotus collection in the world, nearly 30 cars, memorabilia, 180 Lotus books, brochures, toys, pedal cars, etc. My first idea was to let the factory have it to build up a museum, like all other car manufacturers. It was a year ago that I offered it to them, but they don't see the importance, and don't have the money; they like to spend it on things like a posh magazine, that stops now, or a shop in London's Regent street, which I am sure will close within a year, losing millions on silly things instead of spending money on their heritage, because there is no future without a past. There are serious Ferrari, Mercedes, Alfa (museums—Ed.) etc. but sadly no serious Lotus collectors. Why? I don't know, they were 7 times World champion, but nobody cares."

Somewhat embittered, he returned to working on his Bugattis, another great marque, but one with many fans for the old models and factory support from the reborn Bugatti marque to those with show cars. (The modern Bugatti company sometimes pays owners of prewar Bugattis to bring their cars to unveilings of new models so there's a solid link with the past.)

The Etna failed to sell at the Bonham's auction at the Goodwood Festival in June 2012, so there's still a chance for someone to own a one-off Giugiaro-designed prototype. Glasius took the author's contact with him to take one last blast at Lotus, "There are no serious Lotus collectors in the world. How is it possible that a brand with so many fantastic innovations, becoming 7 times World champions, doesn't have a load of collectors? I don't know the answer. Maybe now the last director of Lotus is kicked out, they come back to earth and will understand that there is no future without a past."

Amen, brother.

Chapter 37
Cobra Coupe (not by Shelby)

Imagine that cheeky A.C., thinking they could outdo Der Snakemeister!

A lot of newcomers to the Shelby marque want to credit Carroll Shelby for being the only one to ever bring a Cobra coupe to Le Mans. Wrong. The fact is that when Shelby first brought a Cobra Daytona coupe to Le Mans for practice in April 1964, there was another Cobra coupe there. One not built by Shelby. One that had, in point of fact, never seen the Shelby factory in Los Angeles.

A.C. Cars Ltd, Shelby's supplier of both frames and body-work, showed up at practice with their own coupe, one that looked nothing at all like the Pete Brock-designed Cobra Daytona coupe that Shelby had talked Ford into funding.

The rival coupe was intimidating. Their car could do over 180 mph. Before the car even got to the track it was infamous for a little stunt on the then-new M1 motorway.

First a little background is in order—the mist-green '64 A.C., SN A98 (its design office designation; though it is also known by its first road designation, BPH4B) was designed by Alan Turner and built to race at Le Mans, by A.C. Cars Ltd. atop a Cobra 289 MK2 chassis, complete with additional tubing for structural support.

The motivation to build the car came after A.C. entered a Cobra roadster at Le Mans in '63 but couldn't get it much past 163 mph even with the "trick" of a semi-fastback hardtop. It was felt a more "slippery" shape would produce more speed.

Now they knew Shelby was going to make a coupe because they were supplying the frames. Why not just order one from Der Snakemeister? Shelby was having several bodied in Italy, which A.C. knew because they had shipped the chassis there.

The first rule of racing for a racecar builder is "never sell a competitor the same car you are currently running." Since Shelby planned to run the Pete Brock-designed Daytona coupe, he wanted to keep all the Daytonas built in his own equipe. That was an affront to A.C, but the fact was they had been running at Le Mans as a manufacturer longer than Shelby (back when Shelby was still a race driver, he raced past A.C.'s of various types on many a track), so they just made an extra Cobra frame and put a body of their own design on it.

When first tested in France, A.C.'s own coupe showed overheating and stability problems, which were quickly rectified. With limited testing and no suitable race circuit available before they could get to France, an early morning run was conducted by contemporary Willment Cobra team member, Jack Sears on the recently completed M1, during which time he surpassed 180 mph. Reportedly he had police permission but, later on, when speed limits were imposed on all drivers of the roadway, people blamed Sears.

Once A.C.'s coupe got to Le Mans in June for the race, it had been tuned to give 350 horsepower, conservative for a Cobra small block engine. The car qualified 13th overall, second in class to Dan Gurney's Daytona coupe, but lost time sorting out a fuel starvation problem (traced to a newspaper found in the fuel tank). Then, 77 laps in, with Peter Bolton at the wheel, a tire blew and the car crashed out. Bolton was relatively unscathed but sadly, once he was clear of the car, a Ferrari came along, hit the wreckage and then spun off and killed three young Frenchmen who had snuck into an off-limits area.

Scotsman Barrie Bird bought the wrecked car, restored it, and, by 1981, it was being run in vintage races. It continues to impress Cobra fans in that it is every bit as fast as a Cobra Daytona, and might have been a way for Shelby to go if Brock hadn't come up with Shelby-American's in-house design, the Daytona. Bird was able to buy the car, and apparently had no rivals because it was known at the time that there was no spare bodywork for a one-off body. But he was willing to tackle the job, which took decades to restore. He got it running, rebodied and competed in vintage events for decades since.

Lesson to be learned? Even a wrecked car can be brought back, and on seeing the wreckage, many a would-be restorer might have hesitated because of the scope of the project. Bird didn't. More power to him.

Chapter 38
Der Cobrameister (Lynn Park's Cobras)

The question is: How many Cobras is too many?

One of the great barn hunters of the late 20th and early 21st centuries is Lynn Park, a guy who remembers a significant moment in his life being the first time he read about the Cobra in *Road & Track* in 1962.

"I wanted one," he recalls,"but I was a college student and couldn't afford one. But I could afford an A.C. Bristol and bought one, and echoing Shelby's earlier efforts in 1961, I put a Ford into it. Mine worked great—it was really fast and drove like a Cobra. Although I learned what Shelby went through as I broke every single A.C. part of the drivetrain until I replaced everything with Cobra parts. I got to learn about how Cobras were built by going over to the Shelby plant in Venice and asking them about my do-it-yourself Cobra."

Park, then an elevator company executive, subsequently began saving his coins for a real Cobra and, by 1971, was able to afford his first real one. Since then he estimates he at least 27 or 28 have come his way, some regrettably sold on, but the best part of the story is that he has kept adding to his garage to house his "keeper" collection, some of which he has owned longer than 40 years.

He took the time to tell your author the story of just four of his Cobra finds, all small blocks. The first is "The School Car," so called because CSX2005 was made so early in the Cobra lifespan that it was used as a student car in the "Carroll Shelby School of High Performance Driving." That was back when Shelby still wasn't too sure he could make money building and racing Cobras so he kept the school open until he was sure he'd hit solid paydirt with the Cobra.

Among the instructors were Pete Brock, who later on not only designed the famous COBRA-COBRA-COBRA t-shirt but the famous Daytona Cobra coupe. Another instructor was John Morton who later raced one of the Brock-designed Daytonas in Europe.

The School Car, CSX2005, the fifth Cobra made, was found in OK condition but Park remembers it was owned by a man named Don Bell who bought it from the School. It had been hit. At one point during it's school career, a journalist who thought he was a better driver than he actually was, put it into the hay bales. The car was repaired and continued to be used at The School. Bell bought the car after The School was done using it and contemplated restoring it during the 40 years he owned it but only got a start in 1971.

Park found the car and convinced his club member (Park heads the COCOA branch of the Cobra club) David Lerian, to buy it. It turns out offering cash money didn't do the trick. No, they first found out what the seller wanted—a Kirkham 427 Cobra ready to go, and David happened to have one so it became the perfect swap. Once David bought the Cobra he took it to restorer Mike McCluskey who gave it a perfect restoration, right down to the original 260 engine and the same type of 50-year-old Goodyear tires that were used at The School.

A second Cobra still in his collection is dubbed "The Professor's Car." This one is CSX2044, the 44th Cobra made. "A professor up in Palo Alto at Stanford owned it," says Park. "He drove it on the street and auto-crossed it. Then one day he was entering his garage and knocked off a muffler and it sat for 32 years while he thought about what he would do with it." Park remembers that the Professor had removed some of its desirability when he decided the stock taillights were too small and hammered tremendously ugly ones from a '56 Ford pickup truck onto the rear. Park didn't become aware of the car's availability until 2001 when the Professor called him to find a buyer. Park said he would buy it.

"He didn't want to sell it to me until such time as he ascertained I was a worthy buyer," recalls Park. "He wanted to make sure I was a true blue Cobra enthusiast and not just a flipper who would own the car one day and sell it the next." A deal was struck—soon after picking it up, Park changed it back to the original taillights, and had the car mechanically restored and painted white. The interior was left untouched.

The third car he likes to talk about is CSX2230, the 230th Cobra made. That car enjoyed the dubious distinction at the Rolex vintage car revival at Monterey in 2012 of receiving the most negative comments regarding its appearance. "True," says Park with a smile, "it looks like it was painted with a paint brush." (One wag opined that "its mere presence measurably lowered the collective value of all the genuine Cobras present.")

The car had been owned by a race promoter, Michael Goodwin (later on to become infamous for being convicted of the murder of Mr. & Mrs. Mickey Thompson). Park recalls, "He raced the car quite a bit at first but sold it in 1971. The next owner parked the car for 40 years, hoping to put it back together but never got around to it. He had a family to raise and car took a back seat. During the 40-year-period the owner called me several times about selling it but it took a long time to make it happen."

Finally one day he called and said he was ready to sell. Park drove over in his pickup towing a trailer and rolled the Cobra onto the trailer. He has restored it mechanically but gets a perverse kick out of taking it to events where it draws more attention than perfectly restored Cobras because, well, damn it, it looks like it was painted with a paintbrush.

And finally there's an infamous car in his collection dubbed "The DirtBag," CSX2307. It has engendered a lot of publicity by virtue of being left unpainted—looking just the way it was bought. It was owned by a famous name, in this case Fred Offenhauser, yes of the same family that was in on the ground floor of Indy racing. Park notes that the odd thing about the car was that a Cobra dealer had been sitting on the car until at least '68, so Park figures the dealer must have been using it himself. Park knows Offenhauser had his fun with the car but there came a point when Fred parked the car and there it sat.

That was in 1975. As Cobras went up in price all over the world, the car sat under a tarp in Temple City, California, only a few miles from where Park resided. During its 21 years "in the wilderness" so to speak, Park heard occasional rumors of others who tried to buy it but who were shooed off by Mrs. Offenhauser, sometimes with a shotgun. "But finally," Park says, "she took a liking to a buddy of mine from Northern California. Unbeknownst to Park this buddy came back down to SoCal and bought the car without Park's knowledge—right out from under his nose so to speak. But Park, though temporarily defeated, didn't give up (true barn-finders don't give up). It so happened that the buyer then announced that he planned to make a racing Cobra out of it. Park knew first hand that there's a big difference between a street car and a racer and he said, "If I find you a racing Cobra, will you sell this to me?" Done and done. Ain't life grand?

The funny thing is, because it still looks like it was rolled out of the garage, and Park is, well, a senior citizen, at almost every traffic light he gets shouted-out questions like: "Hey, old, man, do you wanna sell that car?" He laughs.

The really weird part about Lynn Park is that, now that a few of his stable sport roughshod patinas (ah, ain't that a great word stolen by car collectors from antique collectors, because to some people "patina" is just a gold-plated word for "dirt") is that he may have sparked a trend. Even at the fanciest U.S. concours, Pebble Beach, for instance, there is now a category called "preservation class" for cars shown as found, patinas and all. These cars are proud testimony to where a car has been and how long and well it's survived—equivalent to a WWII B-25 that's shown at an air show still sporting the original bullet holes it got while bombing a munitions factory in Germany in 1944. Which is a better indicator of the life and times of the beast in its original era—a vehicle that's been polished and repainted or one that's still wearing the paint it wore when it rolled out of the factory?

On that last car, Park did make a few changes but all under the hood, changing the water pump, rebuilding the car, replacing the fan belt and all the fluids and of course fixing the exhausts.

Quick question? How do you start a car that hasn't been started in 40 years? Answer: Marvel Mystery Oil. It might smoke at first after adding that fantastic liquid, but the more you drive it the more the smoke disappears.

One of the greatest pleasures Park had with Dirtbag was when he toodled over to Carroll Shelby's office in Gardena to show it to the Head Snake himself, Carroll Shelby. "He was all over it," Park told *Motor Trend*. "He just loved it. You'd be amazed at how many people have come to look at it when restoring their own car. It's become like a restoration pattern. It's the kind of thing where you say, 'Wait a minute, maybe I shouldn't touch this.'"

Another reaction people have when they find it's an original is to ask, "When are you going to restore it?" Park just smiles, and then delivers the zinger: "Never; because this one's done."

Lessons to be learned? In a nutshell, Lynn Park is the model of a guy who decided, early on, to concentrate on just one marque. Oh, you can find a hot rod in his garage but, in the main, for 40 plus years, he has kept accurate updated files on the 998 Cobras made in the Sixties in the hope that one or another will become available and, when it does, he hopes to find out sooner rather than later and hopefully just in time to put the money together to buy it.

Another smart move was, back in the mid-'70s, when big block Cobras cost almost twice as much in the collector car market as small blocks, was his decision to specialize in the small blocks. "If you really look at the list of race victories," says Park, "it was almost all small blocks as far as the factory team, so I figured that eventually the small blocks would appreciate as much as the big blocks." By making that decision when there was still a big price spread between the two, he was able to buy twice as many Cobras. Now small blocks and big blocks are worth approximately the same—$600,000 without a racing history. Add more for the history. "Far-sighted" ain't the word for it!

Chapter 39
A Wolf in Sheep's Clothing (Ghia Cobra)

It looks like a rare Fiat, but goes like a Cobra (for a good reason).

Sometimes something you see is not what it looks like. Ever hear the phrase "a wolf in sheep's clothing?" Well that would have to apply to a rip-roarin', butt-kickin', 427 Cobra chassis and engine that has been hiding under a Fiat body for decades. Since new it has been terrorizing British roads.

First some background: A.C. Cars was one of the oldest automobile manufacturers in Great Britain, having presented its first model at an auto show in 1903. In 1961, ex-racecar driver Carroll Shelby, with the mantle of having won the 24 Hours of Le Mans for Aston Martin, asked AC Cars to build him a roadster with a V8 engine. Basically he was having the chassis of the A.C. Ace-Zephyr changed in minor ways to accommodate a Ford V8.

A.C. started with a 221-cubic-inch V8 but then Shelby tried it out first in America with a 260-cubic-inch V8 and that became the production car. Eventually the small block had a Mk. II version in 1963 with the 289-cubic-inch (4.7 liter) V8. It still had the leaf suspension front and rear but at least had the important update of rack and pinion steering.

In 1965, Ford wanted to build the ultimate Cobra and started a new chassis design that was still two basic ladder tubes, but with coil springs all around. This became the Mk. III. Some were even fitted with 428 engines, weaker than the side oiler 427 but the customers weren't told (the car was still called the 427). Though Ford had backed the small block 289 Cobras in racing they lost interest in promoting the Cobra by the time Shelby went to the big block 427, preferring instead to spend their money engineering the GT40 mid-engined cars so they could win the 24 Hours of Le Mans.

So the 427 was sort of a turkey as far as sales. When Shelby failed to get enough made, the car was refused homologation by the FIA to become a production car; consequently, no racer wanted it because that meant they would have to race against prototypes. Fortunately Shelby thought of converting some of the racecars back into street cars and those became the legendary S/C models. In 1967, Carroll Shelby stopped importing cars from Britain and concentrated again on Ford's GT40 program and on the Shelby Mustangs.

There were only three body choices in Cobras as far as Shelby was concerned. One was the small block roadster, one was the small block Daytona coupe, of which only six were made for racing only (and not sold to other teams) and the third was the 427 Cobra roadster. Somehow, some way, one "loose" chassis over in the UK got a different body. That is our subject car.

In the book *Essential AC Cobra* by Rinsey Mills, he shows a picture of an A.C. Cobra bodied by Ghia that looks like a Karmann Ghia on steroids. It is believed that the chassis, CSX3055, came from John Willment, a Ford dealer who raced GT40s and would have some contact with FAV Ford Advanced Vehicles. Either A.C. had stopped making Cobras by the time he got this or he thought a coupe would be interesting. Some suggest the chassis was CSX3055. John Willment fitted a modified body from a 1950s Fiat 8V (it was a V8 but since Fiat mistakenly thought Ford had copyrighted the word "V8" they called their V8 an "8V").

The car was for sale in England by Paul Baber but then ended up at a shop called Autoputer in Florida. It also sat on a California used car lot and is now said to be back in the UK where it has made an appearance at Goodwood. The engine is said to be a Holman-Moody 427 with twin four barrels. The car might have been sold by his shop before completion.

Somehow the name Lady Campbell is associated with it, she being the wife of the speed record setter famous in the Fifties. It is difficult to believe an aristocratic lady would want to drive such a beast but there you are (actually it took all of five minutes to find her on the internet in Janurary 2013, in Lake Gregory, California; she told your author the car was intended to be a surprise for her, but when also offered an E-type Jag, she chose the Jag instead and never took delivery of the Ghia-bodied A.C.).

I present this beast only as an example of how sometimes a great car can be hidden under another body. At different times in this car's checkered career, it has been available cheap but probably the right 427 Cobra fan didn't run the numbers against what registers there were at the time (surprise, there was a Cobra register before SAAC existed, from a club based in Grosse Pointe, Michigan) and realize this car was a real 427 Cobra underneath. Not only that, but maybe a racing Cobra chassis.

Could it be rebodied as a thundering 427 Cobra? No doubt. Is it worth more in this sheep's body (fans of Italian coachwork would say "yes")? Now that there are collectors paying big bucks for Fiats and Alfas with the same Supersonic body (one 8V Supersonic taking over a million at a recent auction). Just the sale of the body would pay for fine new Cobra bodywork to be hammered out. Ah, decisions, decisions....

Chapter 40
Harley's Honey (1954 Oldsmobile F88 Concept Car)

Yes, he planned to build a GM rival to the Corvette.

Standing 6 feet, 6 inches (with his hat on), Harley Earl was running GM's styling department back in the Fifties, and pretty much Lord of all he surveyed. He had begun at GM back in 1927 when they didn't even have a head stylist. He was given a VP slot in 1940.

He quaintly called his office the "Art and Color Section" when he arrived in Detroit. GM had hired him because the man had pizazz. After earning a degree in Engineering from Stanford, he had worked in his father's carriage modification shop in Hollywood, which segued into doing custom cars for movie stars like Fatty Arbuckle and cowboy star Tom Mix.

The cars he designed were more flamboyant than anything made in Detroit, which was why GM hired him and gave him almost anything he wanted as he built an empire that other top designers in Detroit were intensely jealous of. He spawned many a show car, almost 40 during his reign. He also created the Motorama traveling road shows that featured dream cars and svelte dancers to make GM regular production cars look oh-so-glamorous (though they never quite looked as good as the dream cars).

Some of the Motorama cars were generic ones like the "LeSabre." Others would carry the name of GM's Divisions. When Chevrolet had the Corvette in production in 1953, a car he had promoted from day one, he got in mind, why stop there—why not market two-seaters in all the Divisions? Hence the building of two-seater prototypes for all the Divisions, including Buick, Cadillac, Pontiac and Oldsmobile.

This car is one of three (some say four) Olds F-88 show cars, each one slightly different, all with fully hidden convertible tops. One website says Corvette doyen Zora Arkus-Duntov was involved, though that's unlikely—he obstructed various efforts on another GM two-seater for decades. Another name involved was Ken Pickering.

The power plant was a 324-cubic-inch "Rocket V8" producing 250 horsepower, and this is a running driving car powered by that engine.

Designed during 1952 and 1953, around the same time as the first Motorama Corvette, the preliminary sketches of the F-88 came from veteran designer Bill Lange. The final design was done in the main Oldsmobile studio under the direction of Art Ross. Ross was legendary for various things, from his 1941 Cadillac egg crate 'tombstone' grill, to the World War II Hellcat tank destroyer.

The car was built on a Corvette chassis, which does not make it a Corvette necessarily, as GM Corporate would build concept cars and sometimes decide what Division's name would be put on the car later. This practice continues to recent times as when the Olds Aurora was developed as a Cadillac but only became an Olds when it was decided the Olds Division needed it more (it didn't save Oldsmobile).

The interior of the F-88 was designed by Jack Humbert (who later moved on to become Pontiac's chief designer). He chose natural pigskin upholstery. His design was unique but had some Olds "cues" such as the bullet taillights and "hockey stick" side trim.

Unveiled at the General Motors Motorama on January 21, 1954, at the posh Waldorf-Astoria Hotel in New York, the 1954 Oldsmobile F-88 was painted metallic gold with metallic green inside the fenderwells. The F-88 shared the stage at Motorama with the Oldsmobile Cutlass fastback coupe, a car whose teardrop rear roof presaged the Corvette Sting Ray "aero" coupe that would appear on a production car almost ten years later. That year the F-88 went to five Motorama shows in several cities.

Once a GM show car completed its Motorama show bookings, company protocol was to send each car over to its sponsoring division. The division's top execs were then encouraged to eventually destroy it, though some were sold. And incredibly some were given away, such as the time Earl gave a two-seater Cadillac "Le Mans" to a Cadillac dealer who was a personal friend. And your author recently saw a picture of another Cadillac Le Mans, this one with a Plexiglas hardtop, pictured outside a Los Angeles arena with caption naming a blonde bombshell movie star actress, Marie "The Body" MacDonald as the owner (sadly, this car was destroyed in a building fire in Pleasanton, California, in May 1985).

It evidently paid to be friends with Harley.

There are reports that the F-88 didn't run when it was a show car, but home movies taken in the summer of 1954 by a 15-year-old Lansing lad show the F-88 being driven by Shriners in a downtown parade, so—from a collector's standpoint—that puts it a notch above all those dream cars that were never running cars in their original era (called "pushmobiles"), like the Pininfarina Cadillac Jacqueline, the Cadillac Town Car, the LaSalle II and many others.

Why didn't the F-88 make it to production? The Corvette –a car that had been spawned by Earl and promoted through Motorama—was proving to be a dog in sales in '54, with sales so low that GM was honestly thinking of deep-sixing the car; but eventually word got out that there would be a V8 option in '55, and its future looked more promising. So the Corvette was saved. In '56 it got a re-styling that made it look leaner and meaner, so it was on its way to eventual profitability.

The F-88 is interesting because it remains a good example of "the path not taken." Usually automakers hide the alternative choices that may have been better cars than the ones they stuck with, which is one reason why many Motorama Concept cars were allowed to fall into obscurity. More's the pity that the F-88 didn't make the cut. The Olds F-88 would have been a better car than the Corvette was in '54, because it offered more luxury. It would have had a V8 as standard instead of optional, and thus would have trounced the Corvette six.

More about the engine: the 324-cubic-inch V8 it had under the hood was from the '54 Oldsmobile Super 99, and had a stock four-barrel carburetor. Compression was 9.0:1, and it was said to top the Super 88's 185 horsepower with its 250 horsepower. Plus, the F-88 had roll-up windows, while Corvette buyers still had to make do with old-fashioned side curtains of plastic and canvas. The Olds version of a two-seater would have had a four-speed automatic, instead of the puny two-speed Powerglide of the Corvette.

Once again, in this car's case we can toss out the old saw, "concept cars were destroyed and not supposed to be sold, yadda-yadda." This car was reportedly snuck out of GM styling in pieces, and ended up in the garage of Errat Lobban Cord, wheeler dealer and former auto builder (before the war he was CEO of the Auburn-Cord-Duesenberg empire).

Reportedly, the car was not sold complete, just sold in of boxes, but what the hey, when you have been an automaker like Cord was, assembling a car of parts is no big thing. At the time Cord received the F-88 he was no longer CEO of an auto company, but may have just wanted the car to study for a possible comeback into the postwar auto industry.

The surviving car, known within GM as the XP-20, has been traced to styling order #2265. When the car was auctioned at the Barrett-Jackson auction in Phoenix, hundreds of internal GM documents and original blue prints came with the car, a big step in authenticating a car whose mere survival is a miracle. That huge pile of documentation could have something to do with the huge dollars it fetched. Many concept cars have appeared at auctions before and since, but seldom do they come with crates full of historical paperwork revealing the gestation process in such intimate detail. It's like being there with the designers and engineers as they made their decisions.

What makes the F-88 controversial is that experts can't decide even on the number made. Most settle on the number three. A long-time owner of the car was Seattle-area auto collector Gordon Apker, who upon receiving the car began to hear rumors of a twin to the car, but then he also heard rumors the twin was being driven around East Lansing and caught fire. Part of the confusion stems to Olds' re-use of the name, as there was a later Mk. II F-88 with a different body and small tailfins, and a Mk. III, none of them related cosmetically or mechanically to this first car.

A magazine called *Consumer Guide*, which often publishes articles about lost prototypes, claims that Harley Earl ordered another F-88 for personal use, one painted red, but that could have been the quad headlamp, tail-finned job that is a completely different design (That car as well deserves another chapter—when we can find out where it is).

Apparently the '54 gold F-88 is the "last man standing" among F-88 early prototypes and it set a world record when auctioned in January 2005 at the Barrett-Jackson auction in Scottsdale, Arizona, for $3,240,000. In fact, the car astounded the snobby collectors of such cars as Ferraris, because here in front of them was an American car commanding the price you would see attached to a Ferrari racing car. The buyer was a Mr. Hendricks, identified as the founder of the Discovery Channel, a channel which devotes itself to enlightenment and history, so here was obviously a buyer with a sense of history.

According to an article on *The Auto Channel*, "Curator of The Hendricks Collection and bidding agent Alan Lewenthal stated, 'Winning this remarkable one-of-a-kind dream car for the Hendricks family and the Gateway Colorado Auto Museum was an amazing experience. As the bidding surpassed $1 million, it was apparent that leading museums and serious collectors had done their homework on the unique role of this vehicle in American automotive history. Standing on the stage to witness the historic auction were Harley Earl's grandson, Richard Earl, and two members of GM's design team from the 1960s. When the other museums dropped out of the bidding we simply had to stay in to the end to ensure that this remarkable work of American automotive art could be enjoyed by the viewing public and students for years to come.'"

Hendricks displays the car in its own room at his Gateway Auto Museum in Colorado. It's hard to believe the owner of a small museum would spend so much money on just one car but that wasn't all he bought. On televised auctions, he is reported to have spent over $4.5 million. You might ask why would someone spend so much on a car that is obscure even in GM histories?

Well, maybe Hendricks saw the F-88 at a car show long ago, and fell in love. Like seeing a movie star onscreen, then meeting her in person and marrying her. The car business in Earl's time was more romance than practicality. Sometimes romance wins…

Lesson for barn-finders? The American car company concept cars are out there waiting to be found. Reportedly, this car was scheduled for the crusher, but the man charged with that job couldn't bear to destroy it and hid it in a barn. The car had a murky past, but all's well that ends well and the car is a museum star today.

Chapter 41
The Hunchback with "Clown Lips" (Ferrari GTC/4)

Wherein the Author takes the 12-cylinder plunge.

The man's wife, an actress who looked Scandinavian, called it "The Monster."

"You've come for the Monster," she said.

"Yes, I have," I said. Meanwhile trying to figure out why she would call one of Pininfarina's most beautiful Ferrari designs—the GTC/4—"The Monster."

I say "most beautiful" but the Italians, with their ever more refined eyes for body shapes (both women and cars) called it "the hunchback with clown lips" because it had an ever so slight rise to the center of the rear deck lid, and up front there was a black rubber bumper surround. Neither feature hurt the car's looks but you know the Italians. They wanted things just right or they would find something to criticize.

I found out later on, once I took the car, it ate money. It wasn't the cookie monster, but the money monster.

During its short-lived original heyday, 1971-'72, the C4 was the more expensive cousin to the Daytona which shared some of the same parts, including the block. But the Daytona had its gearbox out back for better weight distribution and was more of a brutal sports car. The C4, with power steering and a gearbox connected to the engine, was "a gentleman's sports car" built, I told newcomers to the model, "for the executive in Milano who wanted a fast sports car so when his secretary said she would go with him to spend the weekend in Lake Como he could get there in a hurry at 100 mph before she changed her mind."

But I am getting ahead of myself. First the joys of the discovery.

The way I came across the car is that I often visited a mechanic in West Hollywood named Al Axelrod. Axelrod had a lot of movie folk customers and one of them—a movie producer up in the Hollywood Hills—had brought this dark green Ferrari (I told the mechanic I'd seen that color on International Harvester tractors when I was a cowboy, but I digress) down from his hilltop house atop Mulholland drive for its annual check-up.

Actually the guy never drove the car but periodically would get fired up to get the car going. And then it wouldn't run because it was neglected for so long. Because it was a heavy car, you could get it down from the Hollywood Hills on gravity alone but if it wasn't running right, it wouldn't make it back up the steep roads to its garage.

I saw spider webs on it and asked, "Is this car for sale?"

Axelrod said, "I'm trying to buy it" and revealed he had been turned down in his first offer because the seller, a movie producer, wanted $25,000.

At the time a pristine C/4 was going for around $45,000.

So I forgot about it. Then a few months later I am in Santa Monica, passing an exotic car lot and I see the same Ferrari out on the lot, while there are two pristine C4s in the showroom. The ones in the showroom are going for maybe $45,000 but, for the tatty green one out on the lot, they said, "Make us an offer." Well because I knew Al, I knew what the owner wanted, and when they weren't looking I copied down the owner's registration info out of the glove compartment (hey, all's fair in love and war). I then wrote his office and they called me back in response.

"I want $25,000," the owner, a movie producer of those kinds of movies which feature scantily-clad ladies and runaway slaves, said.

I knew from what Al said that the owner was touchy; and would yank his car out of any shop if the bills started to approach a critical mass. So I took a chance and trash-talked the dealer: "Look," I said, "they are treating your car terrible over there, letting it get all dirty while they shine up the nice ones inside. And I'd love to pay your price but the fact is I only have $16,000 so let's say we split the difference and I pay $19,000?"

He went for it. The beauty of it was, that, by divine providence, I had coincidentally sold my 308GTS a few months before for $29,000 (losing a bunch since I had paid $45,000 for it brand new, but then I had driven it over 50,000 miles), so I had a lot of bargaining room left which I didn't have to use.

I went to the producer's office right at the end of the "strip" part of Sunset Strip and sat and looked at movie posters while waiting to see him. We talked and I handed him the check. I could tell, by the number of employees and the projects he was working on, that 19 grand would maybe cover his expenses up to about lunch.

That afternoon, I went up to his house to pick up the car. That's when the wife, who looked vaguely like some Swedish film star, said her famous monster line and pointed vaguely toward the garage, actually a car port that seemed to stretch into the horizon with many, many cars. Now from past experience in buying cars, I knew before I even arrived that this could be one of those "you can have the car but we can't find the key" deals.

This could happen because the owner had a lot of cars, or maybe even the dealer who last had the car on consignment made the key get lost so the owner would sell the car to them later.

Not to worry. This wasn't my first rodeo, so I arrived with a flatbed tow truck. I laid out the chain, attached it to the bumper and began to yank it out.

Now it turned out that the car had a steering wheel lock so, without the key to unlock the wheel, it yanked the car toward the house. When it came to rest against the house, I kept pulling and the house began to cut a salmon-colored groove in the car while the car began to cut a dark green groove in the house.

(Author's note: when somebody heard this story, they asked me, "Didn't the tow truck have a dolly?" Ah, you live and learn...) Finally, when the car was about half way along the house, the Latina maid found the key and I unlocked the steering wheel. I was not about to give up on this treasure, fearful that at any moment the producer would realize, "Hey, all I have to do is detail this car and it's worth twice as much."

I flat-bedded it down the hill to LeBrea Ave. where Bruno Borri, my Italian mechanic, regarded it dubiously. He knew these were among the most complicated Ferraris. You could start at one end and before you got to the other find six things to fix, maybe seven. I left the car and three days later Bruno called.

"Hey, it's got no compression in two cylinders." Bad news. I knew a four cam V-12 was one expensive engine to rebuild, maybe more than I had paid for the whole car. They knew I was a Ferrari neophyte and that my 308 hadn't needed much because I bought it new. "But we try, we shim the valves, we work on it," Bruno said.

Two days later he called. "We got compression. You come and pick it up."

Now these particular Italians ran things like in some back alley in Salerno. You didn't get a written estimate. You didn't get a bill when you picked the car up. You just left your car and when you came back, you fanned out a spray of $100 bills and hoped they wouldn't hurt you too bad as they plucked out of your hand the number of C-notes they needed. The amount could even depend on how Bruno did on picking nags at Santa Anita that day.

Now the funny part was, Bruno wanted me to test drive it. Not out in the country but right there, on La Brea Avenue. Now this is, you understand, a road full of traffic, with a stop light every couple blocks. But Bruno was a racing mechanic. He could only tell if a Ferrari was running right if he could hear all 12 cylinders screaming in full song, at say 7,500 rpm.

Dutifully I drove a couple blocks away, and ran it by their

shop at 6,000-7000 rpm. I did this three or four times and finally saw him give me the OK sign. I interpreted this to mean something like "Go with God, my man."

I couldn't stand the International Harvester Green paint for long and painted it Ferrari red or what cynics call "resale red." I kept the unique tartan cloth upholstery inserts because it was so contrary to what you expected in a Ferrari. I mean plaid—who was I, Jackie Stewart?

I drove the car for the next three years. It only broke down a couple of times, once when a throttle cable snapped. I managed to tie a wire to the carb linkage and accelerate by pulling on the wire from the driver's window. Once it overheated. And once, early on, the first time I took a trip to a Ferrari event in Santa Barbara, it developed a profuse leak between two of the six sidedraft twin throat Weber carburetors whereupon I discovered a design flaw—when it had such a leak, it would drip raw gas on the hot exhaust headers immediately below (I wondered how many C4's had burned up with this arrangement). A Swiss mechanic at the same event merely spliced another hose to get a new section to replace the leaking one.

My wife at the time, who was only 4 feet, 10 inches, couldn't reach the pedals so, though she liked the idea of driving a Ferrari, she in fact never drove it.

The Ferrari left my life as many a good car goes—through divorce. She wanted it as part of her settlement and since I could sell it to her for the going price at the time—three times what I paid for it– and not have to pay taxes on the profit (no taxes between spouses) I went for it.

I think about that C4 sometimes. I truly miss it. In fact, due to the low numbers of Ferraris produced up to that time, it's got an easy serial number to remember, only five digits and with the wonders of the internet, it's not hard to find, I just go on Google and type in the serial number and there she is, on one used car lot or another, usually priced more toward $200,000 (but still lagging behind Daytonas which were its cheaper brother back in the day). But, though it slipped my grasp, there's those fond memories you can't take away, like driving down Pacific Coast Highway toward Malibu, taking those big sweepers at 100 mph. It had the best exhaust note of any Ferrari made for the street.

But I couldn't own it now. Bruno closed his shop. Going to a Ferrari dealer of the present day and hearing prices like $100 an hour for labor would give me a heart attack. And parts? Hey, give me a break, they only made roughly 500 of them. There aren't any body parts left over except from wrecked ones.

Fortunately the engine was used in the first 365GT4 and 400GTs, when they were still carbureted so it's theoretically possible to get engine parts from European dealers (the 400GTs never having been legal U.S. models). I'll bet that movie producer misses it too. He told me when I brought the check to his office that he had bought the car when he went to the Cannes Film Festival. He wanted something snazzy to drive around, up and down the Croissette, and down to St. Tropez. He did that. His mistake was bringing it home.

Lessons learned? Make one search point for a rare car mechanic's shops, preferably ones near expensive neighborhoods (that particular one, if you walked out the shop door, and looked North, you saw the Hollywood Hills). Look for a car with a pedigree but neglected. When you get close to a target, get your money ready. Try to find out what they want for it before you make your offer. Find a guy that's got more toys than he needs. A guy with a wife that hates the car...and, oh, don't forget to bring a flatbed. Capiche?

Chapter 42
The Four-Door Ferrari (Pinin)

An experiment that somebody believed in.

I know, I can hear you saying: "But Ferrari didn't make four-door cars." Well, they tried, building one prototype and sending it up the flagpole to see who salutes.

This is a story about that car. Maserati can make a four-door car (they do, the Quattroporte). Aston Martin can make a four-door car. And they do.

But not Ferrari. Some things are still sacred.

The car was the 1980 Pinin, named after Pinin Farina, the head of the carrozzeria known as Pininfarina. The 1980 Turin Motor Show marked the 50th anniversary of Pininfarina, and Ferrari fans were eager to see what special concept car would be unveiled. Some were disappointed when it was a four-door Ferrari. Chassis number 99788, the Ferrari Pinin had a wheelbase only five centimeters longer than the Ferrari 400 four-seater coupe, and its predecessor, 365 GT4 2+2. It was a very subdued design, credited to Diego Ottina, who was working under the direction of Leonardo Fioravanti, the man responsible for some of Pininfarina's greatest Ferrari designs since the '60s, including the 365GTB/4 Daytona.

They were able to get a very low height hood by having a flat "pancake" engine from the mid-engined Ferrari Boxer. Very impressive was the flush glass, hiding the A- and B-pillars, which from a distance gave you the impression of wraparound glass running around from C-pillar to C-pillar.

It also had what were called 'multi-parabolic' lights designed in conjunction with Lucas, flush to the body and using three lenses, the middle one the same color as the bodywork. Of course for aerodynamics, the wipers retracted under a panel to help with streamlining (didn't we see that in the 1968 Corvette?), and the five-spoke wheels were angled like the blades of a turbine to funnel cooling air to the disc brakes. Interior appointments were much plusher than production Ferraris, with special tan Connolly leather wrapping most surfaces, and all passenger comfort controls were computerized. The rear-seated passengers also had their own controls including a second radio to be used with headphones. I know, you can order headphones, etc. in today's cars but we're talking 33 years ago here. At the dawn of time so to speak.

But the Pinin was killed off before it reached production.

Fiat, who owned Ferrari, was developing a whole slate of cars, and couldn't be bothered with such a rare car that would only sell a couple hundred a year like the 400GT. The prototype didn't run. It was a pushmobile, so most people thought that soon after 1980, the car would be headed for the crusher; but you sell a car to a car dealer, and what d'ya know, sometimes he resells it. In this case they sold it to Jacques Swaters, the famed head of the successful Ecurie Francorchamps Belgian racing team and a close personal friend of Enzo Ferrari. He didn't care if it didn't run, it was still a show car, right? So, in 2005, he took the Pinin to the Essen Motor Show, which is a sort of "retro" event devoted to the cars of the past.

In 2008, Mr. Swaters sold the Pinin to its current owner at RM's Ferrari –Leggenda e Passione auction. In 2011 the same auction house featured it at its London auction. Its highest bid was £400,000, but that wasn't enough for its sale. Because the Pinin was not originally manufactured as a drivable car, RM pointed out in their catalog description that they were selling the car "as an item of memorabilia" and not as a car. Perhaps that way they wouldn't have to worry about if it would meet the emissions and safety laws of any country. Who knows? Maybe it would end up just as a static display at one Ferrari dealer or another, but that thought didn't reckon with the driving ambition of some collectors to have a one-off driving Ferrari.

The last buyer (whose bid won it at auction) wanted a running car and commissioned former Ferrari Technical Director Mauro Forghieri's Oral Engineering to carry out the necessary work. This is the legendary man who ran Ferrari's racecar development in the Sixties, so it wasn't a formidable task to him; and it wasn't as difficult as if it had been a one-off chassis. The car was basically a stretched 400GT aft of the front bulkhead, and already had a rear suspension and differential, while the engine bay had been adapted from the mid-engined 512BB's rear sub-frame. The front suspension was comprised of short wishbones with the springs welded in place.

Oral Engineering found a complete 512BB engine, which had to be moved forward in the engine bay, further than originally planned, to actually work. A 400GT gearbox was also found. Other work included strengthening the chassis, fabricating a fuel tank, manufacturing a wiring loom, fabricating a radiator, and installing fully functioning suspension and brakes. In other words, all the owner saved was the building of a chassis, but the rest of the car still had to be made to make it a running car. One problem: fixed side windows and the lack of a ventilation system made it difficult to drive on a hot day, so you saved this one for cool concours. A conventional dashboard also had to be made as the experimental one was for show use only.

How much is such a car worth? In 2012, the car was offered for sale at Bonhams Auction in Monaco, seemingly the right place to sell a one-off Ferrari. In the catalog, the estimated value was projected to be $620,000–$740,000, but it left the auction unsold.

Lesson to be learned? Like some of the other show cars found in this book, it takes a heap of work to make a pushmobile, the star of the stage at many an International Auto Show, into an actual running car.

You would have to tally the purchase and restoration costs against the eventual auction sales price to see if a buyer could make out here. We applaud the spirit of those who wanted to make it a running car, to carry Ferrari's dream further than Ferrari was willing to do themselves. But be forewarned, this is a dangerous path to tread unless your goal is not appreciation but an attempt on consummation of your flat-out love for the car.

Romance is something we can believe in.

Chapter 43
The Bail Jumper's Ferrari
(1955 Ferrari 121 LM)

An immigrants tale…
wherein the car survives but
the owner doesn't.

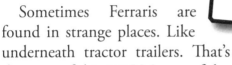

Sometimes Ferraris are found in strange places. Like underneath tractor trailers. That's the story of this 121LM, one of the rare six-cylinder racing Ferraris. Yes, a six. Ferrari also made four-cylinder racecars.

Some background is in order. The Ferrari 121 LM was powered by a Lampredi-designed six-cylinder engine. The engine had been created by utilizing the successful four-cylinder engine and adding two-cylinders to the 2-liter four. The result was called the 306 and was used during the close of the 1954 season. The '306' was really just a developmental version of what would come in the years that followed. The results of testing and experimentation were the Type 118 and Type 121.

The Type 118 was a 3.7-liter engine and fitted into what became known as the 376 S. The Type 121 was a larger 4.4-liter unit, officially known as the 446 S, and it too powered Ferraris constructed by Scaglietti.

The names of the 376 S and the 446 S were later changed to the 118 LM and the 121 LM. There were three versions of each constructed. One of the 118 LMs was later modified to 121 LM specifications. A single 118 LM was entered by the factory into the Buenos Aires 1000 km race and was joined by several privateers. This was the first major race for the 118 LM and expectations at the factory were high. Sadly, the car was black flagged off the course when the driver took a wrong route back into the pits. Two privateers were able to finish in the top two positions for Ferrari.

The next major race was the Mille Miglia, where Ferrari fielded one 118 LM and three 121 LMs. The Ferraris were met with strong competition from other prominent marques such as Mercedes-Benz and their 300 SLRs. To make things worse for the Ferrari team, a Mercedes-Benz was being piloted by Stirling Moss. From the start, the 300 SLR took an early lead. This would be short lived, as the powerful Ferraris soon overtook the underpowered Moss. But the lead would not last, as the tires they had chosen were not adequate for the large, six-cylinder engines, and by the close of the race, all three 121 LMs had crashed. The 118 LM managed to hang in there and finished the race in a respectable third place. Stirling Moss went on to capture the checkered flag.

The Ferrari team next set their sights on the 24 Hours of Le Mans. During practice, Eugenio Castellotti qualified his 121 LM as fastest in the field and thus earned an excellent position on the starting grid. The strategy was for the 121LMs to hang back and let the other break. During a 24-hour race, a lot can happen. Sadly, this was to be one of the most devastating races in history, as a SLR went out of control and flew into a grandstand killing 80 spectators and causing injury to many more. The driver was also killed. The race was allowed to continue, which gave the ambulances easier access to and from the track. A Jaguar D-Type went on to win the race. Mercedes-Benz withdrew not only from the race but from motorsports. A Ferrari 121 LM was holding third before it was forced to retire. Ferrari ended the season just one point short of winning the World Championship. At the close of the season, Ferrari sold their six-cylinder works cars and began working on new V-12 engines.

SCUDERIA PARRAVANO

The 121LM was considered a tricky car to drive, though Carroll Shelby did well with one when it was owned by Tony Parravano, a mysterious Italian-American sponsor who had a big Ferrari team in Southern California. Ironically, Parravano had a tiff with the IRS before he up and disappeared. The Feds made a move to padlock his shop and impound his cars, but he had an advance tip and made a run for the border with a convoy of Ferraris. Some of them got stopped, including this car, which was sold at a parking lot sale by the IRS (other accounts say it was U.S. Customs).

At one point, Parravano was labeled a bail jumper and a WANTED poster was hung in post offices to no avail. He had disappeared. Totally!

The first known owner after the Parravano fracas with the IRS, according to the authoritative source barchetta.cc.com, was somebody named Roland Grandmaison of the San Diego area, in 1958. Next the same source lists it being raced by an equipe run by Jack Brumby and being run in three races, all with drivers who later became famous—Ken Miles (who raced for Shelby), and two Indy drivers, Tony Bettenhausen and Troy Ruttman. In '59 it ended up being owned by racing mechanic Bob Sorrell, who knew the car, having been Parravano's mechanic. His race sponsor career was pretty much of a non-starter except for one race—the Times GP of Riverside, run with Rodger Ward at the wheel in 1959.

The way the car was discovered was this: In the 1980s, a British car restorer was ordering parts over the phone from Pete Civati, an Italian-born mechanic in Los Angeles who repaired Ferrari engines. Civati was acquainted with the son of Sorrell, Parravano's ex-mechanic, who apparently now owned the car. The younger Sorrell had let Civati know that he not only had parts but a whole car, and was in a financial bind. He owed the government money. Sorrell and his aged mother lived in a tiny house in nearby Inglewood, a house jammed with papers, books and car parts.

The Englishman had a local contact in Los Angeles, a retired airline pilot who knew Ferraris and who knew Civati. He wired an initial deposit to his friend who went over and paid the mechanic and then the Englishman flew over to pick and choose what he wanted in person. He arrived, and once they had the parts, and the engine, which was at still another location, it was off to see the car iteself. So they all piled in an old Pontiac station wagon with trailer attached and headed for Norco, about 60 miles east. When they arrived at a piece of desert scrubland littered with

214

old cars and assorted junk, Sorrell pointed out an old battered aluminum-bodied Ferrari parked under a tractor trailer.

It was about 105 degrees and the Englishman, used to cooler climates, no doubt felt like the Englishman who had discovered King Tut's tomb. He could see from 50 feet that it was a rare 121LM, one of three made. He was pleased to see the car had a chassis and body but of course you wouldn't expect an interior after several decades out in the open.

The car was towed out from under the tractor trailer and loaded aboard a car trailer for the trip back to the West side. The Englishman was happy with the deal, especially with all the extra parts the seller was throwing in: wheels, tires, gearboxes, and so forth. He had half a dozen Ferraris back at the shop that could use these parts. At first the Englishman was going to ship the car back to the UK, but then decided he couldn't afford to ship everything, so he called another Englishman dealing in Ferraris in California, and a customer was quickly found for the car and engine. Essentially, this deal made it akin to the first Englishman getting the parts and the shipping of those parts, for free.

Would anybody have been able to buy the car? Probably not. There were others in the Ferrari community who would've jumped on it in a nanosecond, but the seller had a bad impression on meeting most of them, thinking they were out to pay him less than he was due.

The personal introduction from Civati to the buyer made the sale possible.

The second factor was the local contact, the retired pilot, who knew both the seller and the buyer, plus Civati.

The car has since been restored and graced many events in the hands of its present owner, a major Wall Street figure.

Now, Question No. 2: could just anybody driving by have seen the car under the truck? Not likely. (And you had to ask, would anybody out in that inland empire town have recognized a Ferrari so rare?)

Lesson learned? Don't be skeptical when someone says, "I saw an old racecar parked out in the desert under a tree, in a barn, in a field, etc." It could be a car like this, easily worth a million dollars today.

Chapter 44
Prototipo (The Original Ferrari Red Head)

What's a little crash and a little fire when the car's a damn Ferrari factory racing prototype?

When you are talking Ferraris, old racing Ferraris anyway, two things matter most—what's the chassis number (so you can see its racing history) and is the engine the correct number? Well, this car certainly scores high in the chassis number department because it was the first Ferrari Testa Rossa built, back in '57. It was the testbed for the 33 others that would follow. Variations won the Le Mans 24 Hour race in 1958, 1960, and 1961.

This is the original Ferrari Red Head (Testa Rossa means "red head" in Italian, a nickname given thanks to the bright red cam covers on this car—Chassis 0666 TR). And why did they have red cam covers? Because when they were developing the engine and had several identical ones, one proved to have more horsepower so they painted the cam covers red, then reconfigured the other engines to match that one.

This car went through hell and high water (burned twice, and crashed heavily at Le Mans in '58) but emerged to eventually fetch the highest money ever paid for a racing errari up to that point—$16.4 million dollars at the Gooding auction in Monterey.

The catalogue entry when it went to auction details its provenance in great detail and is hence repeated below to explain why the car broke the world record price by nearly 40 percent. Though to be fair, some of that was paid because the auction company, in their catalogue, had a sound recording of the car running through the gears. What man who loves cars can resist that?

First some history is in order. The Testa Rossa was borne out of the jousting of Ferrari against Maserati though Jaguar, Porsche and Aston were catching up.

Ferrari wanted to design a new car and it was obvious that the four-cylinder 500 TRC wasn't fast enough to score an outright victory at Le Mans. So using the example of how Aston developed their DBR1, Ferrari laid out a front engine, three-liter sports car that would be a team car for Ferrari but also be something American buyers could handle. America was their new market. The development began in early 1957 with the car presented here, 0666 TR. 0666 TR was constructed on the tipo 525 chassis, using the usual De Dion tube, transverse leaf-spring suspension in the rear, and A-arms and coil springs up front. Race drivers have some reason why Ferrari built these cars right-hand-drive—something about that was better for European tracks.

They already had a good engine, the 250GT powering the Tour de France berlinettas. The bodywork was similar in style to the 290 MM models of 1956. This particular car, 0666 TR, made its debut at the ADAC 1000 km Nürburgring in Germany, recording the sixth fastest time in qualifying. The drivers for that race were the boyish-looking and bespectacled American Masten Gregory, known as "the Kansas City Flash," along with Oliver Gendebien. Ironically Gregory got misdirected after practice and thought he wasn't driving. He went to his hotel room only to be summoned at the last minute to race. He got into the car and was soon running as high as 6th. He came in eventually, handing the car over to Olinto Morolli, a relatively untested driver who had no previous time in the car and was an incredible three minutes slower per lap! The fast pace under Gregory's driving at the beginning got it to 10th overall by the finish. Still, it was an impressive finish for a new car.

It next appeared at the Swedish 6-hour Grand Prix in Kristianstad, running an experimental 3.1-liter engine that had recently been tested at Le Mans. Gendebien and Maurice Trintignant were the drivers, but the engine didn't last.

By the time 0666 TR returned from Scandinavia, the CSI had confirmed the new three-liter limit for the 1958 season. At that point Ferrari took off the full envelope body and Sergio Scaglietti, who was the in-house racecar body builder for the factory, built a new body with a huge open area behind the front wheels. This became known as the "pontoon fendered" Ferrari. And the final engine was put in the tipo 128 LM Testa Rossa motor (No. 0666 TR, Internal No. GES N 6) mated to a four-speed gearbox. In October 1957, the car was taken to Genoa and put on a steamer for South America for the Venezuelan Grand Prix at Caracas. This was a key race, Caracas the deciding race of the 1957 World Championship season. Ferrari sent along two 335 S models, as well as its TR prototype. Count Wolfgang von Trips and Wolfgang Seidel brought 0666, to 3rd overall behind the larger 4.1-liter four-cam Ferraris. The Maseratis were left in the dust, and Ferrari took the Championship.

Ferrari decided to leave the car in the hands of its South American distributor, Carlos Kaufman, so he could take it to Buenos Aires for the first race of the 1958 season, the 1000 km on January 26. There it was a Ferrari parade, because there were no less than four additional Testa Rossas, two Scuderia Ferrari team cars and two private entries—0666 TR piloted by Von Trips; and Gendebien and Luigi took a 2nd overall just behind the winning TR of Phil Hill /Peter Collins.

Next came a home country race. The Targa Florio in Italy is a race consisting of 40 laps around a 45-mile long course through the Sicilian countryside on ancient roads first built by Romans. Ol' 0666 was fielded in what was to be its last race as a team car. For this race, the two fastest team cars, 0666 TR and 0726 TR, had been fitted with a temporary carb set-up—six Solex twin-choke carburetors. With those it cranked out

330 horsepower but the power band was narrow.

Scuderia Ferrari put a German, Wolfgang Seidel, and an Italian in the car but on the very last lap Seidel went off the road while holding fourth, and went into the rocks. He recovered, and got back on but the hole in the oil sump lost all the oil and the car quit almost within sight of the finish line.

THE AMERICAN ADVENTURE

In June 1958, 0666 TR was sold to Luigi Chinetti Motors of New York, to be run by his team, called the North American Racing Team (NART). In those days American sports car teams ran their cars in the "American color" scheme, white with blue stripes. Chinetti had two good drivers, up-comer Dan Gurney and Bruce Kessler, a moneyed driver out of Beverly Hills.

The car went back to Le Mans but there was a big storm that washed out a lot of cars. Kessler was a victim of the bad visibility and late in the evening of the first day, hit a privately entered D-Type Jaguar, and the Ferrari burst into flame. The rain put the fire out, Kessler survived, but the car had to be rebuilt with an all-new body.

In the '59 season Ferrari had three new Testa Rossas, called TR59s, and signed American Dan Gurney as a driver. Chinetti, feeling his own TR wouldn't be competitive without Gurney, sold the car for $12,500, a princely sum in those days, enough to buy a 3-bedroom house in the 'burbs.

The man with the money to buy it was Rod Carveth, a privateer from San Carlos, California. His experience included racing an Aston Martin DBS. He wanted to be in a really serious racer and this car was his way in. After buying it, he entered 0666 in the 8th Annual 12 Hours of Sebring on the 21st of March, though it was listed as an official NART entry with Carveth and Gil Geitner sharing the driving. It was raining hard, and while running in the top ten the car ran out of gas and rolled to a dead stop past the pits. Carveth gamely pushed the car four miles around the track to the pits. But once under way again, only an hour later he hit a barrel that damaged the headlights and could no longer run in the dark.

Next the car was taken to the Nurburgring in Germany for the 1000 km. While running in the last lap and holding eighth, Geitner spun at the Karussel, spun the car into a ditch, and was unable to extract the car from the ditch in time to get back into the race.

In June of that year, 0666 was back at Le Mans for the second year but all the TRs had trouble that year, and the engine failed in the middle of the night while running at top speed down the Mulsanne straight. The car was almost lost to America when it was in Australia but came back to Carveth's shop to compete in regional SCCA events such as the Laguna Seca Examiner Grand Prix.

Now you would think a Ferrari that could handle Le Mans could handle some little Northern California track, but even with the skills of Phil Hill, the Le Mans gearing was all wrong for the twisty and hilly NorCal course so the car didn't even qualify.

Carveth got the message and changed the gears for an April 1960 race at Cotati Raceway near San Francisco, where Chuck Howard managed to finish 3rd overall with a win in the 1,500-plus Modified category. From there, it ran at a Port of Stockton SCCA Regional event, Carveth finishing 5th in the B–E Modified race. The final race of that season was at Laguna Seca, and 0666 TR finished 10th overall. About that time it got a styling addition—a new hood with a clear plexiglass bubble over the row of carburetors.

In 1961, Carveth and Charlie Parsons entered the 3-Hour Enduro at Cotati, winning over 44 other cars. Then racer Lew Florence took it to a sixth overall at Vacaville on August 20th. After a second outing at Cotati in November, the car was retired for the season.

It came back for the 1962 season at a small race at Stockton where Carveth ran his last race in the car, finishing 11th. The car was still competitive, but the problem was now that mid-engined cars had taken over, and front engine cars were obsolete. Carveth saw the writing on the wall and put a "For Sale" sign on the car's window. The next buyer was a man named Bev Spencer.

A wealthy California entrepreneur, Bev Spencer was brought up in the car business and ran Spencer Buick, a firm founded by his family in San Francisco. He had started racing a 300SL gull-wing and then moved through a variety of Ferrari street cars, such as a: 166 MM, a 212, a 340 America, a 410 Superamerica, and a California Spider to name a few. He was a good friend of Phil Hill who asked him why he didn't buy a racecar, hence his purchase of 0666.

In May 1962, Spencer drove the short distance to the shop of Carveth and bought the TR. While it was bought to race, it became a wild street machine. He eventually sold it to buy an even more legendary car, a 250GTO. Steve Earle, who founded the Monterey Historic races, put the TR up for sale. The last known race for 0666 was in May 1964 at an SCCA event at Santa Barbara.

After that race the original engine needed a rebuild. The engine was taken out and traded to racer Pete Lovely with a package of Lotus racing spares, leaving the Testa Rossa engineless in a garage.

COBRA DREAMS

Now back in those days, when Ferraris were no longer competitive, there was a habit in America of stuffing in a V8. In this case the owner took it to a mechanic in Covina, California, who had some humongous V8s and a good ol' 427 7-liter FE-series side-oiler was installed. As awful as this sounds, it was a good installation, though surely the lump of cast iron engine weighed twice as much as the Ferrari aluminum block aluminum heads V-12.

The man who had bought it apparently didn't enjoy it as a Cobrarri or whatever you want to call it and thought it might be worth more as an insurance casualty than it was and tossed a match into the interior. He collected the insurance money but the car wasn't burned that bad as photos taken at the time still show the body intact and only the seats, dash and doors burned.

On September 27, 1970, two college professors from Chapman College in Orange, California, bought the car. The professors had opened a sideline business, a dealership to sell exotic cars because, as Betz explained, "we had so many we didn't know what to do with them." So Charles Betz and Fred Peters purchased the Testa Rossa, which had gone to mechanic Pete Civati of Los Angeles. It took them a full decade to restore the car.

By the late 1980s, the restoration was complete and 0666 TR began earning concours trophies like it had once collected racing trophies. In 2002, after three decades with the Testa Rossa, the duo sold the car to a new owner who ran it several seasons as a vintage racer and then commissioned Dennison International to complete a restoration that would bring 0666 TR back to its original team car appearance and specification.

Eventually the car got the original, matching-numbers engine and a correct rear differential getting as close as you can get to being 100% original. It won a prestigious First in Class at Pebble Beach, a deserving honor for this legendary car. When the car was sold by that owner at an auction at Pebble Beach, the sale was accompanied by a collection of racing components that includes four wheels and tires, a differential, ring and pinion, drive gears and a racing fuel cell, as well as a complete, spare race engine that was reported to produce over 300 horsepower.

The buyer at Pebble also got a large stack of archival material, including pictures shot at every major race, and the books that featured the car. Plus there was a letter included, signed with Enzo Ferrari's famous purple ink signature (the *Commendatore* didn't want anybody forging his signature so he had his own special ink made).

Lesson to be learned here? Burnt-out racecars, as sad and

sorry as they look, can be a good investment. These professors had done their homework and knew the car's significance. They weren't bothered by the fact the car had been crashed. Or burned. Or re-bodied. Or that the original engine was gone. They knew they could put in another correct-type engine for that model. Eventually they sold it and another owner, at huge investment, reunited it with its correct engine and went further than the Professors would have gone.

Chapter 45
Down to the Frame (Ferrari PF Cabriolet)

By far the scariest word in any car collector's lexicon is: "fire."

Those new to Ferraris, who have come so far as to be able to recognize a Ferrari California Spyder (the original, not the one they make now) might not be aware that the California Spyder was preceded by a model that looked similar called the PF Cabriolet, "PF" for Pinin Farina the coachbuilder and designer. They were built in two series.

The first series were hand-built in a special workshop at Pinin Farina facilities (back then the firm's name was two names, Pinin and then Farina, later combined). By 1959, Pininfarina had changed the car's name and had standardized the Cabriolet in what came to be known as the Series II. Although selling in smaller numbers than coupes, Ferrari tried to keep a cabriolet model on the order list at all times.

Before 1959, these tended to be custom made. By 1957, the successful 250GT 'Tour de France' berlinetta coupe had been introduced and that car made a good platform for a convertible because of its strong separate tubular frame chassis. It also boasted large finned drum brakes, a double wishbone front suspension, and the reliable Colombo-designed 60-degree V12 engine.

Pininfarina, by then Ferrari's most frequently chosen coachbuilder, was commissioned to make the first design, and started with chassis 0655GT. That car made its debut at the 1957 Geneva Auto Show, and was the car that set the pattern for forty more of the same basic design.

Even though they were series-produced, the delight of this model is that they still have those little custom touches that make Fifties Ferraris more interesting to the style-minded fan compared to modern Ferraris— variations in side vents, bumpers, interior dashboard and luggage stowage, outside mirrors, etc. This example is number 34 of the series, and was the show car for the 1958 London Auto Show at Earl's Court.

For just over a decade—stretching from 1953 to 1964—Ferrari produced the 250 series and they would become the company's mainstay. All the 250s shared the same basic Colombo Tipo 125 V-12 which featured an aluminum block, aluminum heads, and was streets ahead of the Jag straight six in weight, power output and number of cylinders. Larger V-12s eventually replaced it, the 275 and the 330.

One example of how much hand work went into the PF Spyders is shown by a price comparison. Back in 1958, a 250 GT PF Spyder cost $14,950 new, and by comparison a 1958 250GT California Spyder, of which more were produced, cost less, at $11,600.

This particular 1958 Ferrari Cabriolet (serial number 1075 GT) with coachwork by Pinin Farina made its show debut painted gold. It came with a factory-installed luggage rack on the truck lid.

The first owner was a private owner in France in 1959, but it then migrated to the U.S., where the first time it popped up in a "For Sale" ad was in '65 with a Californian selling the car. Ironically, at some point back then it was displayed at the Pebble Beach Concours where it was awarded a second in class in "European sports cars over $7,000" (today it would have to be in a category of "cars over $700,000"). Then it went to a San Francisco dealer who sold it for $6,000 to a couple in the city and it was off the grid for 18 years.

Flash forward a couple of decades to 1984 when Said Marouf of LaJolla, a seaside city North of San Diego, bought it and had it repainted red. Marouf is a world-class connoisseur and bought a car perfectly fitting the ambiance of La Jolla, where some roads run along the sea and the air and scenery are most generally perfect. The town could double for Monaco in some respects. But Marouf was a racer through and through, and eventually traded it to Dick and Marian Teague for a car with more brio, one that could be raced, a Ferrari 250GT short wheelbase berlinetta.

THE FIRE

Now those familiar with car designer names might recognize the name of Dick Teague, a Packard designer before the war who eventually became design chief of American Motors (and designed another car in this book, the AMX/3). Teague retired in '83 and moved back to his native California where he planned to enjoy the ideal country life in a town called Fallbrook, known for its avocado farms and vineyards.

But as nice as it is to live out among nature, there is one problem with country living—wildfires. In 1998, some local firemen touched off a controlled burn of a barn, and left the scene thinking they had extinguished the fire. They didn't. The result? About 5,000 acres charred, plus 49 homes and 49 outbuildings burned to the ground. It took only minutes for the Teague home to burn, including all the mementoes from his many decades of being a car designer. Plus, in the garage, the PF Spyder.

A month later the famed Ferrari hunter Tom Shaughnessy bought the remains of the car. The whole top half was burned, including the glass all around, the wiring, the cloth top, the interior, the tires and even the wheels, but Shaughnessy had been collecting parts for years before this, and had many of the parts so he was not intimidated. There was a nearby coachbuilder in Orange County who could replace the bodywork. They began, even having to make a new instrument panel. Four years later, the car wasn't done yet. A new buyer hove into view, Mr. & Mrs. Peter McCoy, Peter a construction executive who also was in the fine arts. He appreciated the uniqueness of the PF cabrio and bought the car.

He sent it off to Motion Products, a tiny body shop in

Neenah, Wisconsin, known world-wide for its work on Ferraris. To read accounts of the restoration, even Motion Products was at first daunted by the scope of the project—they had hardly ever received a car so burnt-out, one so far gone. Fortunately, the engine had already been rebuilt and was running by 2006 on an engine stand at a show in Monterey so that moved the project forward. Finally, a former Ford PR man, John Clinard, and his wife Linda volunteered to make their virtually identical PF cabrio available to serve as a guide for the bodywork. The modern method of scanning was used, administered by Frank Kaiser of 3D Imaging, who only needed one day to do it. Once that was done, a plywood buck was made and shipped to Motion Products, who had already saved almost 75% of the original bodywork.

The result of this second 20-month restoration was a prize-winning car, winning a First in Class at Pebble Beach, the very same event it had won a prize in decades earlier. Then in 2009 it won Outstanding Ferrari at the Amelia Island concours and many more awards since.

Lesson learned? Burnt-out cars are scary to look at but damage may not be as bad as you think, especially if they have a stout steel-tube frame. And in a vintage Ferrari, the chassis, a valid i.d. plate on the cowl and the title are all you need to start in your rebuild. In this case, the rebuilding was speeded along by the first buyer after the fire having lots of parts; and the second buyer having a twin of the car available to capture the body lines in 3D for the modern way of building a classic body.

So everything came together to make this car whole again—a buyer funded and dedicated to bring it back and a reference source that was only a few serial numbers away. So in short, burned out is not always "destroyed." Some cars are worth bringing back!

Chapter 46
Dirt is Good (Lancia Aurelia Spyder)

Of course classic car collectors call it "patina."

This is a story of a very *schumtzig* car. When the Gooding auction-house had their Scottsdale auction in 2013, they featured lots of shiny cars and one very dirty one. The be-grimed car was an old Lancia B24 Spyder America. It turned out to be one of the event's top sellers.

First a little history on the car… Lancia produced their first car, with a unit body, in 1922. They were among the first to use narrow-angle V engines. In rallying, they ruled the roost in the Sixties and early '70s. It was an "in" car and American Formula One champion Phil Hill used to say that when he went to Europe to race he discovered the other GP drivers had Lancia Aurelias for their personal cars. The Aurelia started in 1950 and went through six series until '58. The chief engineer was engineer Vittorio Jano who had designed V-6 engines for Ferrari.

Although the coupes were good looking, the sexiest Aurelias were the soft-top roadsters. This car at Scottsdale was introduced in January 1955, and formally called the "B24S Spider America," as the United States was the target market.

Styled and built by Pinin Farina, the B24S's V-6 had a displacement of 2.5 liters and cranked out 110 horsepower. The 4-speed manual transmission was mounted in back for more ideal weight distribution, as a transaxle, with the rear drum brakes mounted in-board next to it. The rear suspension was De Dion with leaf springs.

The B24S Gooding featured had the advantage of being "Holy Grail" status by virtue of being a one-owner car. It was owned by John Jang who had been so bowled over by it in 1956 that he traded his Porsche Cabriolet for the Lancia, which cost a heady $5,600 at the time. He drove the Lancia for seven years in Northern California, racked up 28,000 miles and parked it in the garage.

Flash forward almost 50 years…

It's December 2012, and the Jangs had an idea. They weren't using the car, so why not sell it? They went out to the garage, and looked it over. The operative question was: who should they call—the junkman or an auction house? They found out that miraculously, the engine still turned freely, the electrical system worked and all the bits and pieces, like the original tools, the jack and the removable Plexiglas side windows, were still there. Plus the tools and manuals. And hey, it was a one-owner car.

They contacted an auction company, not just any company but one particularly experienced in classic sports cars—the company founded by David Gooding. Gooding bought the car, telling the Jangs it would be in their 2013 Scottsdale auction. The auction company estimated the car's value at $400,000 to $450,000. Why so much? For some reason the Spyders, with their wraparound windshield and removable side windows, are more prized than later versions with a conventional windscreen and roll-up windows. You might consider them stylistically to be baby Ferrari California Spyders. They look that good. And just 240 Lancia Aurelia Spyders were built which scores high on the rarity scoreboard.

Gooding did something unusal then. Instead of attempting to refurbish the car, he left it dust caked, with its original patina, as if to say, "this is precisely how we found it in the barn." It sold

Gooding was wrong when they projected the value though. When the auctioneer slammed down the gavel, the car fetched $803,000. Ironically, on the same weekend, across town at the RM Auction at the Frank Lloyd Wright-inspired Biltmore hotel, they had a jet black pristine 1955 Lancia Aurelia B24S America Spyder that they sold fro $825,000—a world record for that kind of a car sold at auction. OK, so they sold it for a little more, but hey, the way I look at it Gooding was ahead— they didn't even have to wax their car!

Chapter 47
Phony and Flashy (1939 Delahaye Type 165 Roadster)

Who woulda thought that nickname is attached to what has been called "the most beautiful prewar car?"

You hear about cars found in barns. You hear about cars found out in fields. How about a one-off car, a French classic built by the most baroque of French coachbuilders, found seemingly abandoned in a single car garage behind a so-so farm house in Fresno, California? It happened.

Fresno is a dirt-poor farming area where even a '55 Chevy pillarless two-door coupe would be considered exotic. But that's exactly the town where, back in 1982, a Los Angeles-based enthusiast of French cars found a 1939 Delahaye, one of the five great French luxury marques before the war, the others being Delage, Talbot Lago, Hispano Suiza, and Bugatti.

First a little background on the maker: Emile Delahaye started producing his first automobiles in 1894 in Tours, France. His first automobiles were single- or twin-cylinder, belt-driven power units. Emile Delahaye departed his company in 1900, just one year before a factory was constructed in Paris. It is unknown why the founder left his company. Four-cylinder engine production under new owners began in 1908 in sizes of 1,460cc and 2,120cc.

Later they went to a 2,565cc V6. Delahaye production was boosted by manufacture under license in America and Germany. By the end of WWI they had switched to mostly doing trucks. In 1934 they went back to doing cars, with two new models, the 12cv and the 18cv. The 12cv was powered by a 2,150cc four while the

18cv was powered by a 3,200cc six. The engines were derived from the truck powerplants. It was in the following year that Delahaye introduced its most famous cars, the Coupe des Alpes and the 135.

The firm's rise to glory in the luxury car world began when they decided to emulate companies like Mercedes and get into racing. Back then, much as now, the thought was if you were going to build luxury cars, you needed to have some racing success to demonstrate your durability. Even with Mercedes and Auto Union dominating the sport, Delahaye managed some success, such as winning the 1938 24 Hours of Le Mans, and that success brought more customers.

What really put Delahayes on the map of luxury car buyers though, was the flamboyant coachwork. You ordered the cars by chassis and then picked a coachbuilder to make the car to your whim, and the most artful coachbuilders were Figoni et Falaschi, Chapron and Letourneur et Marchand.

Despite creating these very special cars Delahaye continued to build trucks. This particular car, chassis number 60744, has coachwork by Figoni & Falaschi (who traders in antique motorcars call "phony and flashy" because of their nearly excessive use of chrome). The two unique parts of the design are a roll-down windscreen and completely covered (with what are called "fairings") front wheels and tires.

It is called the Type 165 and this model came with a V-12 engine, a detuned version of their racing engine used in the Type 145 racecar. This particular car was built to represent France at the 1939 New York World's Fair, an exposition that was promoted with the slogan "Dawn of a New Day." But Delahaye could not get the 12-cylinder engine finished in time, so an empty 12-cylinder magnesium type 145 racing crankcase was thrown into the car for its world debut, including its twin spark plug heads and engine-turned cam covers. The plan was that they'd put the running engine they had in Paris into it when it comes back after the fair.

Well, wouldn't you know, something happened—World War II.

The car remained in the USA after the show closed in 1940.

U.S. Customs impounded it for the duration of the war. In fact the car was stranded at customs for the next six years! So it was a real conundrum—here you had arguably the world's most beautiful car, but it had no operating engine.

But fortunately, one man with vision had seen the car. He was Roger Barlow, who had seen the car at the World's Fair and tracked down its whereabouts, buying it for the then-princely sum of $3,000 from the French Consulate in New York. He then transported the car to the West Coast. He was planning to start a car sales operation and figured this car would draw the movie stars he hoped to sell cars to. He had more ambitions than selling cars. During the war he had made films for the Army, and the car operation was intended to be only a stepping stone because what he really wanted to do (like everyone else in Hollywood) was be a director! Step one was to sell flashy cars, so he purchased it at public auction and took it to his Beverly Hills dealership.

Later that year, he made it operational by installing a special high-powered Cadillac V8 engine originally intended for a tank, and sold it for $12,000 to businessman Vivan Corradini. Some say the car then went back to New York but the '80s discoverer of the car thinks its next port of call was Hawaii where in 1951 a Naval Lt. named Nevels purchased the car from a used car lot in Honolulu. In 1953 Nevels, needing a more proper and reliable family car, sold it to an enlisted man in Hawaii.

The enlisted man brought it to California because the next owner of record was a Fresno, California, tow truck operator who had assumed ownership after it was abandoned by the enlisted man's widow at a shop where it had either been left for restoration, or just to get it running. At the point the tow truck driver glommed onto it, it was minus its engine and transmission.

Al Brewer, a Fresno-based heavy-duty tow truck driver, purchased it from the garage for $1,200 in truly derelict form. Today that amount wouldn't even cover the cost of one wheel of the car!

Fast forward to the 1970s. Jim Hull, a furniture designer, is racing his Bugatti at the Monterey Historic Races. His green

Delahaye, which he planned to show at Pebble Beach the next day, is sticking out of his truck. A spectator sees the Delahaye and starts a conversation with Jim's wife, saying in effect that he knew of a Delahaye in his home town of Fresno, California. Jim's wife signaled Jim to come over and the man repeated his claim. Jim asked a key question: "Did it have enclosed front fenders with skirts?"

When the man replied in the affirmative, Jim got excited. There were only a few Delahayes that had that feature—particularly those bodied by Figoni et Falaschi, the most flamboyant of all the French coachbuilders. Jim got the man's phone number and, before leaving Monterey, called. No answer. He called several more times during the weekend but the guy wasn't picking up the phone. Jim began to fret the man was realizing the car might be worth something and had decided not to reveal its location; but Jim didn't give up. He called many more times and finally the man answered and wouldn't say he remembered exactly where it was but he ended the conversation by giving him two clues: "It's near the airport and there's a big yellow tow truck parked outside."

So on the way home from Pebble Beach, Jim stopped in Fresno, drove to the airport and began doing a circular search pattern. It took all morning. He finally spotted the yellow truck and found it hard to believe the little frame house behind it could be sporting a luxury car like a Delahaye. But there it was, the car sticking out of the garage—it being a couple feet longer than the garage.

It took quite a long time for the man of the house to answer Jim's knocking but finally he answered. Jim was not invited inside the house but figured, hey, maybe the guy is embarrassed he's not set up for visitors, so the home owner came out and Jim got the idea of taking him over to his truck to show him his own Delahaye. That opened up a discussion of Figoni et Falaschi. The day ended with the man saying that he appreciated Jim's visit but the fact was that he really was not interested in selling the car. Case closed? Not quite.

Jim kept on the case, periodically keeping in touch with the tow truck operator. Finally, four years later, in 1985, Jim got the call he was waiting for—the man said he could come up and see the car again and to bring his car hauler. They agreed on a price of $30,000—a high price at the time for a car with no engine, no transmission and no information on how to find these items considering Delahaye was out of business. This was the price of three brand new Detroit-made cars at the time.

Once Jim got the car out of the garage he saw how much work it was going to take. Jim had, since first seeing the car, taken on a partner, Peter Mullin, with the goal of restoring several French cars. By coincidence, Jim had also located a Delahaye engine—a 4.5-liter triple cam, aluminum block V-12, one of approximately two to four such engines ever built.

This had surfaced in the collection of Jim's friend, Count Hubertus von Doenhoff of Germany, who also owned a V-12 Delahaye, a coupe. Upon checking the numbers, Jim found that this engine was the exact one originally planned for the New York Worlds Fair Delahaye back in '39 so purchase of that engine allowed the car to be united with its engine.

Flash forward another ten years, and a small fortune is spent on restoring the car. Changing marital circumstances caused Jim Hull, who still owns the original green Delahaye that started his passion for the marque, to sell out his interest in the 165, but not before he had at least seen it restored and exhibited at Pebble Beach, where it won a First in Class award. After WWII, Delahaye tried to recapture their former glory but sales were a trickle and the last cars bearing their proud name were seen in 1951.

Lessons learned? Next time you hear about a classic-looking car in some low-rent neighborhood, don't be snobby and turn up your nose. Check it out despite the incongruity of the description of the car vs. its location. It might be worth it.... Oh, and Jim figures the car is now worth upwards of $20 million dollars.

Chapter 48
"TIGER, Tiger, Burning Bright"
(Lister Tiger)

Wherein Shelby pulls a fast one.

Think of the Sunbeam Lister coupes as Roote's Cobra Daytona coupes.

Take a car that was touched by Carroll Shelby, the famed creator of the Cobra, and even if it is not a Cobra, it is worth more by being able to be linked to Der Snakemeister.

Such is the Sunbeam Tiger.

Actually, in the early '50s Rootes made prosaic family cars but around '53 they introduced the Alpine, a two-seater with the first hint at sportiness. Even Stirling Moss raced one!

In '69 they put the same name, Alpine, on a newer two-seater with a unitized steel frame. The engine was a four rated at 78 bhp. It was successful as a racecar and reached early potential with Harrington modified coupe versions in the 24 Hours of Le Mans.

Then Sunbeam's West Coast USA distributor, Ian Garrad, decided that, with Shelby's factory just down the road, why not go over there and see if they could have him work the same magic on the Sunbeam as he had on the A.C. Ace? So, for a reported $10,000 Shelby made a quick conversion, stuffing a 260-cubic-inch Ford V8 into an Alpine. Ken Miles, then still an outside vendor not yet with Shelby, also did a prototype, for peanuts. Both inspired the factory's production version, the Tiger.

It was ready in time for the 1964 New York Motor Show where it was displayed along with Ford's own Mustang.

The Tiger used the same advanced monocoque chassis as employed by the Alpine. Thanks to the Ford V8's relatively small size and low weight, it could be installed fairly easily. It was mated to a sturdy Borg Warner four-speed gearbox. Suspension was by double wishbones at the front and a live rear axle. Disc brakes were only fitted to the front wheels, with drums bolted to the rear. Visually the V8-powered Tiger was difficult to distinguish from its four-cylinder counterpart. Slightly wider wheels, twin exhausts and the 'Tiger' badge on the side tipped off the car's identity.

To promote the car, Sunbeam decided to make two coupes for Le Mans. They sent two roadsters to an outside contractor, Brian Lister, famous for his own racecars, to be converted. Aluminum coupe bodies were created by Williams and Pritchard. Shelby shipped them two supposedly race-prepared 260 engines. Why not 289's as the later Tigers got? Shelby convinced them that the 260s would be able to do the job. But, in the race itself, both entries retired early with engine problems, leading some to suspect that Shelby didn't want the Tiger coupes to beat his Cobras. Evidentially Rootes were a bit naïve, having never heard that racer's rule: "Never sell the competition something that will beat your own cars." It wasn't that the 289 was not available, as A.C. had used them in two Cobras that raced at Le Mans in '63.

Graham Vickery, of the Sunbeam Tiger Owners Club in the UK (www.sunbeamtiger.co.uk) feels that it was a combination of his Lordship wanting to use the same engine in the racecar as in the street car and inexperience with a V8 that was responsible for the double disaster. Vickery wrote your author: "Lord Rootes had personally ordered 260 engines from Iacocca on price or maybe Ford wouldn't sell him the 289. So he wanted the LM cars to have a motor the same as the production model. It is thought that what did it for the motors at Le Mans was the lack of oil baffles in the sump since the drivers noted oil pressure falling on corners. It is hard to believe that Shelby's shop didn't know they were not supplying the sumps that were needed.

We now understand that there was no one or hardly anyone in the Rootes Competition Department at that time who had any experience of V8's. The engine mechanics were old boys who'd only ever worked with 4-cylinder motors. No one knew anything about competition V8's! Still they got replacement motors from Shelby, so he must have accepted responsibility!"

Your author, a biographer of Shelby, imagines Shelby no doubt shed a crocodile tear or two when he heard the Tigers went out of the race…

The 'standard' Tiger roadster proved to be popular in U.S. SCCA racing, because engine parts were available at every auto parts store.

In 1967 a 'Series 2' Tiger was introduced, which used the 289-cubic-inch version of Ford's V8. Unfortunately production was halted shortly after because Sunbeam's parent firm was bought by Chrysler, who just hated having to sell a Ford-powered car and even warranty it! But over 7,000 Sunbeam Tigers were made, seven times more than Shelby made Cobras, including 536 Series 2s with the hotter 289 engine.

A LE MANS RACING CAR FOR $1,500

There was a rather long window of opportunity to get one of the two Sunbeam-Lister Tiger Le Mans cars for a dirt cheap price, and that was right up to the early '70s, when historians were still sorting out the significance of everything Carroll Shelby touched.

The Sunbeam Lister fastbacks went unrecognized for their provenance as the vintage car historians waxed eloquently on the FIA Cobra, the USRRC Cobras, the Ford GT40 MK. I, II, & IV, the King Cobras and God knows what all.

Their general theme: If Carroll Shelby so much as touched it, it was gold. The poor Tiger factory racecars were left out in the cold. Chassis: B9499998 (registered for the road as License Number: ADU 180B) Sunbeam Lister Le Mans #9 is a case in point. This machine stayed a bit longer at the factory but in 1965 was raced by a Sunbeam (Rootes Group Motors) staffer by the name of Bernard Unett who prepared and raced the car to a second slot in the British Autosport Championship of '65. Unett was known to Team Fraser Race boss Alan Fraser and they came together for the '66 season but the rules changed that year disallowing GT's (coupes). So the main race components of the #9 car went into a production car (the 'Monster,' itself a successful racer) and the racecar was put into storage and forgotten.

In 1971 the #9 car was 'found' by Ted Walker (who runs a business selling old race photographs called Ferret Photographs) in a barn at Henley on Thames in England. Ted passed the news to John May who paid a few hundred pounds for his 'barn find' and later, once acquired by Jaguar man Ken Dalziel in 1974, was re-constructed and put back as a racer for John May to race at Silverstone in 1978. It left for the U.S. in 1979 (where it met up with the 'Monster' Tiger and was restored with many of the components that had been removed in 1965). Come 1982 it moved to the East Coast of the U.S. into Syd Silverman's 'Lister' collection. There it stayed not competitively used much for 20 years before making the return journey via a West Coast auction in 2001 into the hands of Darrell Mountjoy.

Following a top-class restoration by the LA restorer Steve Alcala, himself a Tiger owner, Mountjoy received an invitation from Lord March of Goodwood to enter #9 in the 2002 Goodwood Revival 'TT,' the 'blue ribbon' historics race event in the UK. During that summer of 2002 the 1971 barn find was raced at the Le Mans Classic by one of its 1964 drivers – Peter Procter—who had come out of retirement to do so and who received the 'Spirit of Goodwood' award from his Lordship in front of thousands of spectators for his drive in the TT (Tourist Trophy).

Darryl Mountjoy finished it out so that it now represents the breed as raced at Le Mans in 1964. It was raced in the 2011 Monterey Motorsports Reunion where it proved it could take a 260 Cobra though not a 289 Cobra roadster or the Brock-designed 289-powered Daytona Cobra coupe.

Lesson learned? Some racecars are more obscure than others. This one had Shelby connections. If you heard of it back then, and digged deep enough into Tiger history, you could have bought a car with the good-as-gold provenance of a 24 Heures du Mans on its racing pedigree, all for a mere $1,500!

Second lesson learned? Who better to be able to recognize an obscure racecar than a man that sells racing pictures? My advice, find these vendors selling racing art and let them know they will receive a handsome reward if they call you first next time they see something in the tin that they recognize from their old photographs.

Chapter 49
The Breadvan (Ferrari 250GT SWB)

In its time, nothing on American roads could catch it.

Imagine if you will that you are with Ferrari. You are their chief engineer. You go to a race, and in the pits you see a car wearing the Ferrari badge that you have never seen before. Worse yet, it's faster than the factory cars, the boss is waiting in Modena for a phone update, and you have to tell him the bad news. Or let's say you are a cop, in say, Nebraska, sometime in the late '60s. You've got a Dodge police car, a 440 that tops out at 140 mph. You see a car go past, some sort of low-slung foreign thing. You give chase, topping out at 140 mph, absolutely pegging the speedo; and what does the guy in the goddamn piece of foreign crap do? He puts it into fourth and rockets away into the horizon. There's nothing on an American road that can catch it.

So are some of what makes up the legend of the 1962 Ferrari 250GT SN2819, a.k.a. the "Breadvan."

First, the back story: Gary Wales, a stockbroker at the time, was one of maybe three guys (okay, maybe four) in Detroit at that point in time (the mid '60s) who knew what a Ferrari was. He and some friends found dealers overseas who regularly sent them "last year's cars," essentially the Ferraris that were hot a couple years ago, but now were oh-so-passe.

So, one time their scout overseas calls and says he's got a line on this car called "The Breadvan." Gary scratches his head. He vaguely remembers a private entry car run by Count Giovanni Volpi's Scuderia Serenissima out of Venice that was odd looking but reportedly faster than stink. "It's on a short wheelbase 250GT chassis," the contact says, trying to persuade him. Okay, short wheelbase berlinettas are great cars, and it's $3,000 (a lot of money then, say in Detroit you could buy a house in the suburbs for $30,000).

The car got its nickname from English reporters because, from the back, it looks no more distinguished than the little van the breadman delivers loaves of bread in. The French would call it "camionette."

It has a very interesting history. You might say it's a car that was built entirely for revenge, i.e, to stick it to The Old Man (Ferrari's nickname).

It originally left the Ferrari factory in Maranello in 1961 as a 250 GT Berlinetta *passo corto* (short wheelbase) "Competizione," participating the same year as a Ferrari factory race-car in the Tour de France with Gendebien and Bianchi sharing driving tasks, before it was bought by Count Volpi di Misurata, a Venetian count. Volpi painted on his shield and race team name (Scuderia SSS) and fielded it in the 1,000 km of Paris with Trintignant and Vaccarella co-driving.

At the time Volpi and The Old Man of Modena (Enzo Ferrari) were *simpatico*, but then came the so-called "palace revolt" at Ferrari where five of the top engineers left the firm all at once, one story being they were tired of Signora Ferrari meddling in the racing team's business. When the engineers left, they scraped together money to start a new car company, called ATS, with the aim of competing with Ferrari with a factory F1 team and GT cars. One of the investors was Count Volpi, another was a Bolivian tin magnate.

Now, as soon as Enzo Ferrari heard about that, he erupted like Mt. Etna. He told Volpi, who at that moment had two Ferrari 250GTO coupes on order, that it would be a cold day in hell before he ever saw those cars. Volpi, in retaliation, then called one of the ex-Ferrari engineers, Giotto Bizzarrini, and said he wanted him to make a faster car than a GTO. Now Giotto Bizzarrini wasn't just any engineer but the guy who had *designed* the 250GTO (engineered and designed it, without a stylist being needed). The Count sent Bizzarrini a short wheelbase 250GT and told him to stop at nothing in his quest to make it a GTO beater—whatever it took, within reason of course…

So Bizzarrini worked on the mechanical bits and the famous body shop of Neri & Boneschi worked on the bodywork. There was never a drawing per se, it was just Bizzarrini telling them "make the roof flat," and "make the tail end chopped off" and the nose "smaller in cross section than the 250GTO." If Bizzarrini had stayed at Ferrari this would have been his proposal for the third stage of GTO (the second body style of GTO, the '64, was designed by Pininfarina). Bizzarrini added most of the features of the GTO that made it successful including moving the engine back and dry sump lubrication, but alas, he was unable to get a 5-speed transmission, settling instead for a 4-speed. (You can bet Enzo was making sure he couldn't order a 5-speed as long as there was a chance it would get into a car that would shame the factory GTOs.)

In some ways, Count Volpi got a car that was better engineered than a GTO. At the 1962 Le Mans, the Breadvan, with much smaller proportions, weighed in at 143 pounds lighter than the standard GTO. Despite the lack of five-speed gearbox, the reduced weight helped the Breadvan stay ahead of the GTOs at Le Mans, until it retired four hours into the race. The drivers were Abate and Davis.

What led to the DNF was an unbalanced driveshaft. Bizzarrini had moved the engine back from where it was in the 250GTO, and that required a new driveshaft and hence the problem. The Breadvan only raced four more times after Le Mans, and managed a class win at Brands Hatch in 1962. It also ran with Scarfiotti at the Paris 1,000 km. In 1965 it ran its last "original period" race, The Coppa Gallenga in Rome. In later years, it was used as daily driver from that period and added to the legend.

The Count did quite a bit of entertaining on the French Riviera, and among the playboys he ran with was Giovanni Agnelli, a Fiat heir and the epitome of the word "playboy." One night Agnelli had no car to go home so he was loaned The Breadvan. Once he had it at his house, someone remarked, "it looks like a funeral hearse," so he told his butler to go out there and paint it black. The butler did the back, roof and sides in black but ran out of paint so the front just had black stripes. Volpi didn't laugh.

Volpi liked driving the car. The weight was so evenly balanced fore/aft that you could, he said, "paint with it," i.e. do any maneuver; but eventually, his interest in his own Serenissima brand (which came out of the ashes of the failed ATS firm) took his attention so he sold the Breadvan. Volpi sold The Breadvan for $2,500 and a Dodge Polara station wagon. His thought at the time was, "I can always buy it back for less later on" because that was before vintage racing with postwar cars became what it is today, a multi-billion dollar sport. You ran an old racecar into the ground and junked it.

ITS AMERICAN PERIOD

Now, we return to our hero, Gary Wales, in Detroit. Wales, a stockbroker, had a little Ferrari business on the side in Detroit, and had already had eleven Ferraris go through his hands. He drove, for instance, the Superfast I to his brokerage job, parking it out on the street, where it would gather crowds. One day their contact in Italy says he's got three Ferraris they can have— a 275GTB, a Tour deFrance Berlinetta, and some oddball old racecar that looked like a station wagon. The price was right so the three partners sent the money and the cars were shipped.

In the book *Rebel Rebel* by Marc Sonnery and Keith Bluemel, a book devoted entirely to the wondrous Breadvan, Wales tells of going to New York with two partners to pick up the Breadvan and two other Ferraris from the dock. The Breadvan had no heater and it was the dead of winter, but Wales drew the short straw and got that car to drive while the other two were in more comfortable GT cars. Wales was driving fast, hoping to get the car home before his buddy in the passenger seat froze to death. They had to stop several times to thaw out his buddy.

At one point, going through New York state on the Tollway at 130 mph, Wales was pulled over by an extremely irritated cop, who had to drive like hell to catch up with him. When he asked why he was driving so fast, Wales pointed to his buddy, who was actually turning blue from the cold, and said, "We're dying here. I've got to get him to a place where it's warm." The cop, though dubious, bought the story but warned him, "Just get that car out of my state." Gary took off for the nearest Howard Johnson's, thawed out his seat-mate a bit, and then stuffed rags into any air intake into the car and they continued….but not without more drama. At one point, the tachometer began buzzing like a low flying Messerschmitt and Gary, frustrated, reached out a ham fist and slammed it. It shut off the tach, and only left Gary a little bloody. (Hey, if you can't beat up your Ferrari, what's it good for?)

Once the three-car convoy got to Detroit they had their own little car show and showed the cars they had brought from Europe. Wales, at that point, had had enough of Detroit-in-winter (think of the German march on Leningrad, only reoccurring yearly). He decided to move to California. He split up his partnership in Ferraris and his prize was the Breadvan. He drove the car to California, hammer down all the way. "It wasn't comfortable," he recalls, "but it was a helluva drive." He passed cars like they were sitting still. It was still the era of no speed limit in many outlying country areas, and gas was a mere 35 cents a gallon; and the car had a 40-gallon-plus gas tank.

Out in California Wales repainted it red, and put racing numbers on the side, with little lights to illuminate the numbers, just like it ran at Le Mans. This of course gave him the opportunity to be the ultimate squelch, because if anybody said, "What, you pretending your car raced at Le Mans?" he could answer back, "As a matter of fact…" But then his house needed a new roof, and hey, gotta keep the home fires burning, so he sold the Breadvan.

Remember, this was before there was the mania of Ferrari collecting, when old racecars were just old cars, and the Monterey Historics hadn't started yet. The first buyer was a mop-topped singer from Detroit who had made it big out on the Left Coast by the name of Sonny Bono (more famous as husband of Cher). He put down a check, but sometime later that day he evidently ran out of gas and abandoned the car. The cops found Wales' contact info in the car and called him, advising him he better come and pick it up as it was blocking traffic, being illegally parked, and he had one shot to retrieve it, or it would go to the car impound lot. It was about then Wales had discovered Bono had written a rubber check! Bono sent some heavies to lean on Wales to stop from taking legal action on the bounced check, but Wales had assembled some heavies on his side including the LA district attorney. The "muscle," when confronted with muscle of infinitely greater means, meekly retired from the field of battle.

Gary sold it again, to a real buyer, Asa Clark, head of the Ferrari Club, who bought it for $4,500. According to Wales' memory, Clark was not a full-time Ferrari guy, but more of a yachtsman. He was, Wales remembers, not really the kind of guy to own the car, not someone who would take the sonovabitch up to the mountain and hang out the tail on turns, or wind it out to 9500 rpm on the straights; go "full chat in top cog" as the Limeys say. That was the way you had to drive the Breadvan to get full use out of it. Like each drive was your last race.

Clark realized it was too much car for him, and sold it to a Ferrari club guy who did in fact drive it like it had been built to be driven, but sometimes came close to putting it off a cliff in the back roads of the mountains around L.A. and in fact stuffed the nose at least once. He offended Wales by taking out the 250GTO-like blue cloth upholstery and putting in leather instead, trying to civilize a car that was made to be a brute.

Your author had a ride in it back in its California days. It reminded me of the 250GTO I had been treated to a ride in when a *Motor Trend* artist, Chuck Queener, borrowed one for a week from Steve Earle back when they were only worth $90,000 and not $45 million. The Breadvan's sound was even better than the GTO because of the whoosh from air being sucked into the Testa Rossa-styled clear bubble air scoop atop the hood enclosing the Webers. That scoop alone, for me, made it "oh-so-exotic."

I remember one night when that Breadvan owner who gave me a ride pulled into a Ferrari Owner's Club gathering at the opening of the L.A. Auto Show. He pulls into the parking lot, does a few doughnuts, and generally upstages every new car that automakers would have in the show. In the book *Rebel Rebel*, by Frenchman Marc Sonnery with Keith Bluemel, that owner was interviewed with many others, telling tales of high velocity late night drives through Southern California that sound terrifying today; but hey, again there was nothing that could touch it (except maybe the odd road-converted GT40 or Lola T-70). He even tells of picking up a girl on Sunset strip with it. The car was so flamboyant it would stop pedestrians dead in their tracks.

That owner sold the car to British car dealer Brian Classic (for 15,000 British pounds, however much that was at the time) who sold it to another Brit, John Harper. The car came back to America in 1985 where Monte Shalett of Oregon bought it on the recommendation of Jess Pourret, a famous Ferrari author in France who said "if not a GTO, it certainly belonged with the GTOs." He was offered the bait that if he bought it, along with the purchase came an invitation to go to a rally featuring 27 real GTOs in France. He bought it. When the rally went to the Ferrari factory as part of the itinerary, Shalett told the authors of *Rebel Rebel* that Ferrari workers poured out of the factory to look at the car. Apparently by that time Ferrari had plum forgotten this car was once thean outlaw built purposely to shame the Ferrari factory team!

The car traded hands until finally it broke the million-dollar barrier. In 2005 it was taken to the Christies auction at the Monterey Jet Center, but was not sold with an estimate of $3,500,000 to $5,000,000. Later, in February 2006, it was purchased by Klaus Werner of Germany.

He had the car completely refurbished, complete with a period-correct nose from Hietbrink Coachbuilding, who used the old-fashioned methods like hammers and sand bags to make the nose match the way the car looked in '62. The interior was once again restored to GTO blue cloth seat covers. He took it to several events, and recalled in the book *Rebel Rebel* how at Mugello in 2008 it was faster than even the 4-liter 250GTOs.

In April of 2010 Ferrari Classiche, an agency Ferrari established to authenticate old Ferraris, issued a "Notice of Attestation" for the Breadvan, which fit in a new class they had established for vehicles that "do not comply with the strict Ferrari Authenticity Certification criteria, (but) have been deemed, as a result of their competition and/or international recognized show history, to be of historic interest." That was an irony of ironies for the car—in effect blessed by Ferrari, because its whole *raison d'etre* when it was built was to be the "anti-Ferrari."

In the book *Rebel Rebel,* Count Volpi is quoted saying something both philosophical and curious: "Really owning those cars is similar to still feeling them and doing with them what cannot be done anymore. In other words, we, I, still own them, even if they're sold. If I bought a stagecoach I would never experience what it was like, because the time had gone and whatever the reenactment wouldn't even get me far from what it was."

I think, no doubt due to translation difficulties, the Count really meant "close to" what it was, but I get his point. Owning The Breadvan in 2013 isn't the same as it was back in the days of no speed limits in lots of U.S. states, when gas was cheap and there was nothing made domestically that could touch it. When the idea of running a full blown tuned-for-Le Mans 180 mph Ferrari on the street was incomprehensible for people who thought a sports car was like a Thunderbird, a boulevardier. Back then, driving a car like the Breadvan on the street was akin to say, flying in to Oshkosh (an old plane event) in an SR-71 Blackbird (and maybe buzzing the field a couple times at Mach 3 before you land).

Lesson learned? Nothing is as cheap as an old racecar when it no longer has a sponsor or a class where it could be competitive. The time to buy is right when its future is in limbo, when it's about to be sold downriver.

Footnote: After he had sold the car, a later owner learned Wales still had the original Italian license plates. Wanting the car to be "original" as per '62, the new owner bought the plates. Wales gave him a "deal" and charged him only $5,000—$2,000 more than he paid for the whole car!

Ain't life grand!

Chapter 50
Rebel With a Cause (1969 L88 Corvette)

*Wherein you're lucky
that you read old car
magazines.*

So you read car
magazines, right? Well, Kevin Mackay of
Valley Stream, New York, has a good story to tell you about the
virtues of reading car magazines.

Back around the early '90s, he was at a swap meet in Pennsylvania when he bought a back issue of *Corvette Corner* magazine that
was several years old, figuring he would read it back at the motel.

He also bought it because of the cover car, an SCCA racer
called "Ol' Rebel." The car had won its class at Sebring and Daytona. Dave Heinz and Bob Johnson were its most famous drivers.

Mackay likes big block Corvettes and maintains many of
them at his shop. He knew that a big block L-88 Corvette with
a racing history was worth getting at almost any price.

Now back to the car: The magazine story said that in 1968
well-known racer Or Costanzo ordered a 1969 yellow L-88
Corvette from Ferman Chevrolet in Tampa, Florida. The car
turned out to be one of four lightweight prototypes, and had
the open chamber heads not available to the public until June
of the model year as well as a dual disc clutch car.

Constanzo and Dave Heinz co-drove the Corvette at the 12
Hours of Sebring three years in a row, accounting for four of
five IMSA wins in '71 and won the first IMSA championship.

How did the car get the "Rebel" paint scheme? As far as Mackay
can figure out, the big dog in Corvette racing back then was John
Greenwood with his "stars and stripes" paint scheme so the natural
enemy of the Union in the south was the Confederacy—hence the

"rebel" flag-color theme for the Florida-based Corvette.

By the way, the car also had the ZL-2 cold air induction hood, a heavy-duty clutch, a smaller flywheel and a heavy-duty cross-flow aluminum radiator plus the K66 transistor ignition with pulse amplifier and a special coil improved ignition control.

All this whetted Mackay's appetite. If it could be found, the car would be truly historic, not just a street Corvette that some wannabe racer had tricked up to look like an old racecar.

Well, long story short, Mackay got hooked on the car so much after reading the story that, despite the coldness of the trail, he found himself dialing "411" to get the phone number of a fellow named in the story, a fellow with the colorful name of Orlando Costanzo who had raced the car from 1969 to 1971.

Amazingly, though the magazine was several years old, he was connected with him immediately. He explained why he was calling, and Costanzo said that, yes indeed, he had ordered and raced the car but that, mid-way through the 1971 season, he had sold the car to Toye and Dana English who put a new team together. They re-named the car "Scrappy" because they were always cutting away at the car to lighten it.

They even got a "secret" sponsor—Goodyear—who wanted them to race on special unmarked tires they were testing. Later on, Goodyear bought a full-page ad in the *Wall Street Journal* touting the team's 1st place in the GT class at the '72 Daytona 24 hour with Dave Heinz and "Marietta" Bob Johnson sharing driving tasks.

The team also did well at the '72 12 Hours of Sebring, taking 1st in GT again and fourth overall. At that race they beat a lot of Ferraris and led the GT class for the entire 12 hours.

Then, as racecars do, it began to slide out of sight, though Mackay diligently tracked it through its next owner, Alex Davidson.

Now Mackay is not your average car hobbyist. His bread and butter is restoring Corvettes. Having gone this far, he couldn't stop looking for the car. He hired a Corvette sleuth, David Reisner, to find the car. It was money well spent. Reisner found that the last owner of record was a South Carolina dentist whose nickname was "Doctor Charlie."

Problem was, nobody could remember his last name. South Carolina probably had a thousand dentists whose first name was Charlie.

Reisner began to check early 1970s state dental association records against SCCA (Sports Car Club of America) driver rosters of the same period. Only one name was on both lists—Dr. Charles West. He called Mackay up with the name and phone number.

Armed with this information, Mackay called Dr. Charles West. The dental assistant asked if he wanted a dental appointment and he said, "no," that he was calling about Corvettes. A second later Dr. Charlie was on the phone.

Good news! Not only was Dr. West still alive and kicking, he still had the Corvette.

Then came a heart-stopping moment—"But it's in the junkyard," the Doctor said.

McKay's heart sank. "Junkyard" brought to mind a vision of a heap of old cars being crushed and melted down, sold by the pound as scrap metal.

Then came some relief—"Now it so happens I own that junkyard," said the Doctor. "And if you're interested in the car I will take you to it."

Well, that was a horse of another color. "Now I'm aiming to go to a wedding this weekend," the Doctor said, "but if you meet me after the wedding, I'll drive you on over."

So McKay hopped on a plane, met the Doctor at the wedding reception and together they set off, the Doc driving his pickup still clad in his tuxedo. It was already dark and the Doc's wife insisted he change to overalls before setting foot in the dirty old junkyard so he acquiesced, but Mackay was already standing by the car. In the light thrown off by the pickup's headlights, he could see the car was there.

"Rough" doesn't begin to describe it. "Rode hard and put away wet" comes closer. It was battered, with cracked fiberglass, missing the distinctive domed hood, missing the engine, missing the transmission—but as soon as he saw the name of one of the previous racecar driver owners on the door, Mackay knew this was the right car. Another clue was the FIA-approved fixed dual headlights in lightweight brackets with their pre-formed plexiglass covers.

"And I got the original order slip from Chevrolet," said the Doc.

"How much do you want for the car?" McKay asked, mentally reviewing what he would have to unload back at home if the price Dr. West named was too high.

"Y'know," said the Doc, "There's this ol' Porsche around here I used to have that I want back. You buy that for me and we'll trade even."

So a trade—not cash—would swing the deal. Duck soup, right? Not quite. Mackay wasn't out of the woods yet. There's Porsches and there's Porsches. Was it a 904? A 4-cam Carrera speedster? Something like that could run over $100,000! Relief came when he found out it was a 911. Nothing special. An old 911. Once contacted, the local owner was willing to sell it for $7,000. So McKay bought the Porsche, did the trade, and towed home his new prize.

Mackay also lucked out in connecting with Walt Thum, a former Rebel car crew member who provided invaluable documentation, photographs and technical assistance. (When you choose to restore an old racecar, it is best to pick the "look" it had in a specific race, so that's where the pictures come in.)

Mackay finished the restoration in 1993. Was he worried it did not have the corresponding block it was built with? "Not really," says McKay, "because this was a racecar. So I figure racecars had their engines changed several times a season, along with rear ends, brakes, etc." He obtained a duplicate L-88 engine, the right gearbox, and the right rear end for big track driving.

The restored car appeared the National Corvette Museum and at the 1994 Bloomington Gold Special Connection. It was even reproduced in miniature by a model car manufacturer.

Eventually Mackay sold the car to Corvette collector Larry Bowman in a package deal including two other Corvettes, the total for all three being over a million dollars. It later went to another owner and periodically comes back to his shop for one thing or another.

Lesson learned? No clue is too old—any clue is a place to start.

And it's a damn good thing Kevin Mackay likes to read old car magazines!

Chapter 51
How To Find Them

IN SUM

If you are inspired enough by these stories to join in the hunt, take the advice of someone who's been (most of the time informally and on spec) in the hunt for over 40 years. Here's some general tips with a few examples from your humble servant's own experience…

SPECIALIZE IN ONE MARQUE.

This has one advantage. If you have a limited amount of room in your house, office or apartment, it makes sense you can't store books and brochures and shop manuals on everything. So choose a marque, be in Chevrolet, Pontiac, Ferrari, Shelby, etc. And become the world's leading expert on it. You can even publish articles on the marque on the net or in magazines or newspapers and obtain even more information from readers of your articles. By specializing you can recognize some of the cars you are searching for on the most scant of information and you can track cars better. Don't spread yourself too thin by being too multi-marque.

The best example is ace barn hunter Lynn Park. He's spent some 40 years chasing Cobras. Oh, he's been tempted by other cars, but mainly Cobras, so much so you can fling a serial number at him and he'll recite the car's history. That's out of 998 cars!

TARGET SPECIFIC CARS

There was a movie with Jack Nicholson and Morgan Freeman called *The Bucket List* where two aging fellows do a lot of wild things so they can cross them off their bucket list before they die. I have the same thing with cars. In my head, I've got dozens of cars floating there on my list (constantly subject to change), hoping no one else finds them first.

I have specialized—narrowed my list down to cars I want or can use to tie in with other things I am writing, or cars I am depicting in oils in my fine art endeavors. By narrowing it down to, say, just five marques, I can still stuff the information I have gathered in a few boxes devoted to each marque.

For example here's a few on my list with reasons why I want it:

- Fiero Spyder—Pontiac showed this, I had a ride, it would be a cute little low maintenance car.
- Bizzarrini GT5300 Strada four-seater—Rumored to be in South Africa. Ugly compared to the two-seater coupe, but it's still a Bitz. Maybe I could shorten the wheelbase and rebody it as a two-seater GT5300 Strada coupe. After all, it would still have a Bizzarrini SN.
- Stutz Blackhawk convertible, bodied in Italy—Plus: easy to find engine parts (Pontiac) Downside: 7 mpg.
- Rolls Royce Silver Cloud drophead coupe with Chevy engine—One was used as a prop car in film, *The Last of Shiela*. It's out there, I want it.
- Intermeccanica Indra—great styling by the legendary Scaglione, nobody talks about collecting them yet. They are the next Iso Grifo in terms of appreciation potential.
- Bentley Blower replica. I saw it advertised for $11,000. On a Ford truck chassis. Kept the ad. Still feeding my piggy bank.
- Ad infinitum....my list changes daily.

START AN ACTION FILE

The word "action" is key here. That means you have to update the file periodically. Fortunately with the internet this is fairly easy to do; but here is one major problem, one that people born after the age of the World Wide Web don't realize. Not everything is on the net. If no one from the Tucker Torpedo club entered their April 1959 club newsletter on the net it's not there.

So I would say step one is to join the clubs in the marques you are interested in and periodically buy all the old club newsletters you can to see if your target cars are mentioned. For instance, one car on my bucket list/target list is the Bizzarrini four seater car. I have traced it as far as Capetown, South Africa. But I haven't heard of it or read of it in 20 years. So that's a cold, cold trail. But it's a starting place. Many cars in this book were found by barn-finders following much colder trails. Bizzarrinis have mushroomed from about $7,000 in the Sixties to about $500,000 to $1 million today so it remains a high priority car. Plus it wouldn't require much to get the engine running. Small block 327 Chevys are in every junkyard from Missoula to Tampa.

RUNNING VS. NON-RUNNING

Now even after several chapters in this book talk about cars bought with no engine, or the wrong engine, or even wrong brand of engine, I have to say in my own personal life, that the cars I bought running, and kept running, I had more fond memories of. Even when I had my Ferrari 365GTC/4 painted I never took the engine out, and even went down to the body shop on occasion and started her up. The cars I never got running (the two Alfa Sprint Speciales and others I have banished from my memory) were no fun, so if you are a beginning or intermediate barn-finder and have a wife who wants to see what enjoyment there is in old cars, get one that's running and keep it running even while it's being painted, tuned, reupholstered, etc. Cars that are what the military calls in a very good state of "operational readiness."

THE PERILS OF THE INTERNET

Remember, the internet is your friend, as far as getting background on cars, but it's also your enemy if you use it unwisely. Why is that? Well, because although you can pick up old trails of cars you are looking for on the net, the trouble is, so can everyone else who views that page.

It's all too convenient to want to get on the net the second you found that potentially valuable old car and brag about what you've found but don't forget not only do all the people that go to that club website read about the car but some of those immediately forward that description you posted of your find to other friends. Friends that have more money. For instance, I found a 1961 Bentley Continental drophead coupe (non-Chinese eye which is rarer) in Venice, California. I could have got on the net, to a Bentley site and bragged about it, but what do you want to bet someone wouldn't have beaten me to it within hours? Someone more bankable. So I kept quiet until the car was on the flatbed heading to my client, the New York buyer who had issued the check to buy it. First I didn't want to betray a client's trust, but also I didn't want people to know about the car and beat my client to it. He had the right of first refusal. If he wanted to resell it as it was enclosed in a truck bound for New York, that was up to him. (In fact, as various cars I bought for him were being trucked coast to coast, the truck would sometimes have to divert as he sold the car sight unseen to a friend in another city).

FREQUENT CAR SHOWS AND WEAR BIG EARS

I go to them all, from Pebble Beach to the local car shows. I also go to auctions, sweeping through Gooding, RM, Mecum and the others in Phoenix every January. Let me tell you an auction story. I am standing at an auction back in the '80s looking at a 300SL gullwing and a middle-aged guy says, "I got one of those." I edged him off to the edge of the crowd, got his number, scraped together $8,000 and bought it. Today they are worth about $400,000 up.

Unbelievably at the same car event another man said he had a gullwing and I went to his house and looked at it. He was a pilot who'd lost his job by sneaking a friend on board for an overseas trip. His car was apart so I didn't buy it, but ironically it would have been the better car. He only wanted $6,500.

So my advice is to go to an auction, car show, whatever, bring a little folding chair and a picnic basket, park your keister near the car you desire and listen for comments like that. Pony up for refreshments and be Hail-fellow-well-met. And take a note-pad and make sure no one else is in earshot when you write down the contact info. Don't portray yourself as a guy buying cars for profit for a quick flip-over. No way, you are the true-blue enthusiast who lives, eats and breathes Checker Marathons or whatever the car is that you parked yourself by. If they sell their car to you, you alone will keep the flame burning for the marque. (And I applaud those restorers who actually do follow up on that frequently made but seldom kept promise: "When I restore the car I will bring it over so you can take a ride in it.")

When I interviewed the always interesting Gary Wales for this book he said that most of his tips on cars he found came from when he was already exhibiting a car in a show. At an all-day concours you have plenty of opportunity to stroll around and talk to other owners and who knows what car they might mention they have seen in their travels. I don't think it's that important *what* you show, as long as you are there, one of the group. And don't worry if what car you enter isn't concours, it's your option to enter it as a non-judged entry so you can be there and enjoy it without worrying if you have the wrong stamp on your radiator hose.

BUY ROSTERS

Every car club has a roster. When I was in the Ferrari Owners Club for several years, I had a stack of Ferrari Owners Club rosters. One day I started comparing one year's entries with those of the next year and found a few people weren't listed in the updated directory. So I paid a letter writing service (this was before computers) to write each of the dropouts a form letter and say, "I notice you dropped out of the club but by any chance do you still have your car?" I bagged three Ferraris and a Bizzarrini that way. So if you are hankering for a particular rare car, join the club and buy rosters as far as they go back.

If you are a skeptic, you might counter, "But what good is that, people move all the time—so the listings will be out-dated." True generally but one time in 1970 I was given a Cobra

Owner's Club roster from a club that pre-existed the huge club there is now. I reprinted a few of those in 2012 and one British owner who was on the roster told me that—of the British Cobra owners listed—three of those listed still had their cars. And this list was over 40 years old! So rosters are worth their weight in gold, even if they had coffee spilled on them.

One way I'd find Ferraris and other exotics in the days before The Internet was to run in ad in *Auto Trader* with a picture of an old Ferrari. Any old Ferrari. I'd say:

FERRARI WANTED: Pre-1975. Beat-up, dented, missing engine or trans. Dents and Rusts OK. Send picture to my address. (Address follows.)

I wouldn't even use an e-mail address. That's because, if the car owners know how to send e-mail they might also know how to look up the value of a car like that on a computer. Sometimes, as a result of these ads, I'd get a picture of another car than the one pictured; sometimes people don't even know what they have. I bagged several collector cars that way back in the '80s.

HANG OUT WITH THE RICH

I know, I know, we should be feeding the poor and whatnot but let's face reality. I see a lot of wisdom in the old line: "A crumb off their table is a whole meal to me." One time at a Ferrari event in Holland I met a wealthy Italian man who, in casual conversation, said he was having his Ferrari 365GTC/4 driven up from Italy for the event. Right away I knew he must be somebody as he was too busy to drive his own Ferrari (after taking me for a hell-raising ride once the car arrived, I doubted he would have made it without crashing). At any rate, during the next few years he was my only connection to the "jet set" as he would fly from country to country on business (commercial real estate), but also indulge in his hobby of buying cars here and there—Ferraris, Bizzarrinis and even old Cadillacs. He would rent a storehouse, park them and I think forget about the place, failing to pay the storage fees. When I last saw him he had a Maserati Ghibli Spyder (cut from a coupe), three or four smashed Ferrari 400s, a Triumph TR8 and a '57 Cadillac in storage in an airplane hanger. I was supposed to go over there and check on them but it was in a neighborhood with a high murder rate so I demurred. I often wonder what became of those cars when he died a few years later. But at any time, I probably could have bid on one or the other because, to him, they weren't that important, like sets of cuff links a cuff link collector would buy. He would sell one to buy another. Now a word of warning from a middle class guy: these wealthy people are mercurial. You could be having lunch with them at a place where a cuppa java is $4.00 and suddenly they get a call and—BOOM—they're gone. My advice: always pack a sack lunch and have transportation money to get home. You have to recognize your "station"—you are only a facilitator to their car hobby but when it comes to their real business, whatever that is, you disappear.

A related thought to that is hang out where the rich hang out. I remember going to Southampton, Long Island, in 1967 or so and here was a Ferrari Lusso at a gas station with its engine lying across the seat. Probably could have got it for four grand if the owner didn't even take it to a Ferrari garage. That's a rich neighborhood where Ferraris were bought like toys and thrown away when the ashtrays were full. You aren't going to find cars like that where the streets are mean.

So where are the rich neighborhoods? A search engine search will tell you that in about 2 minutes. I'd say Scarsdale, New York, is a good start. And islands are good because if nobody on the island wants to buy a car, the seller sometimes gives up. I met an Englishman named Colin Crabbe who got into Cuba and bought two XK-SS Jags. Nobody in a country where the average income is $200 a year could afford them. He could. He came. He found. He bought.

KEEP YOUR FINDS CONFIDENTIAL
This is the hardest part because I have to burden you with

sad tales of a couple of betrayals, although it reveals my naiveté. But what the hey, you paid good money for this book so you deserve to learn from my private agonies. I look at a lot of cars and often used to take someone with me. One time I was at my house entertaining a friend from the Iso club (Italian car, Corvette engine) and I casually mentioned I had just seen an Iso being serviced at a gas station nearby. He jumped up and said let's go look at it. So he and his buddy, who was also staying at the house, and I all climbed in my car, drove four blocks and discovered the car. Amazingly, the gas station owner gave us the owner's contact info. I forgot about it until my client in New York asked if I knew of any Isos. I had lost the number of the owner of the car so I called the guy who had been a guest at my house. "I don't remember any Iso," he said. "But your buddy was with us, he might remember," I pleaded. Nope. He was firm that it never happened. This was, mind you, before digital camera days or I'd have images of it. Anyhow I am sure if I pursued it through the club I'd find the car as not too many had silver leather interiors and I will eventually find out how the car went from that service garage to the present owner. No sin goes unpunished!

Then the same thing happened with a friend of the friend who betrayed me (who I will always wonder was an implanted agent). Through one of my *Auto Trader* ads, I had found a Ferrari, an early '50s Ghia-bodied one with a Corvette engine. True it was bastardized but I am talking Ghia-bodied Ferrari and those are rare on the ground. The price was $40,000, a fair price at the time, in the '80s. I went to the location with a fellow from Holland who was staying with me. When we were at the Ferrari owner's house I saw the owner of the car give the Dutchman his card. I knew right then I'd made a fatal mistake bringing my "friend" along because when I got back to the Ferrari owner a few weeks later with a cashier's check from my New York client to buy the car he asked, "Didn't your friend tell you—he came back and bought it?" I could again trace what happened to that car but it's all too obvious—the Dutchman had hung out with me until the moment he heard I was on the trail of a good car and then claim-jumped me. Ah, you live and learn (and if I ever catch up with him, he's owed at a minimum a knuckle sandwich).

BE CAREFUL WHO YOU SEND TO INSPECT A CAR

Now the problem is you often find a car that's a long way off. People say, "why don't you find a club member in that area to inspect the car for you?" Seems logical. They know that model of car. But automatically if you turn the car down that club member either buys it himself or tells other club members and they buy it. I had one Cobra barn hunter tell me he sent a local to inspect a racing big block Cobra in another state. The guy reported back to him that it wasn't such a great car. But then who buys it? The same guy who he sent to inspect it! So I would say get the money ready and fly there yourself.

KEEP PRIVATE YOUR WRITTEN RECORDS ON LEADS

Still involving the same general area, Italian cars with Corvette engines, I also was a member of the Ferrari club and the Owner's Club directory back when the club was foolish enough to have each member's home address with a list of other cars they owned. One fellow had a Bizzarrini listed. Well, once I made the mistake of loaning this old roster with that listing to the same shark that was in the club. For months I kept praying he wouldn't read that "other cars owned" list below each name. I asked for the book back and subsequently bagged that Bitz for $18,000 (apart but complete). I passed it on for a mere $500 profit because I knew it would get back to the claim jumper that had claim-jumped me before. He'd flip out when he discovered he had that Bizzarrini owner's name in front of him for months and never knew it because he hadn't even taken the time to read the roster diligently.

This claim-jumping saddened me so much I no longer look for cars actively, just take note when I see one, and I no longer have a customer who's waiting to pay me for finding one. The internet has changed barn finding. It's much more of a dog-eat-dog thing now if you're trying to make a living because it is now he-who-is-bankable wins. You can no longer leisurely send snapshots like I did and wait weeks to see who wants it. It's an internet world and the purchase has to take place almost simultaneously with the discovery, which also greatly increases the chance of making a mistake.

That is not to say that cars can't be found. To the contrary, they are all over the place. (And new ones, in the form of concept cars, are being created by automakers every year.) It's just you have to be very careful who you impart information to or all your hard work in finding the car—even decades of looking for one—goes out the window. You have to be very, very careful, to the point where you just can't take your friends with you to inspect a barn find. It is only common sense. If you were a businessman, say selling chrome plating, you wouldn't take a social friend with you on a business call, would you? It wouldn't be considered very professional. So if you want to make the "life changing sum" I talked about in the introduction, remember, buying old cars is business, business, business—so don't take someone along who could be a claim jumper.

GAUGING THE SCOPE OF YOUR DISCOVERY

There will be cars you come across that are too much to restore—way beyond your scope. But fortunately, there is a breath of fresh air in the concours community known as the "barn find" or "preserved" section where the cars are permitted to be displayed as found. Maybe they don't have the mouse nests on the seats anymore but they have the original patina, and God bless the owners for bringing those cars because we can learn a lot more about a car's history seeing it as it was found than we can seeing it all dolled up and freshly painted, re-upholstered, re-chromed and waxed.

And now that there is the internet, that's the good thing about it, that you can merchandise a car from the minute you bought it (you get to Starbucks for the wi-fi connection, plug in your laptop and post the pictures; but be sure not to post them with license plates or identifying the city or state—it might be better to photoshop those out first). And really it's not a good idea to advertise the car until you have:

1.) title in hand
2.) actual physical possession of the car

CARS WITHOUT TITLE

Ah, this is a sore area. I was reading about a guy that took a Corvette to an auction where it was pulled. That's because another guy read about this Corvette, which had been part of a famous Le Mans race team, and said, "Hey, I own that." Now I don't know if he established how it had left his family's hands but you want to be sure, you buy a car with clear title.

On the other hand, some people have a car and no title. So then if the owner dies, you have to contact the executor of the estate and see if the estate can issue you a signed and witnessed bill of sale. And some states will see if there's a car registered by that VIN, and if not, issue you a title based on that bill of sale signed by someone authorized to settle the estate.

I remember shooting pictures of a '56 Corvette at a car show and when I wanted to print the VIN in the story the owner suddenly clammed up. His car had been bought with a disputed title and he wanted his car in the magazine but not enough to alert the former owners who might claim it was never sold.

TITLE CLARIFICATION

If the seller honestly owns the car he shouldn't mind faxing a copy of the title. How do you know what a title looks like from another State? I would try to find another title from that State or call the State DMV and check out if it is a real title in that name. Or go on a forum for another make of car (Corvette forum, etc.) and ask what a title looks like from that State. You'll find out in 5 minutes.

Also I would recommend buying only if it has the seller's name on it so that they are authorized to sign it off. Now some say "Mr. *or* Mrs. so-and-so" and that's OK if it says "*or*" because that means either one of the two signatories can be authorized to relinquish ownership. If it says Mr. *and* Mrs. you got a problem because what if the Mister wants to sell and the Mrs. doesn't? If she won't sign, you got a whole 'nother person to bargain with. If it's owned by a company how do you know the seller is authorized to sell that company's property? It's worth straightening all this out if the car's valuable enough but if the car is hundreds or thousands of miles away you can do a lot of advance straightening before you ever get on the airplane. Any obfuscating activities on behalf of the seller ("My ex-wife no longer talks to me" etc.) are your clue that this one should be a "pass."

Life is too short to have to deal with that.

HAVE A PLACE TO PARK IT

Now let's say you are a successful barn finder, in that you found a treasure guaranteed to escalate in value if only it can be stored like a fine old wine. Ah, but then you need a "whine cellar" of sorts, a place to put it. Don't even attempt to buy one if you live in an apartment, and have one open parking slot and that's it. Cajole a relative with country property (yes, and old barn would do), or canvas the local garage rentals and see who will allow you to store it until such time as you can come up with enough money to make it a running driving car. The next step after that is finding a shop to take it and give it what it needs (or rather what you can afford). Perhaps in another volume I'll tell the sad story of selling my first gullwing Mercedes for $2,500 (that's no misprint!) because my father wouldn't let me park it in the garage where he wanted to park his 1964 Pontiac Catalina. So I sold it rather than leave it out in the Michigan winter to suffer. Oh, pop apologized later, when he realized the gullwing's significance, but it was too late. The car was gone. So part of you acquisition plan is determining where to store it before you take delivery.

LATE MODEL CARS

How could a car you buy new go up in value?

This is one of the fondest hopes of car collectors—if they buy a car new, it will be reliable, they can drive the wheels off it and if it's the right car, sell it at a profit. Well, it doesn't happen. There are so few exceptions that you can count them on one hand. Say the Ferrari Enzo. Cost over a million new, now worth more. Same with the McLaren F1. But those are rarified cars, let's get down to the average working man's new car. The only Detroit-made car of the last decade I can find in 2013 that's worth more than it cost new is the Pontiac Solstice coupe. Why? Because just as Pontiac started making the coupe, with its lift-off roof panel, the whole Pontiac Division disappeared. So only around 1,000 were made. One car dealer is advertising a 2006 for $22,000 while the used Solstice ragtops are a mere $11,000. So there's a car you could buy even for $22K, drive for ten years and sell it for more than you bought it for because it's rare. But what if you bought a Buick Reatta convertible in its time or a '76 Eldo convertible? Both were stashed away by those with grandiose dreams of appreciation and are just used cars now, falling in price. I monitor a number of late model cars but I can't say they are good barn finds. So few become so anointed...

GREY MARKET CARS

The U.S. is a country with standards regarding what cars you can import. Now some countries let in any ol' car, but the U.S. has a pretty high wall; a new car has to meet our emissions and safety standards. Ironically, that makes cars that don't meet the standards, that are "walled off" from the U.S., that much more desirable by collectors.

Now that there is the "cars 'n coffee" type informal car meet, I find one of the types of cars that is really interesting at these events is the foreign car that was "snuck in" by hook or by crook.

On my list are a number of different Alfas, like the Junior Zagato—the engine parts are easily found as it was the same engine as offered in some legal-in-the-U.S. models but the problem is when you need body panels, rubber trim, the windshield, etc. Which is the problem with gray market cars—you can get the car but can you get the parts?

And then there's the problem of being able to register it. Back in the '80s there were a number of gray market conversion shops making Boxers, Ferrari 400s, Alfa Montreals or other illegal cars legal by installing various components. Some of these were fly-by-night operations and in one case I know of the owner of the shop went to jail for lying to Uncle Sam. But ironically if the car you're looking at was registered once legally in the U.S. after its conversion, it could already be "grandfathered in," i.e. legal now. I'd still veer away from any car in the U.S. that still has foreign title and plates though because even though the DOT now has better things to do than go around confiscating gray market cars, there is still the potential they could.

SALVAGE CARS

Some states have salvage titles which are put on cars sold from junkyards so the general public is protected from buying a car that might have been "put together" from wrecked cars in a way that you can't detect from curbside. Now it is possible to go to a non-salvage title state and retitle it and it comes out "clean" but if the buyer discovers in its former State it was a salvage car you might be sued for fraud. Still there's several million-dollar cars in this very book that in fact were bought out of junkyards including the Bugatti Royale cabriolet, the Rebel Corvette, and of course everybody has heard of the Motorama show cars found in a junkyard within rifle shot of the GM Tech Center. So sometimes you got to take a chance.

RACECARS

There's a new kind of event that's spread across the U.S. and even foreign countries, called the "cars 'n coffee" where owners of interesting cars meet early in the morning on a Saturday or Sunday in some parking lot and walk about looking at whatever shows up. Most of the events end at 9 a.m., about which time the wife wants her hubby home so she can began issuing the day's orders. I think some of the most interesting cars at these events are former racecars, especially with the old racing number still on the car. Accordingly, I recently stopped by an independent Porsche shop in Riverside, California, and looked at the 20 or so cars parked out back and fell in love with an old 911, still with its racing numbers, roll bar, wide wheels and tires. The perfect car to take to a cars 'n coffee. The shop employee present warned me it had an illegal plexiglass windscreen, and no heater and defroster (which you need out on the road) but I put that possibility—an old racecar—on my wish list because, who knows, you could do a little documentation and find out it ran at Sebring or Daytona. Suddenly you got a car with a story. And 911 cars are pretty modular—engines from decades back and forward could bolt right in.

Just be forewarned with racecars—the car may not have been street registered, so it's difficult to satisfy the DMV with a racer's logbook. Plus it may be a mish-mash of parts (engines changed several times during a season and even during a race). But damn it, being able to answer that question, "Hey has that thing ever raced?" by pulling out a scrapbook and saying, "As a matter of fact…" is a worthwhile moment.

CUT CARS

On occasion I find a car that was born as a sedan or two-door coupe but it's been cut into a convertible. These can still be valuable if it's a rare enough car, and especially if the automaker once made their own convertible version of the car "in period." For instance, Rolls made the Silver Cloud two-door convertible at the same time as they made their four-door sedans and indeed the early ones were cut from sedan shells. But when you come to cars that were never convertibles, it's a more difficult decision, say the Ferrari 400GT, the Porsche 928 and the like. Sure, they look great and the craftsmanship may be worthy of the original automaker, but in the end, they're just customs.

One saving grace can be if the original automaker did in fact make one or two prototypes for VIPs. For instance, Ferrari did make two, count 'em, two Ferrari 400 convertibles, as experiments and actually sold them after the experimenting was over. So those original two would be worth a lot; all the ones cut in private shops are worth much less but still somewhat "blessed" because Ferrari did make two that paved the way. Ironically you could score big here buying a coupe that's been cut into a convertible (think of the cut Daytonas) and making it a coupe again. Alas, the shops that did the cutting mostly likely threw the roofs away!

FOREIGN COUNTRIES

How does the film *Raiders of the Lost Ark* start? Harrison Ford is digging a valuable gem out of an idol's eye in some jungle. Likewise, Americans have this persistent fantasy they can go to some far-off foreign land, find some valuable car and wrest it away from locals who don't know any better.

Well, it's true and the same things happen in reverse where the foreigners come to America and buy treasures that we didn't realize were that valuable. I remember when I told a Japanese man where he could buy a Ferrari GTO for under $100,000. He did (from Steve Earle, founder of the Monterey Historics). Now it's worth $45 million (and that's the last time I divulge where a valuable car is).

I would say, having traveled the world in the '80s, that there are treasures to be found in foreign countries, the ultimate one being Brunei where Prince Jeffri salted away some 3,000 cars including Ferraris, Bentleys, Rolls Royces, Lamborghinis and such in long term storage. Google Sultan of Brunei and you might even find a list.

For starters I'd say if you don't have a local contact in the foreign country you plan to search in, it's no use going. Why? Because just getting it out of the country could involve local authorities who have to be, uh, persuaded. And then getting it back to the U.S. you have to be prepared to pay customs duties. For a good local contact, I'd say car club, though they might then alert all their club members a Yank is trying to buy their treasure out from under them. Or at least someone in air freight who knows how to fill out the paperwork and get it on a plane. When wheels are up, with your cargo in the hold, you can relax a little.

I myself went to a country in the South Pacific where in less than two weeks I found a Ferrari Boxer, a SS100 Jag, a gullwing Mercedes and heard rumors of coachbuilt Rolls. But it was one of those countries where the wealthy who own these cars don't need to sell them and nobody else can afford to buy them. So they aren't often advertised. I would say if your business brings you in contact with local business leaders, that's a start. Say, you are an oil pipe salesman and you are stationed in Dubai where you play polo with the bigwigs who own all the airlines, shipping companies, etc. But if you know not one person in that country, I wouldn't advise becoming an exporter with something as expensive as a car.

PAYMENT

I prefer cashier's checks. If they ask for cash only, you are opening yourself up to robbery. I remember when, with an investment partner, I was trying to buy a Lancia Zagato. I told the seller I'd meet him in the bank lobby, figuring the bank would stop him from snatching the $20,000 we had assembled in cash. But the seller kept calling and postponing until, wouldn't-cha-know, the bank had closed. Then he was ready but we smelled a set-up, because then we would just be in a parking lot with no bank personnel protection. We passed.

BUYING PROTOCOL

My patented technique was to get the cashier's check ready and fly to wherever the car was with no warning. That's because the owner usually has long promised six friends he will "call them first if he ever decides to sell." When you are there, on their doorstep, check in hand, he forgets all about calling. I would urge them to go to the bank to see if the bank manager would take the check. Usually they were only too happy to oblige (though in one case the seller was such a local goof that the bank manager doubted anyone would pay him $30,000 for an old car...). Then I would pull out a bill of sale which would be signed (have a duplicate, one for you, one for him), the seller would sign off on the title, I would take the keys and with a tow truck following, go to the house and take the car away. I would not say where I was taking it. Once clear of the house I would ask the tow truck driver where the nearest rental yard was with closed units. We would drive there, I would unload the car, roll down the door and padlock it. I would send the padlock key by Fed Ex to a national shipping company that would pick it up next time they had a truck rolling through the area. I would never, never keep the signed-off title in the car because once you do that, whoever wants to steal the car can go register the car in their name.

BUY OFF-SEASON

One of my buys was a Ferrari V-12 during a snowstorm in Tahoe. I was following a tip sent by my East Coast buyer, two Doctors who were partners in the car who wanted to sell. It was a clean, running driving car, just not a sexy model (I think GTE). At any rate, I looked at the car, started the engine, handed them the check and they handed me a bill of sale and the title. I told them I'd send a tow truck when the storm broke, then trudged through knee-deep snow to a restaurant to celebrate. Now there are other guys who probably knew of the car, and who had the money but thought, "Hey, there's a big storm coming. The roads will be closed." (As they often are in Tahoe.)

The same applies to hot weather. Imagine Palm Springs in August, when it's 120 degrees in the shade, and you're buying an old sports car from a widow who refuses to go out into the un-air-conditioned garage. You inspect the car, start it up and make an offer. You can get through this. Wear a hat, shorts, t-shirt, sunblock and drink plenty of liquids. Do you think Lawrence of Arabia complained about the heat?

Someone who waits until the weather's nice to follow up a barn find tip is a dilettante. If you're a serious barn finder, you go when the tip comes in. You wait, and the car will be gone.

A WORD OF CAUTION

Why do I remove the car from their premises forthwith? Because sometimes owners have buddies with the same car and the buddy might say, "Hey, if he hasn't picked up the car yet, let me switch those Borrani wire wheels, I always liked your wheels better, etc." and for God's sake you don't want the seller being tempted to take that One Last Drive; whereupon they could smash your car to smithereens. The moment they sign off the title and pluck the check from your hands, it's your car.

FOR THE NEXT EDITION, WE INVITE YOUR INPUT

Yes, this book is just the start. There will be a second volume and I, the author, and my publishers welcome submissions on rare cars you want to nominate as a barn find. Not one that you yourself bought necessarily. Just one you find interesting. What you send can be an old newspaper clipping or magazine story, or just your own self-written tale of a significant find.

But we have to have some basic criteria or the book would be too big. The main criterion will be cars that, if fully restored, would be worth say $100,000 and above, what the author deems worth a "life changing" amount (at least enough to put a down payment on a middle class home). Otherwise we would be flooded with entries and this book would have to be 1,000 pages thick (for instance, there are no less than ten 1965 Mustangs parked in driveways within a mile of my house).

If you have a car to nominate for Barn Finds 2, we need three essential things:

- picture of the car as found or close to the condition it was in when it was discovered

- approximation of the price paid when found by the barn finder or their customer
- names of people in the chain of ownership

An interesting note: When I described this book as it was being written to a colleague, he said, "there's no chance of finding a rare car whose owner doesn't know what it could be valued at." I say "rubbish" to that because even though some rare cars may be escalating in value, not everyone in fact is a car enthusiast. Some people inherit a car, and even in the computer age, not everyone knows how to use a search engine. If they did they would see what that make and model is selling for at actions and maybe even get the wrong idea on value, confusing their unrestored hulk with a fully restored auction star. The biggest changable factor in the collector car world is the car owners. The cars just sit there, unmindful of all the drama that's taking place in the lives of their owners—births, deaths, disease, marriages, dismissals from their job, divorces (how many great cars were sold because a wife wanted a kitchen remodeling?), criminal incarcerations, you name it. You might approach the car owner just as that old hulk in the garage is the least important thing in their lives and they've been praying for a way to get rid of it.

If you want to mail your information on your nominee, write:

Wallace Wyss—Barn Finds 2
C/O Enthusiast Books
1830-A Hanley Road
Hudson, WI 54016

We can't return anything you send on a car you nominate, including words or pictures, CD-Roms, flash drives, etc., so PLEASE don't send what you can't afford to lose, and there's no guarantee it will be used. But wouldn't it be neat if your all-time great barn find story becomes a chapter in the next edition? We'd like to see it there too!

Oh, and Good hunting....

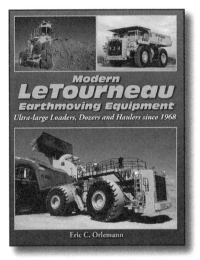
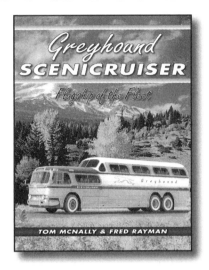
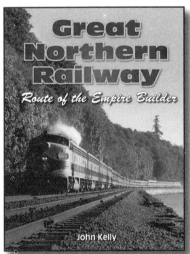
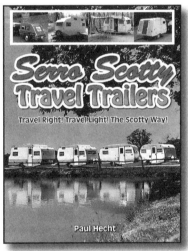